STUDY GUIDE

Joseph Amodeo
Sheridan College

PRINCIPLES OF MARKETING

Fifth Canadian Edition

Philip Kotler
Northwestern University

Gary Armstrong
University of North Carolina

Peggy H. Cunningham
Queen's University

Toronto

Copyright © 2002 Pearson Education Canada Inc., Toronto, Ontario. For sale in Canada only.

All Rights Reserved. This publication is protected by copyright, and permission should be obtained from the publisher prior to any prohibited reproduction, storage in a retrieval system, or transmission in any form or by any means, electronic, mechanical, photocopying, recording, or likewise. For information regarding permission, write to the Permissions Department.

0-13-060747-9

Acquisitions Editor: Kelly Torrance
Developmental Editor: Paul Donnelly
Production Editor: Mary Ann McCutcheon
Production Coordinator: Deborah Starks

1 2 3 4 5   06 05 04 03 02

Printed and bound in Canada

Contents

PREFACE

This Study Guide is offered as a tool to augment the student's reading and understanding of *Principles of Marketing*, Fifth Canadian Edition.

The Guide offers a comprehensive chapter-by-chapter review of the text that includes summaries and overviews, self-testing in the form of multiple choice and true/false questions, and case studies that encourage critical analysis and application of fundamental marketing concepts.

Each chapter in the Guide consists of the following components, which have been designed to take the student through the text in a coherent manner.

- Chapter Overview
- Chapter Objectives
- Chapter Topics
- Chapter Summary
- Key Terms
- Multiple Choice Questions
- True/False Questions
- Applying Terms and Concepts
- Answers

To properly understand marketing, students must place themselves in the role of the consumer, industrial buyer, and marketer. In this way they will comprehend the true power and depth of marketing. By considering marketing from these three views, students will see how marketing touches every aspect of their world; from the toothpaste they use, to how they spend their time on a Saturday night. This text will show that marketing is about more than just selling. Marketers must now take into consideration such things as: legislation, consumer rights, and the environment. Students will have an understanding of marketing as a career that will prepare them for a vast number of jobs.

With competition growing from industries around the world daily and the knowledge and the demands of the consumer along with it, marketers must be ever vigilant as they strive for customer relationships that will grow over time as products improve and customers buy. Add to this the growth of international markets and the expansion of computers and the student will see the need for skilled educated marketers.

Joseph Amodeo B.A., M.Ed., Ed.D.
Professor

Chapter 1

Marketing in a Changing World

Chapter Overview

Companies are built on success and that success is based on marketing. Marketing is based on attracting new customers, keeping old ones and expanding product depth and width. In our global world companies must see beyond their own frontiers as the world is open to them through improved technology on an ever-increasing scope. Sound marketing is the backbone to a company's success or failure. Today's emerging companies share both a strong focus on and a heavy commitment to marketing. Modern marketing seeks to attract new customers by providing superior value, and to retain current customers by delivering satisfaction. Sound marketing is critical to the success of all organizations: large or small, for-profit or non-profit, domestic or global expansion.

Many people view marketing as only selling or advertising. But marketing combines many activities, including marketing research, product development, distribution, pricing, advertising, and personal selling, all designed to serve and satisfy customer needs while meeting the organization's goals. Rapid changes can quickly make yesterday's winning strategies obsolete. In this century, marketers will face many new challenges and opportunities that were beyond the grasp of their predecessors. Success will belong to the firms that are market-focused.

Chapter Objectives

1. Define marketing and discuss its core concepts.
2. Discuss the relationship between customer value, satisfaction, and quality.
3. Compare the five different marketing philosophies and the role they play.
4. Forecast the role of the marketer in the new century.

Chapter Topics

What is marketing?
- Needs, Wants, Demands
- Products and Services
- Value, Satisfaction and Quality
- Exchange, Transactions, and Relationships
- Markets
- Marketing

Marketing Management
- Demand Management
- Building Profitable Customer Relationships

Marketing Management Philosophies
- The Production Concept
- The Product Concept
- The Selling Concept
- The Marketing Concept
- The Societal Marketing Concept

Marketing Challenges in the New Millennium
- Growth of Non-Profit Marketing
- Connections with Customers
- Marketing on the Internet
- Global Connections
- The Changing World Economy
- Connections with Values and Social Responsibilities
- The New Marketing Landscape

Chapter Summary

1.   Marketing and its role in the economy.

Marketing is the blend of ideas that come together to provide a product or service to a customer, the process by which individuals and groups obtain what they need and want through creating and exchanging products and values with others. Economic roles include meeting needs, wants and demands; creating products; creating value and satisfaction; facilitating exchanges, transactions, and mutually beneficial long-term relationships; developing markets; meeting societal needs; increasing consumer choice; and providing fair profiles and meeting ethical beliefs.

2.   The five marketing management philosophies.

Production Concept: consumers favour products that are available and highly affordable.
Product Concept: consumers favour products that offer most values, performance, and innovative features.
Selling Concept: consumers will not normally buy enough products on their own.
Marketing Concept: delivering needs and wants more efficiently than competition.
Societal Marketing Concept: company determines customer's needs and wants and society's best interest.

3.   The major forces now changing the marketing landscape and challenging marketing strategy.

A growth in non-profit marketing seems to meet new needs. Rapid globalization marked by geographic dispersion of purchasing, manufacturing and marketing activities results in marketers being a new breed keeping abreast of changes in every corner of the world. The changing world economy marked by a decline in real buying power and the increase of two-income households in the US. Increased demand for social responsibility including more ethical business practices and more attention to the environmental consequences of business decisions. These decisions being effected not only by profit but also by social and governmental needs. A new marketing landscape characterized by extremely rapid change.

4.   The marketing management concept.

Marketing management is the analysis, planning, implementation and control of programs designed to create, build, and maintain beneficial exchanges with target buyers for the purpose of achieving organizational objectives. Marketing management seeks to manage demand efficiently and effectively so as to help consumers obtain value in their transactions, resulting in satisfaction for the customer and profit for the company

5.   The relationship between value, satisfaction and quality.

Customer value is the difference between the value of customer gains from owning and using a product and the costs of obtaining it. Satisfaction depends on a product's perceived performance in delivering value relative to the buyer's expectations. Quality, especially in the form of TQM, is a company's commitment to constant improvement. Satisfaction comes from delighting and surprising customers with more quality, which heightens their perceived sense of value. Customer satisfaction is linked to quality; thus companies strive to improve quality and customer satisfaction. Such practices are the only formula for long-term success and result in connecting for a customer's lifetime.

Key Terms

Customer Value	(pg. 9)	Customer Satisfaction	(pg. 10)
Customer Satisfaction	(pg. 10)	Needs	(pg. 6)
Demands	(pg. 7)	Product	(pg. 7)
Demarketing	(pg. 14)	Product Concept	(pg. 17)
Exchange	(pg. 11)	Production Concept	(pg. 17)
Internet	(pg. 23)	Relationship Marketing	(pg. 12)
Market	(pg. 12)	Selling Concept	(pg. 18)
Marketing	(pg. 6)	Societal Marketing Concept	(pg. 19)
Marketing Concept	(pg. 18)	Transactions	(pg. 11)
Marketing Management	(pg. 14)	Wants	(pg. 6)

Multiple Choice Questions

1-1   Multiple

The basic part(s) of the human makeup consists of:

1.   Social needs
2.   Physical needs
3.   Psychological needs
4.   1 and 2
5.   All of the above

1-2   Multiple

Ogo lives in a small rural community in Tanzania. Resources are scarce, therefore in order to satisfy his families needs he will:

1.   Try to reduce their desires
2.   Try to reduce their needs
3.   Satisfy their needs with what is available
4.   Find or develop objects that will satisfy their needs
5.   1 and 3

1-3   Multiple

The importance of physical goods lies in

1.   The satisfaction of owning them
2.   The satisfaction they provide
3.   The benefits they provide
4.   The desires they satisfy
5.   None of the above

1-4   Multiple

Fabiana is looking for a new microwave. She is on a limited budget, but values quality and performance above price. Which of the following concepts will she apply in choosing the appropriate microwave?

1.   Customer value
2.   Consumer preference
3.   Product quality
4.   Product value
5.   Customer satisfaction

4

1-5   Multiple

Which of the following systems of commerce allows a society to produce much more than it would with any alternative system?

1.   Transaction
2.   Exchanging
3.   Relationship marketing
4.   Open markets
5.   All of the above

1-6   Multiple

Guida's 15-year-old car has just broken down and she says she has been towed for the last time. She will pay cash for her new car. This form of purchase is known as:

1.   Transaction
2.   Exchanging
3.   Relationship marketing
4.   Markets
5.   Bartering

1-7   Multiple

People satisfy their wants and needs through:

1.   Purchasing products
2.   Purchasing services they require
3.   Buying improved goods
4.   Satisfaction with other similar products
5.   All of the above

1-8   Multiple

Marketing management involves:

1.   Managing customer relationships
2.   Managing supplier relationships
3.   Managing demand
4.   1 and 2
5.   1 and 3

1-9   Multiple

Long weekends result in overcrowded park grounds in provincial parks across Canada. Park officials could use which of the following techniques to reduce the overcrowding situation?

1.   Marketing management
2.   Demand management
3.   Demarketing
4.   Negative marketing
5.   None of the above

1-10   Multiple

Companies operating under which philosophy run the risk of focusing too narrowly on developing and advertising one product and failing to produce enough to meet the newly increased demand?

1.   Production concept
2.   Product concept
3.   Marketing concept
4.   Societal marketing concept
5.   Selling concept

1-11   Multiple

Non-profit organizations spend a lot of money promoting their organization to the public. They are sometimes more concerned with receiving donations than with providing the best service. They are applying which type of company philosophy?

1.   Production concept
2.   Product concept
3.   Marketing concept
4.   Societal marketing concept
5.   Selling concept

1-12   Multiple

The societal marketing concept argues that the pure marketing concept overlooks the possible conflicts between _____ and _____.

1.   Short-term wants and short-term welfare
2.   Short-term needs and long-term welfare
3.   Short-term wants and long-term welfare
4.   Long-term wants and long-term welfare
5.   Long-term wants and short-term welfare

1-13   Multiple

The social and managerial process by which individuals and groups obtain what they
need and want through creating and exchanging products and values with others is called:

1.   Commerce
2.   Economics
3.   Sales
4.   Marketing
5.   Purchasing power

1-14   Multiple

The term "global connections" refers to:

1.   Dealing with associate firms
2.   Providing product around the world
3.   Conducting research globally
4.   Using international markets to establish pricing
5.   All of the above

1-15   Multiple

_____ is the analysis, planning, implementation, and control of programs
designed to create, build and maintain beneficial exchanges with target buyers for the
purpose of achieving organizational objectives.

1.   Demand management
2.   Marketing management
3.   Sales management
4.   Corporate management
5.   Consumer management

1-16   Multiple

Which of the following explains the use of the Internet?

1.   The marketing concept
2.   The use of relationship marketing
3.   The use of physical resources
4.   The use of corporate databases
5.   A global web of computer networks

1-17   Multiple

With the expansion of jet travel to every country, fax machines and the Internet are characteristic of what new challenge to marketing?

1.   Rapid globalization
2.   The changing world economy
3.   The call for more socially responsible marketing
4.   The micro-chip revolution
5.   1 and 2

1-18   Multiple

The fact many Canadian households need both spouses to work to maintain the buying power of a single-wage earner from a generation ago is characteristic of:

1.   The new world order
2.   The "want it now" consumption syndrome
3.   The changing world economy
4.   Inflation
5.   Rapid globalization

1-19   Multiple

When a merchant appears in a central location called a marketplace, the total number of transactions required to accomplish a given volume of exchange:

1.   Increases
2.   Decreases
3.   Remains the same
4.   Fluctuates over time
5.   Unable to determine from the information given

1-20   Multiple

Programs designed to constantly improve the quality of products, services, and marketing processes fall under which of the following concepts?

1.   Customer satisfaction
2.   Customer value
3.   The exchange process
4.   Total quality management
5.   All of the above

1-21   Multiple

Which of the following entities is not considered a product entity?

1.   Person
2.   Place
3.   Organization
4.   Ideas
5.   All of the above are considered product entities

1-22   Multiple

Which of the following situations provides potential marketing opportunities for firms?

1.   Changing customer values and orientations
2.   Economic stagnation
3.   Environmental decline
4.   Increased global competition
5.   All of the above provide opportunities

1-23   Multiple

Which of the following companies would definitely not set up shop on the Internet?

1.   Jim's Fix-it Centre
2.   Carl's Roofing and Plumbing
3.   IGA
4.   Canadian Airlines
5.   All of the above would probably set up shop on the Internet

1-24   Multiple

Most large marketing companies like Coca-Cola and Nike undertake marketing research to understand their customers and to be able to cater to their needs. Which of the following questions is not usually answered after they have conducted their marketing research?

1.   Why
2.   What
3.   Where
4.   How
5.   All of them are answered

1-25   Multiple

The marketing concept of the firm is very important to its survival. The focus of the marketing concept is:

1.   Market
2.   Integrated marketing
3.   Customer needs
4.   Profits through customer satisfaction
5.   Providing value

1-26   Multiple

Which philosophy in business is typically practised when marketing unsought goods?

1.   The marketing concept
2.   The selling concept
3.   The production concept
4.   The product concept
5.   The societal marketing concept

1-27   Multiple

Looking for growth markets in other countries, as Coca-Cola and Pepsi have done, is characteristic of which trend?

1.   Rapid globalization
2.   The need for increased profits
3.   The slow growth rate of the North American market
4.   The increasing ethnic diversity of senior managers in major corporations
5.   All of the above

1-28   Multiple

Basic needs such as food, clothing, and safety refer to:

1.   Social needs
2.   Physical needs
3.   Physical wants
4.   Individual needs
5.   Social wants

1-29   Multiple

A(n) _____ consists of a trade of values between parties.

1.   Sale
2.   Exchange
3.   Transaction
4.   Market
5.   Barter

1-30   Multiple

The _____ holds that achieving organizational goals depends on determining the needs and wants of target markets and delivering the desired satisfaction more effectively and efficiently than the competition.

1.   Production concept
2.   Product concept
3.   Selling concept
4.   Marketing concept
5.   Societal marketing concept

True/False Questions

1-1   True/False

Needs are states of perceived depravation.

1-2   True/False

Customer satisfaction is the extent to which a product's perceived performance matches a buyer's expectations.

1-3   True/False

Exchange is the core concept of marketing.

1-4   True/False

Exchange marketing is part of the larger idea of relationship marketing.

1-5   True/False

In our society the pace of change and the ability to change is a competitive advantage.

1-6   True/False

It costs more than four times as much to attract a new customer as it does to keep an existing customer satisfied.

1-7   True/False

The Internet cannot be used as the technology for a model doing business.

1-8   True/False

The goal of the marketing concept is to build customer satisfaction into the very fabric of the firm.

1-9   True/False

It is difficult for new firms to develop techniques to deliver more value to customers.

1-10   True/False

The World Wide Web has given companies access to millions of new customers at a fraction of the cost of print and television advertising despite the huge costs of setting up a Web page.

1-11   True/False

Marketing myopia occurs when sellers are so taken with their products that they focus only on existing wants and lose sight of underlying customer needs.

1-12   True/False

To qualify as an economic exchange, the buyer must offer the seller money for a product or service.

1-13   True/False

The societal marketing concept holds that the organization should determine the needs, wants and interests of target markets.

1-14   True/False

The changing world economy is the primary reason for the emergence of "hybrid products," where design, material purchases, manufacture, and marketing may all take place in different countries.

1-15   True/False

Successful marketing companies find customers to purchase the products they have produced.

1-16   True/False

A market is a set of actual, not potential, buyers of a product.

1-17   True/False

Organizations that are market orientation based are more profitable than their production based rivals.

1-18   True/False

The selling concept holds that the organization should determine the needs and wants of consumers and undertake large-scale selling efforts.

1-19   True/False

Purchasing your textbooks is an example of relationship marketing.

1-20   True/False

A new car, a car cleaner, and a car wash are all considered products.

Applying Terms and Concepts

To determine how well you understand the materials in this chapter, read each of the following brief cases and then respond to the questions that follow. Answers are given at the end of this chapter.

Case #1   Handyman Hardware and Lumber[1]

Thomas Steenburgh began the Handyman's store in 1979 after determining a huge do-it-yourself market existed for hardware and building supplies. His research showed that as plumbers, electricians, carpenters, and others began charging more in the mid-70s, many homeowners decided to do their own repairs and remodelling. And if their work wasn't quite perfect, homeowners could at least take satisfaction in knowing they had done the work themselves and that they had saved money. Steenburgh's research was consistent with the findings of the Do-it-Yourself Research Institute, based in Indianapolis, which estimated that do-it-yourself sales would grow from $6.4 billion in 1970 to $63.5 billion in 2004, thereafter increasing approximately 8% per year.

---

[1] *Principles of Marketing*, 3rd Edition, Kotler, Armstrong, Warren (Prentice Hall) – pg. 7.

Steenburgh's concept of retailing was to stock a wide variety of name-brand hardware and building supplies in what was essentially a warehouse. He spends virtually no money on fixtures and allows customers to use handcarts to select their own merchandise, which they bring to a centralized checkout area. The stores are open from 7 a.m. to 10 p.m., Monday through Saturday. Handyman's main form of advertising consists of flyers and inserts in local newspapers. When a Handyman Store is opened in a city, its prices are reduced to a minimum. The usual practice is to post a local competitor's catalogue or flyer at the store and offer the customer the same or comparable goods for 20% less. Prices are kept low because they buy direct from the manufacturer and sell for cash or approved cheques only. The company also saves money because its stores serve as its own warehouse; each store is between 75,000 and 100,000 sq. ft. What merchandise does not fit on a shelf or rack is stacked on the floor, sometimes up to the ceiling.

One area where Steenburgh will not skimp is personnel. Since 85% of his sales are to do-it-yourselfers, he typically hires 30 to 40 salespeople for each store and trains them in do-it-yourself tasks. These salespeople liberally dispense free how-to pamphlets and practical advice on projects from start to finish.

Steenburgh's philosophy of selling quality products at a low price with good advice has served him well. Sales per square foot have averaged between $250 and $275 at each of its 19 stores with projected profits this year of $22 million.

1.   What type of people are involved in marketing activities at Handyman Stores?

_____

_____

_____

_____

2.   How does each of the above people contribute to the marketing activities?

_____

_____

_____

_____

3.   How does Steenburgh implement marketing management in his stores?

_____

_____

_____

_____

4.   What product(s) is Handyman selling to its consumers?

_____

_____

_____

_____

5.   Identify Handyman's marketing philosophy and list the reasons for your decision.

_____

_____

_____

_____

Case #2   First Nations Cola

Mike Birch is from Cross Lake, Manitoba, a small isolated reserve community located 850 km north of Winnipeg. The only way to reach the reserve in the summer is by airplane and, in the winter, by a winter road. Mike decided since there was only one store in town, and it charged above average prices, many needs were not being met. He decided to bring in a trailer to sell soft drinks, chips and chocolate bars. His most successful product was the soft drinks, because the Aboriginal population consumes them at 4 times the national consumption rate. He realized that since this was an issue on his reserve, it must also be an issue on other reserves. Mike, therefore, decided to start First Nations Cola so Aboriginal people could have a beverage to call their own. Since its inception, his company has expanded to cover not only reserves, but also urban centres like Winnipeg. He also entered the international market by exporting to Europe and bottling in the US under license. He went after the European market because of its fascination with the Aboriginal culture. This is an excellent example of how an entrepreneur saw an unmet need, capitalized on it, and made a profitable business.

1.   In your opinion, why was this a good opportunity to capitalize upon?

_____

_____

_____

_____

2.   Describe the profitable customer relationship.

_____

_____

_____

_____

3.   Describe the marketing philosophy you feel Mike Birch used.

_____

_____

_____

_____

4.   What new potential markets should Mike Birch investigate?

_____

_____

_____

_____

Case #3   Coca Cola International[2]

The Coca-Cola Company is the world's leading soft drink maker and sells its brands in more than 200 countries. In fact, Coca-Cola outsells Pepsi three to one overseas with the largest growth occurring in Latin America and Asia. Both Coca-Cola and Pepsi are concentrating on the Asian market, as it holds almost half of the world's population and the growth opportunities are tremendous. However, Pepsi will find it difficult to compete against Coca-Cola in these markets because Coca-Cola invested heavily in bottling plants and has demonstrated it understands local market needs and marketing tactics. Coca-Cola has used its resources and creativity to become a very profitable multinational company.

1.   Which marketing management philosophy is Coca-Cola using? Why has it been so successful?

_____

_____

_____

_____

---

[2] *Principles of Marketing*, 4th Edition, Kotler, Armstrong, Cunningham (Prentice Hall) – pg. 25.

2.   What do you believe is the primary need being satisfied by Coca-Cola?

_____

_____

_____

_____

3.   Do you believe this move into Asia and Latin America is socially responsible?
        Why or why not?

_____

_____

_____

_____

Case #4   Pet Insurance Company of America[3]

George Smrtic founded the Pet Insurance Company of America (PICA) three years after the death of his shetland collie, Priscilla. It seems that the 11 year old Priscilla developed heart and lung trouble and rather than spend the estimated $1,200 for treatment he had Priscilla put to sleep.

Smrtic reasoned that since Americans are inclined to insure themselves and many of their possessions, they might also be inclined to insure their pets—especially since pets are seen by many as an integral part of the family—in some cases more loyal, obedient and loving than certain family members.

Smrtic researched the concept of pet insurance and found there are in excess of 110 million dogs and cats in approximately 65 million households in the US. He also found that Americans spend $15 billion a year on pets for everything from air-conditioned dog houses and designer clothing, to toys, vacations, and more recently, beefy-flavoured beverages and ice cream treats. Smrtic's research, including data collected from the American Veterinary Society, pet owners, and individual veterinarians, indicated that dog owners spend $95 per year on veterinary care while cat owners spend $78 per year. Smrtic also found not only that people's attitudes toward pets are changing, but also that increasingly sophisticated and expensive medical treatments, including chemotherapy, cataract operations and heart pacemakers, are now available.

The basic policies, which are underwritten by the Black Hawk Data Group of Dallas, sell for $49 with a $300 deductible clause. For $90 per year, the deductible falls to $100. Each policy insures the pet against catastrophic illness and/or accident. Not covered are routine procedures such as examinations, office visits, inoculations and neutering.

----

[3] *Principles of Marketing*, 3rd Edition, Kotler, Armstrong, Warren (Prentice Hall) – pg. 9.

The policies currently available, only on dogs and cats, are sold only through veterinary offices with the veterinarian acting as an agent for PICA.

Sales to date have been excellent, with over 70,000 policies providing $3,000,000 of coverage on approximately 100,000 dogs and cats. Competition from two other firms is minimal in that the market is expanding by 20-30 per cent per year. PICA, which is licensed in 47 states, expects to begin offering policies on pets other than dogs and cats within a year.

1.   What is the marketing concept used by PICA?

_____

_____

_____

2.   The product provided by PICA is an intangible item. Why is it still considered a product?

_____

_____

_____

3.   How would PICA expand its insurance products to other pets?

_____

_____

_____

_____

4.   What type of business transfer would an insurance policy qualify as?

_____

_____

_____

_____

5.   How could PICA use the Internet to expand their business? Are there any
       concerns with this mode of media for PICA?

       _____

       _____

       _____

       _____

Case #5   Can Changes Ever Happen at the CBC?

The CBC has always fought with its need to be the radio station that holds Canada
together. By depending on taxpayers' money it has always been in a nonenvious position.
The government is constantly cutting its funding while the media finds it an easy target to
attack. Its concern has always been to provide radio and TV for Canadians across the
entire country even in remote areas where it is the only station available. This in turn has
put the CBC in a position to come up with creative marketing in order to stay in
existence. The problem becomes even more complex when one realizes that all decisions
are a combination of funding requirements, donations and management, consisting of
government appointments on how decision are made at the CBC.

In our capitalistic society with its market-directed economy, the buying market has the
major say about what stays and what goes, because they "vote" with their dollars. If
people like a product, they will buy more of it. This puts the CBC in a unique position:
should it survive because some Canadians feel it serves a need, or be dropped because it
needs tax payer money to survive?

1.   What are the main characteristics of a market-directed economy?

       _____

       _____

       _____

       _____

2.   What role does marketing play in providing customer satisfaction in a market-
       directed economy?

       _____

       _____

       _____

       _____

3. How does a market-directed economy differ from a planned economy?

    _____

    _____

    _____

    _____

4. Identify the types of goods and services resulting from the decisions made by
    government officials in a market-directed economy. Explain why they cannot
    easily be made in the marketplace.

    _____

    _____

    _____

5. If the CBC wanted to start a relationship-marketing program, what would be its
    main focus?

    _____

    _____

    _____

    _____

Case #6   Honda

Honda, like all car companies, is faced with heavy competition as it strives for continued
success. To this end the marketing division of the company in each country looks at many
factors. And in Canada the story is the same. Their growth in the future will be built on
satisfied customers returning with their friends and family to purchase new Hondas and
in turn expanding their purchasing capabilities to include other Honda products from
generators to outboard motors. They have developed a strong community-based mentality
for the company and staff and realize their social responsibilities to the community and
the host country.

1. What kind of marketing is Honda pursuing and why?

    _____

    _____

    _____

    _____

2.   How will social responsibility help in future sales?

_____

_____

_____

_____

Multiple Choice Answers

1.	Correct Answer:	4	Reference:	pg. 7
2.	Correct Answer:	5	Reference:	pg. 7
3.	Correct Answer:	3	Reference:	pg. 10
4.	Correct Answer:	1	Reference:	pg. 11
5.	Correct Answer:	2	Reference:	pg. 12
6.	Correct Answer:	1	Reference:	pg. 12
7.	Correct Answer:	4	Reference:	pg. 7
8.	Correct Answer:	5	Reference:	pg. 14
9.	Correct Answer:	3	Reference:	pg. 15
10.	Correct Answer:	1	Reference:	pg. 17
11.	Correct Answer:	5	Reference:	pg. 17
12.	Correct Answer:	3	Reference:	pg. 19
13.	Correct Answer:	4	Reference:	pg. 7
14.	Correct Answer:	2	Reference:	pg. 10
15.	Correct Answer:	2	Reference:	pg. 14
16.	Correct Answer:	3	Reference:	pg. 18
17.	Correct Answer:	1	Reference:	pg. 23
18.	Correct Answer:	3	Reference:	pg. 26
19.	Correct Answer:	2	Reference:	pg. 13
20.	Correct Answer:	4	Reference:	pg. 12
21.	Correct Answer:	5	Reference:	pg. 10
22.	Correct Answer:	5	Reference:	pg. 20

23.	Correct Answer:	5	Reference:	pg. 23
24.	Correct Answer:	1	Reference:	pg. 9
25.	Correct Answer:	3	Reference:	pg. 18
26.	Correct Answer:	2	Reference:	pg. 17
27.	Correct Answer:	1	Reference:	pg. 24
28.	Correct Answer:	2	Reference:	pg. 7
29.	Correct Answer:	3	Reference:	pg. 12
30.	Correct Answer:	4	Reference:	pg. 19

True/False Answers

1.	FALSE	Reference:	pg. 6	Topic: Needs, Wants, and Demands
2.	TRUE	Reference:	pg. 9	Topic: Value, Satisfaction, and Quality
3.	TRUE	Reference:	pg. 11	Topic: Exchange, Transactions, and Relationships
4.	FALSE	Reference:	pg. 11	Topic: Exchange, Transactions, and Relationships
5.	TRUE	Reference:	pg. 21	Topic: The Internet
6.	TRUE	Reference:	pg. 14	Topic: Building Profitable Customer Relationships
7.	FALSE	Reference:	pg. 24	Topic: Marketing Technology
8.	TRUE	Reference:	pg. 18	Topic: The Marketing Concept
9.	TRUE	Reference:	pg. 30	Topic: Rapid Globalization
10.	TRUE	Reference:	pg. 23	Topic: The Internet
11.	TRUE	Reference:	pg. 17	Topic: The Product Concept

12.	FALSE	Reference:	pg. 11	Topic: Exchange, Transactions, and Relationships
13.	TRUE	Reference:	pg. 20	Topic: The Societal Marketing Concept
14.	FALSE	Reference:	pg. 26	Topic: The Changing World Economy
15.	FALSE	Reference:	pg. 14	Topic: Production Oriented
16.	FALSE	Reference:	pg. 12	Topic: Markets
17.	TRUE	Reference:	pg. 17	Topic: The Production Concept
18.	FALSE	Reference:	pg. 18	Topic: The Selling Concept
19.	TRUE	Reference:	pg.19	Topic: Market Based
20.	TRUE	Reference:	pg. 10	Topic: Products and Services

Applying Terms and Concepts Answers

Case #1   Handyman Hardware and Lumber

Question #1
- Handyman
- Store personnel
- Customers

Question #2
- Handyman – the store sells what it advertises, they live up to their name of quality products and provide all the services they say they do, and the profits from the store pay for the advertisements in the papers and flyers.
- Store personnel – they sell their expertise and knowledge and obviously suggest products the store carries in order to help someone complete the task at hand.
- Customers – if they are satisfied with the service and products they received at Handyman's and they are content with the finished job, they will tell others of their experiences and suggest that they go to Handyman's for any required home repair projects.

Question #3
- Steenburgh knows it is very important to have customer loyalty. For this reason his marketing plan is to provide quality products at low prices. This is evident in the marketing strategy of showing the competitors' prices and beating them; also the no frills atmosphere lets consumers know that they are not spending money on

unnecessary things so they get the lowest price. He ensures his staff are very knowledgeable and qualified to be "professionals" in their departments so consumers get quality service and a complete experience.

Question #4
- Hardware and building supplies
- How-to pamphlets
- Free how-to advice
- They are selling a complete package so they can be a one-stop-shop destination location which will give them a competitive advantage over other stores.

Question #5
- The market concept
- The key to Steenburgh's success is determining the needs and wants of target markets and delivering the desired satisfaction more effectively and efficiently than competitors.
- Low prices, quality products, name brand merchandise, convenient hours, large selection, free advice and knowledge, how-to pamphlets

Case #2   First Nations Cola

Question #1
- Aboriginals had a greater than average consumption rate.
- The local convenience stores were charging high prices.
- They could identify with this cola and therefore customer loyalty would not be difficult to maintain.
- Many companies would not fly products into reserves because of the expense.

Question #2
- They can identify with the product as it was started and is run by an Aboriginal person.
- Their logo is Aboriginal.
- The product has a similar taste to the national brands, so this is a minor issue.

Question #3
- First Nations Cola uses the marketing concept as they see a need and try to satisfy it by making it available to all reserves.
- They market the product as an Aboriginal product, and people feel pride in the product and are extremely loyal.
- The customers are obviously satisfied as the company is growing and moving into new markets.

Question #4

- Europe—capitalize on their fascination with First Nations' Culture.
- The US reserves and Aboriginal Peoples
- Australia and South America have many Aboriginal people; these could be very profitable markets.

Case #3   Coca Cola International

Question #1

- The selling concept
- The organization has taken on a major promotion effort.
- There is a huge potential market in Asia and Latin America so Coca-Cola must get loyal customers now, they are selling an image that will maintain loyalty.

Question #2

- The primary need is an image, not the drink.
- This is seen as a "cool" product, which is a treat. Disposable income in these countries is not very high; therefore this is a luxury item, which sends a certain image to those around you.

Question #3

- It is, for the reason that you are providing a country with a good product that satisfies a need.
- It could not be if Coca-Cola is bottling product in these plants at sub-standard working conditions and wages.
- It could not be if the marketing would convince the people that Coke is so important that they must buy it rather than a meal.
- It is, because it is bringing joy and contentment to the people of these countries.

Case #4   Pet Insurance Company of America

Question #1

- Marketing concept
- Smrtic has identified a need and a want and has been able to provide it to consumers in a more efficient and effective manner, as he has a lower deductible and is planning on expanding coverage to other pets and not limiting it to dogs and cats.

Question #2

- A product can be a tangible or intangible item.
- Intangible items are referred to as services and are just as important a product as they satisfy needs and wants in a way that satisfies customers.

Question #3
- PICA could expand its service to other pets through veterinarians, pet stores, or even flyers to communities where pets are predominant, like the suburbs.
- As PICA is growing, they now have more income being generated, therefore they can spend more on advertising, and it would probably be beneficial to them to start a television or radio campaign to make consumers aware of their services, and to convince them that a pet is just as important as a family member, and therefore should be insured.

Question #4
- It would be considered a transaction.
- It involves a trade between two parties that involves at least 2 things of value, and agreed-upon conditions—money for financial coverage at the necessary time
- The agreement only covers certain conditions and they are known at the time of signing and paying for the agreement.

Question #5
- They could build a Web page so consumers can look and see what PICA is all about.
- They could provide all necessary logistical information on the Web page so consumers know how to contact them.
- They could also use vets' home pages and have links to their Web site to increase exposure and the chances that their ads will be seen.
- Issuing policies over the Internet is not possible as people must understand the terms and conditions of the agreement before they sign.

Case #5   Can Changes Ever Happen at the CBC?

Question #1
- The people have a major say in what gets produced because they "vote" with their money.
- If they like a product they will demand more programming.
- To be able to compete with the vast production of the United States
- Supply and demand especially in remote areas where there is one choice only
- Competition helps to increase the quality of a product and reduce process

Question #2
- Consumers have the opportunity to get what they want through more use of cable.
- They also acquire knowledge about these goods and services.
- Benefits of having programming designed both for regions and for Canada-wide.

Question #3
- In a government-run media the government decides what to produce, who will produce it, when and where it will be produced and the prices they will charge.
- In a market-directed economy, these decisions are made not as a result of the profit motive, but by government funding and not customer satisfaction.

Question #4
- Government officials in a market-driven economy make decisions about:
  - What will be aired
  - Scheduling
  - Censorship
  - Funding
- These decisions are made by the government because people in the marketplace have shown lack of interest in giving more of their tax dollars to the CBC.

Question #5
- Creating, maintaining a strong Canadian nationalism
- Reliable amounts of products
- Assortment of products through more than one source
- Information where you can get more products

Case #6   Honda

Question #1
- Honda is pursuing relationship marketing, with the goal of developing a long-term relationship between the product and the consumer. This acts to deliver more value to the consumer as the company begins to assess the true value of the client to the company.

Question #2
- The public's image of a company is directly related to sales of the company. Corporate ethics and social responsibility enter into every business decision. Many companies like the Royal Bank, the Body Shop and Saturn build their reputation by distinguishing themselves by being more civic-minded and accepting their social responsibilities, which in turn build sales.

Chapter 2

Strategic Planning and the Marketing Process

Chapter Overview

Strategic planning sets the stage for a company, be it be large or small. Marketing contributes to strategic planning and the overall plan defines marketing's role in the company. Although formal planning offers a variety of benefits to companies, not all companies use it or use it well. Strategic planning must define and build on a company's mission statement and guide it through their decisions. The firm's business portfolio acts as a building block that reflects the strengths, weakness and opportunities to a company. The ability to grow in many different businesses, both related or not, is a sign of a strong business strategy. Many discussions of strategic planning focus on large corporations; however, small businesses also can benefit greatly. Small companies with a strong foundation in strategic planning and the marketing process are the giants of tomorrow, especially in the technology growth fields. This can be shown by such cases as Nortel, Apple and Wal-Mart and their different approaches and the results that followed.

Chapter Objectives

1.   Explain company-wide strategic planning and its four steps.
2.   Discuss how to design business portfolios and growth strategies.
3.   Explain functional planning strategies and assess marketing's role in strategic planning.
4.   Describe the business process and the forces that influence it.
5.   List the marketing management functions, including the elements of a marketing plan.

Chapter Topics

Strategic Planning
- Defining the Company Mission
- Setting Company Objectives and Goals

Designing the Business Portfolio
- Analyzing the Current Business Portfolio
  - The Boston Consulting Group Approach
  - The General Electric Approach
- Developing Growth Strategies
- Planning Functional Strategies
- Strategic Planning and Small Business

The Marketing Process
- Target Consumers
  - Market Segmentation
  - Market Targeting
  - Market Positioning
- Marketing Strategies for Competitive Advantage
- Developing the Marketing Mix

Managing the Marketing Effort
- Marketing Analysis
- Marketing Planning
- Marketing Implementation
- Customer Relationship Marketing
- Marketing Department Organization
- Marketing Control
- The Marketing Environment

Chapter Summary

1. The strategic planning process and the four steps of strategic planning.

Strategic planning is defined as the process of developing and maintaining a strategic fit between the organization's goals and capabilities and its changing marketing opportunities.

The four steps in the strategic planning process include
1. Defining the company mission;
2. Setting company objectives and goals;
3. Designing the business portfolio;
4. Planning marketing and other related strategies.

2. Comparing and contrasting the BCG and GE portfolio matrix models and their limitations.

The BCG consists of Stars, high-growth high-share; Cows, low-growth high-share; Questions Marks, low-share high-growth; and Dogs, low-share low-growth. Strategies include build, hold, harvest, or divest. The GE Planning Grid consists of two dimensions: industry attractiveness and business strength. Dimensions are an index rather than a single measure. BCG may rely too much on market share while GE Grid may rely too much on formal planning.

3. The marketing management process and the forces that influence it.

The marketing management process involves helping each business unit of the company reach its strategic objectives in relation to creating value for target consumers while fulfilling company goals. Factors influencing the process are target consumers (central), marketing mix decisions, planning, implementation, analysis and control procedures, and micro and macro environmental forces.

4.   The sections of the marketing plan, their strategic function and what each section contains.

Marketing plans should have eight sections. The executive summary provides a brief overview of key points. Current marketing situation presents relevant background. Threats and opportunities identify factors affecting the product. Objectives and issues define share, profit, and sales goals. Marketing strategy presents the broad approach. Action programs specify how to proceed. Budgets give P/L estimates. Controls measure plan progress.

5.   The marketing implementation process and how companies implement, organize, and control their marketing efforts.

Marketing implementation turns strategies into plans and actions specifying who, where, when and how. It requires an action program, an organization structure, decision and reward systems, human resources planning, and fit with the company culture. Controls must provide objective feedback measures for all these areas.

Key Terms

Business Portfolio	(pg. 56)	Market Targeting	(pg. 74)
Business Unit Strategy	(pg. 50)	Marketing Audit	(pg. 82)
Corporate Strategic Planning	(pg. 49)	Marketing Control	(pg. 82)
Cost Leadership	(pg. 62)	Marketing Implementation	(pg. 79)
Customer Intimacy	(pg. 63)	Marketing Process	(pg. 72)
Differentiation	(pg. 62)	Marketing Mix	(pg. 72)
Diversification	(pg. 60)	Marketing Strategy	(pg. 50)
Focus	(pg. 62)	Mission Statement	(pg. 53)
Functional Strategy	(pg. 50)	Operational Excellence	(pg. 63)
Growth-share Matrix	(pg. 56)	Portfolio Analysis	(pg. 56)
Market Development	(pg. 60)	Product Development	(pg. 60)
Market Penetration	(pg. 60)	Product Leadership	(pg. 63)
Market Positioning	(pg. 74)	Strategic Business Unit (SBU)	(pg. 49)
Market Segmentation	(pg. 74)	Strategic Planning	(pg. 49)

Multiple Choice Questions

2-1   Multiple

Strategic planning is useful to all organizations because it:

1.   Encourages management to think systematically
2.   Forces management to sharpen its objectives and policies
3.   Helps with performance standards for control
4.   Helps the company to anticipate and respond quickly to environmental changes
5.   All of the above

2-2   Multiple

A clear _____ acts as an invisible hand that guides people in the organization so that they can work independently and yet collectively toward overall organizational goals.

1.   Company objective
2.   Company goal
3.   Mission statement
4.   Business portfolio
5.   Vision

2-3   Multiple

Mission statements should be:

1.   Specific, realistic, motivating
2.   Specific, realistic, simplistic
3.   Realistic, motivating, simplistic
4.   Motivating, simplistic, specific
5.   None of the above

2-4   Multiple

Which of the following is a good objective for a company?

1.   Increase our market share
2.   Increase our market share by 15% over the next 2 years
3.   Increase our market share by 15%
4.   Increase our market share over the next 2 years
5.   Increase our market share indefinitely over the next 2 years

2-5   Multiple

André owns a fishing, tackle and grocery store. Sales in the fishing equipment have been booming, however, the grocery merchandise is not moving and there is substantial waste. He decides to drop the grocery products to concentrate on the fishing and tackle trade. André has used _____ to make this decision.

1.   Strategic business unit
2.   Business portfolio
3.   Portfolio analysis
4.   Strategic business planning
5.   Clarification of company goals and objectives

2-6   Multiple

Procter & Gamble is a large multinational organization specializing in many different products. As can be expected it is comprised of many different strategic business units (SBU). Which of the following would qualify as a SBU?

1.   Beauty products division
2.   Bounty towels
3.   South American division
4.   1 and 3
5.   All of the above

2-7   Multiple

The major activity in strategic planning is business portfolio_____.

1.   Marketing
2.   Cash cows
3.   Product development
4.   Analysis
5.   Dogs

2-8   Multiple

Which of the following is NOT a problem with matrix approaches to strategic planning?

1.   They provide little direction with respect to future planning
2.   They can be time consuming
3.   They can be costly to implement
4.   They can be misleading with respect to consumer value
5.   They can be difficult to define

2-9   Multiple

Reebok is developing many new products for different segments of the market. They have especially designed a new marketing campaign for seniors and children. Which quadrant of the product/market expansion grid are they focusing on?

1.   Market penetration
2.   Market development
3.   Product development
4.   Product expansion
5.   Diversification

2-10   Multiple

Eltron Electonics is a successful new company specializing in only 4 electronic components for a major supply house. Their research and development is their future. They should be focusing on:

1.   Relationship marketing
2.   Developing a matrix approach
3.   Considering new products for the future
4.   Market segmentation
5.   Market segment

2-11   Multiple

In the past 3 years, the city of Winnipeg has been flooded with new bagel stores opening up on every corner. These new stores are following the _____ approach to a marketing strategy.

1.   Market-follower
2.   Market-leader
3.   Market-nicher
4.   Market-challenger
5.   Market-penetrator

2-12   Multiple

Through _____, the company turns the strategic and marketing plan into actions that will achieve the company's strategic objectives.

1.   Analysis
2.   Implementation
3.   Planning
4.   Control
5.   Managing

2-13   Multiple

Competitive strategy depends on a company's

1.   Research
2.   Position in an industry
3.   Adopting more than one mission statement
4.   Size
5.   Market management

2-14   Multiple

Typically, answers to the questions, "Who is our customer?" "What is our business?" and
"What should our business be?" are found in which of the following?

1.   The product concept
2.   The company mission statement
3.   The company goals and objectives
4.   The organizational culture
5.   The personnel manual

2-15   Multiple

The components of successful strategies for Strategic Business Units are:

1.   Market size and growth rate
2.   Differentiation, cost leadership and focus
3.   Strategy and growth potential
4.   Relative market share
5.   Globalization

2-16   Multiple

All the following statements about formal portfolio planning tools are true except:

1.   It is sometimes difficult to measure market share and market growth
2.   Portfolio approaches classify current businesses not future ones
3.   Portfolio approaches alleviate the need for managers to use their judgement in
      determining what resources to give each SBU
4.   Formal planning approaches can lead management to place too much emphasis on
      market-share
5.   None of the above

2-17   Multiple

In terms of business functions, the marketing department seeks to take the consumer's point of view. But this can create conflicts with other departments. Problems marketing creates for other departments include:

1.   Increased production costs
2.   Disrupted production schedules
3.   Increased inventories
4.   1 and 2
5.   All of the above

2-18   Multiple

To successfully communicate and deliver the company's desired position to the consumer, the company:

1.   Must emphasize advertising in support of its positioning strategy
2.   Must focus its promotional efforts on personal selling
3.   Must place its greatest efforts on producing the desired product efficiently
4.   Must focus the entire marketing program in support of the chosen positioning strategy
5.   Must split the focus between the personal selling and product efficiency

2-19   Multiple

Growth of companies depends on Customer Relationship Marketing, an example of:

1.   Maintaining and enhancing relationships with existing clientele
2.   Representing the seller's view of the marketing tools used to influence buyers, not the view of the consumers
3.   Designing new products for new markets
4.   Establishing profits
5.   Being able to adapt to different geographic regions

2-20   Multiple

When you are starting a small business or you currently own a small business, all the following situations can be remedied or even prevented by developing and actually implementing a sound strategic plan except:

1.   You have taken on too much debt
2.   Your growth is exceeding your production capacity
3.   Your engineering design is not stable and does not meet industry standards
4.   You are losing market share to a competitor with a lower price
5.   All of the above can be solved with a proper strategic plan

2-21   Multiple

Which of the following is not considered a step in the process by which small firms create their strategic plans?

1.   Identify the major elements of the business environment
2.   Purchase all necessary resources in order to compete successfully
3.   Describe the mission of the organization in terms of its nature and function
4.   Develop a set of long-term objectives that will identify what the organization will become in the future
5.   Identify the major driving force that will direct the organization in the future

2-22   Multiple

In a solid marketing plan, all the following areas are covered in the current market situation except:

1.   Information about the market
2.   A product review
3.   A review of the competition
4.   A review of the distribution
5.   All of the above are covered

2-23   Multiple

Ideally the best company mission statements will be:

1.   Product-oriented
2.   Production-oriented
3.   Market-oriented
4.   Employee-oriented
5.   Company-oriented

2-24   Multiple

In setting marketing objectives to reach goals, which of the following is true?

1.   Increasing sales is a better strategy than increasing profits
2.   Marketing strategies must be developed to support marketing objectives
3.   Increasing profits is best achieved by reducing costs
4.   Increasing profits is a better strategy than increasing sales
5.   Customer satisfaction, not sales or profits, is the priority

2-25   Multiple

Under the BCG growth-share matrix, the market growth rate provides:

1.   A measure of market attractiveness
2.   A measure of the company's strength in the market
3.   The primary information for investment/divestiture decisions
4.   A measure of profitability for all products
5.   None of the above

2-26   Multiple

Heinz has decided their new hot dog sauce division has not been performing well and is using too many resources. They decide to phase this SBU out and use the resources to develop a new product. This move would be considered a _____ strategy.

1.   Build
2.   Harvest
3.   Hold
4.   Divest
5.   Product

2-27   Multiple

The General Electric strategic business-planning grid evaluates business on the basis of:

1.   Macro and micro environmental factors
2.   Market share and growth ratings
3.   Industry attractiveness and business strength
4.   Profit margins and demographic trends
5.   Tangible and intangible products

2-28   Multiple

Nike has just introduced into the market its first ever orthopedic sandal for seniors and people with arthritis. This situation is considered:

1.   Product development
2.   Market penetration
3.   Market development
4.   Diversification
5.   None of the above

2-29   Multiple

Nike has decided to bring back the "flip-flop" sandal. They will cater their advertising to seniors, as this is a comfortable shoe that is easy to put on. This situation is considered:

1.   Product development
2.   Market penetration
3.   Market development
4.   Diversification
5.   None of the above

2-30   Multiple

Levi's realizes they have very different markets with very different needs, characteristics and behaviours. The process of dividing up the different markets is referred to as:

1.   Demand forecasting
2.   Market segmentation
3.   Market targeting
4.   Market positioning
5.   Market segments

True/False Questions

2-1   True/False

Strategic planning is not useful at all in a fast changing environment.

2-2   True/False

Because long-range plans extend many years into the future, they only need to be revised every 3 years.

2-3   True/False

No matter how small a business is, time should be invested in strategic planning.

2-4   True/False

Mission statements are best when guided by an almost impossible dream.

2-5   True/False

The purpose of strategic planning is to identify ways in which the company can best use its strengths to take advantage of attractive opportunities in the environment.

2-6   True/False

Market penetration, market development, product development and market expansion are the four different quadrants in the product/market expansion grid.

2-7   True/False

The Boston Consulting Group classifies all its products according to growth share.

2-8   True/False

Marketing has the main responsibility of achieving profitable growth for a company.

2-9   True/False

Designing competitive marketing strategies begins with a thorough competitor analysis.

2-10   True/False

The marketing mix consists of product, place, performance, and promotion.

2-11   True/False

Marketers must continually plan their analysis, implementation and control activities.

2-12   True/False

Successful marketing implementation depends on how well the company blends the five elements—action programs, organization and structure, total quality management, company culture, and the pay scale.

2-13   True/False

Building strategies are based on environmental and political concerns.

2-14   True/False

Diversification often involves buying new businesses unrelated to the company's current products and markets.

2-15   True/False

The company's mission needs to be turned into detailed supporting objectives for only the top level of management.

2-16   True/False

The BCG growth-share matrix plots relative market share to industry attractiveness.

2-17   True/False

Whereas most small ventures start out with extensive business and marketing plans used to attract potential investors, strategic planning often falls by the wayside once the business gets going.

2-18   True/False

Advertising refers to the activities surrounding the communication of a company's offer and its efforts to persuade target customers to buy.

2-19   True/False

Customer intimacy provides customers with a constant flow of reduced prices on products.

2-20   True/False

Hiring a consultant is an element of a successful implementation program.

Applying Terms and Concepts

To determine how well you understand the materials in this chapter, read each of the following brief cases and then respond to the questions that follow. Answers are given at the end of this chapter.

Case #1   Cyberdesk

The Cyberdesk is an ergonomic, stylish computer desk created to fill deficiencies in the marketplace for computer furnishings. The market for computer desks, like the rest of the home computer industry, is growing rapidly as the PC becomes a part of people's everyday lives. Currently, products offered by established furniture manufacturers leave a great deal of room for improvement regarding features and style. Through superior design, Cyberdesk seeks to penetrate the growing computer furnishings market.

Cyberdesk will be structured in the form of a "virtual company," under which it will perform the functions of design, distribution, and sales, while outsourcing production to an independent manufacturer. The production process will flow through a "pull-system," whereby manufacturers will commence production based upon Cyberdesk receiving a confirmed customer order. Upon completion of production, the product will be shipped directly to the customer. This system minimizes working capital requirements by minimizing investment in inventory, and by allowing a framework by which purchases from manufacturers can be financed—namely by securing financing with receivables.

Through strong cooperation with suppliers, sound working capital management policies, and intense sales efforts, Cyberdesk will be able to effectively compete in the marketplace and achieve high profitability.

Cyberdesk will require a little in the way of overhead and capital investment, and will be funded initially through $50,000 in equity from the four founders and a $50,000 loan from the Business Development Corporation. Due to the nature of the organization, with its low initial investment and overhead requirements, all sales over a marginal break-even point (1,500 units in year 1) contribute directly to profit and strong returns.

The Cyberdesk will offer superior features, quality, ergonomics and style to those who place value on these qualities. Thus, Cyberdesk's marketing effort will target home and small office users, professionals, and enthusiasts. This will be accomplished by achieving floor space with high-end furniture and computer retailers. As well, an Internet home page and advertisements in appropriate personal computer magazines will be utilized to generate sales and product awareness. Subsequent sales efforts will seek to penetrate the market by focusing on national office furniture retailers in Canada and the United States, and by pursuing opportunities to design customized desks for computer manufacturers.

1. What do you believe would be a good mission statement for this company?

    _____

    _____

    _____

    _____

2. Which developing growth strategy is Cyberdesk using? Do you believe that it is the appropriate one?

    _____

    _____

    _____

    _____

3. What are the 2 different segments that Cyberdesk is trying to attract? Are they different?

    _____

    _____

    _____

    _____

4.   List some of the places where Cyberdesk should display and sell their product.

_____

_____

_____

_____

5.   What do you believe could be some barriers for Cyberdesk to enter this new market?

_____

_____

_____

_____

Case #2   Atlas Drugs

Atlas Drugs is a drug manufacturer supplying drugs to wholesalers for resale to institutions. For the past ten years sales have steadily grown but they have now hit a wall and the decision to expand into the United States has been made. Established contacts and the research they have produced seem to give positive indications to potential sales. Their plans for growth include getting into the consumer market and entering institutional sales in the United States. Management seems to be their biggest stumbling block with little expertise in expansion. As growth becomes evident management will be faced with a number of questions. Proper planning and a strong strategic plan will lead to them being a major competitor in this new market.

1.   What types of organizational problems would you expect this firm to encounter as a result of utilizing a functional approach in its marketing?

_____

_____

_____

_____

2.   Briefly evaluate each of the following organizational formats in light of the firm's product/market situation and likely requirements.

A.   Geographic Organization

_____

_____

_____

B. Product Management Organization

_____

_____

_____

_____

C. Market Management Organization

_____

_____

_____

_____

D. Product/Market Management Organization

_____

_____

_____

_____

3. On the basis of the analysis above, which organizational format would you recommend?

_____

_____

_____

_____

Case #3   Don Seville Rum

In 1859, Don Jorge Seville began distilling and selling rum in Kingston, Jamaica. Initially, the townspeople carried his rum away in pails and tubs. Later, when Don Jorge began to bottle the rum, he had the labels marked with the likeness of a seagull, to assist illiterates in identifying his brand.

The seagull is still on each bottle of Don Seville Rum, and the company is now run by descendants of Don Jorge. The rum's secret formula hasn't changed, but just about everything else about the company has. Seville is now a worldwide operation with sugar cane plantations in Jamaica and bottling plants in Puerto Rico and Martinique, ocean-going cargo ships based in Trinidad, office buildings, warehouses and advertising agencies in Mexico and the USA, and a trucking firm in Spain. While most operations were somehow originally connected with the production and distribution of the rum, others, such as the development of a 124-acre luxury resort on the island of Antigua, are totally unrelated. The 11 semi-autonomous firms making up the Seville empire have sales estimated at $1 billion.

Don Seville is the world's largest selling rum, with an estimated 60 percent of the market. In the United States, Don Seville accounts for 75 percent of total rum sales. Although impressive, Miguel Serrales, a great-great-grandson of the founder, has found the sales and profitability figures to be disappointing. While hard liquor sales in the USA decreased by 4.5 percent in recent years, rum sales increased by 2.3 percent. In view of this trend, Serrales had hoped that sales and profitability would have been higher. However, Serrales noted that increased competition from two firms, who promote their product as premium rums, has recently begun to erode Don Seville's sales.

After considerable study, Serrales ordered the development and ultimate distribution of Caribe as Seville's own entry into the premium rum market.

Caribe will sell for $3 more per bottle than Don Seville. Projected sales this year are for 85,000 cases of Caribe and 7.6 million cases of Don Seville.

In 1978, Seville engaged in a promotional campaign designed to increase the public's awareness of rum. It was at this time that a change was taking place in American drinking habits. Drinkers switched from heavier whiskeys to lighter spirits such as rum. By 1990, rum accounted for 9.2 percent of the distilled spirits consumed in the USA, compared to 2.1 percent twelve years earlier. It was during this period of time that sales of Don Seville rum increased dramatically.

1. The symbol of a seagull, which appears on each bottle of Don Seville rum, is an example of a brand. The brand should be considered part of which element of the marketing mix?
   A. product
   B. promotion
   C. place
   D. price
   E. both (A) and (B)

2. The development of the luxury resort by Seville on the island of Antigua is an example of:
   A. market development.
   B. product development.
   C. market penetration.
   D. diversification.
   E. both (A) and (C)

3.   When Seville introduced Caribe rum to compete in the premium market, it was engaged in:
       A.   market penetration.
       B.   market development.
       C.   product development.
       D.   diversification.
       E.   none of the above

4.   The various businesses making up the Seville organization are known as its:
       A.   business portfolio.
       B.   strategic plan.
       C.   company mission.
       D.   marketing concept.
       E.   marketing mix.

5.   Using the Boston Consulting Group approach to portfolio analysis, Don Seville Rum would be considered a:
       A.   star.
       B.   cash cow.
       C.   question mark.
       D.   dog.
       E.   none of the above

Case #4   Barth Enterprises

William Barth started Barth Chevrolet in 1974 after having worked as a sales manager for two other dealerships. He had a simple philosophy of meeting his customers personal transportation needs at a fair price. Barth Chevrolet was a success, so much so that he eventually opened dealerships which cover General Motors full range of automobiles and pick-up trucks. Barth opened a Pontiac/Buick/GMC dealership in 1978 and an Oldsmobile/Cadillac dealership in 1984. Barth's latest dealership was a Saturn franchise opened in 1992. Each dealership sells new and used automobiles, vans, pick-up trucks and sport utility vehicles. Lease and rental programs are available for customers who do not wish to purchase vehicles outright.

Also part of the Barth Transportation Network is a Honda Motorcycle and all-terrain vehicle (ATV) centre opened in 1991. With the exception of the motorcycle shop, now run by Barth's 28 year old son—a motorcycle enthusiast and main impetus for the shop—Barth engaged in careful and extensive research to identify customer needs, wants and demands and their relative satisfaction with existing dealerships. Research in each case indicated considerable consumer dissatisfaction with existing dealerships. This led Barth to start the Chevrolet and Saturn dealerships from scratch, but he acquired the other dealerships by buying out the previous owner. Barth pioneered the now-common practice of free shuttle service for service customers, and offered a free loaner if the work took more than one full day and a service department open from 7 a.m. to 9 p.m. on weekdays and to 5 p.m. on Saturdays. Additionally, each dealership has a fully stocked parts department for the do-it-yourself and local service stations.

Sales at each dealership have increased steadily despite the periodic downturns in the automotive industry. Barth attributes this success to his philosophy of treating customers fairly and to a pricing strategy of selling vehicles for an average of 10% over invoice. Sales per dealership have averaged 2,000 vehicles per year as opposed to the industry average of 975. Profitability has averaged 18% before taxes. Barth sets realistic quotas for each dealership and then allows his dealership managers considerable flexibility in achieving the goal. A liberal profit-sharing plan and autonomous dealership management have resulted in a successful organization controlling 46% of the local market.

The motorcycle franchise, however, is not as successful as the auto dealerships. Although it is marginally profitable, the operation experienced only a 2% increase in sales last year, while the market expanded by 12%. The shop currently controls less than 10% of the local market.

1.   Using portfolio analysis, characterize and evaluate each of the following: motorcycle/ATV dealership

_____

_____

_____

auto dealership

_____

_____

_____

_____

2.   Comment on Barth's strategic planning related to the automotive dealerships.

_____

_____

_____

_____

Multiple Choice Answers

1.   Correct Answer: 5   Reference: pg. 49

2.   Correct Answer: 3   Reference: pg. 53

3.   Correct Answer: 1   Reference: pg. 53

4.   Correct Answer: 2   Reference: pg. 74

5.   Correct Answer: 3   Reference: pg. 56

6.   Correct Answer: 5   Reference: pg. 49

7.   Correct Answer: 4   Reference: pg. 56

8.   Correct Answer: 4   Reference: pg. 58

9.   Correct Answer: 1   Reference: pg. 60

10.   Correct Answer: 3   Reference: pg. 58

11.   Correct Answer: 1   Reference: pg. 54

12.   Correct Answer: 2   Reference: pg. 79

13.   Correct Answer: 2   Reference: pg. 61

14.   Correct Answer: 2   Reference: pg. 53

15.   Correct Answer: 2   Reference: pg. 62

16.   Correct Answer: 3   Reference: pg. 56

17.   Correct Answer: 5   Reference: pg. 61

18.   Correct Answer: 4   Reference: pg. 74

19.   Correct Answer: 1   Reference: pg. 64

20.   Correct Answer: 3   Reference: pg. 62

21.   Correct Answer: 2   Reference: pg. 49

22.   Correct Answer: 5   Reference: pg. 72

23.   Correct Answer: 3   Reference: pg. 53

24.	Correct Answer:	2	Reference:	pg. 50
25.	Correct Answer:	1	Reference:	pg. 56
26.	Correct Answer:	4	Reference:	pg. 56
27.	Correct Answer:	3	Reference:	pg. 49
28.	Correct Answer:	1	Reference:	pg. 60
29.	Correct Answer:	3	Reference:	pg. 60
30.	Correct Answer:	2	Reference:	pg. 74

True/False Answers

1.	FALSE	Reference:	pg. 49	Topic:	Strategic Planning
2.	FALSE	Reference:	pg. 49	Topic:	Strategic Planning
3.	TRUE	Reference:	pg. 53	Topic:	Defining the Company Mission
4.	TRUE	Reference:	pg. 53	Topic:	Defining the Company Mission
5.	TRUE	Reference:	pg. 56	Topic:	Analyzing the Current Business Portfolio
6.	FALSE	Reference:	pg. 56	Topic:	Developing Growth Strategies
7.	TRUE	Reference:	pg. 56	Topic:	Business Portfolio Planning
8.	TRUE	Reference:	pg. 58	Topic:	Developing Growth
9.	TRUE	Reference:	pg. 50	Topic:	Marketing Strategies for Competitive Advantage
10.	FALSE	Reference:	pg. 72	Topic:	Developing the Marketing Mix
11.	TRUE	Reference:	pg. 77	Topic:	Managing the Marketing Effort

12. FALSE	Reference:	pg. 79	Topic: Marketing Implementation
13 FALSE	Reference:	pg. 60	Topic: Business Strategy
14. TRUE	Reference:	pg. 56	Topic: Developing Growth Strategies
15. FALSE	Reference:	pg. 84	Topic: Setting Company Objectives and Goals
16. FALSE	Reference:	pg. 56	Topic: The Boston Consulting Group
17. TRUE	Reference:	pg. 49	Topic: Strategic Planning and Small Business
18. FALSE	Reference:	pg. 72	Topic: Developing the Marketing Mix
19. TRUE	Reference:	pg. 63	Topic: Customer Intimacy
20. FALSE	Reference:	pg. 50	Topic: Strategic Business Units

Applying Terms and Concepts Answers

Case #1   Cyberdesk

Question #1
- To continually design and distribute functional, ergonomic, stylish computer desks that meet the needs and desires of home and office computer users.

Question #2
- Product development
- They are offering a new or modified product to current market segments. There is no company that specializes in computer desks; therefore they are fulfilling a need.
- This is a new company with very little capital and exposure, therefore they must focus on their product in order to make a name for themselves and become profitable. This is the best strategy for that.

Question #3
- The two different target markets are enthusiastic professionals and home and small office computer users.
- They are different because the home computer markets want a functional affordable desk that will meet their needs; the professionals, however, will probably be looking to spend a little more money and they will be wanting more amenities than the first group.

Question #4
- Office Supply Stores
- Computers Stores
- Home Furnishing Stores
- Home Depot and Revy Stores
- Over the Internet
- Trade and Computer Magazines

Question #5
- Economies of scale
- Intense competition for retail space
- Large capital investment required to enter the manufacturing industry
- Establishing distribution channels
- Many competitors

Case #2   Atlas Drugs

Question #1
- They have probably experienced inadequate planning for specific products and/or markets
- Some of the products have been stressed while others have been neglected
- Functional rivals may inhibit coordination efforts

Question #2
A.   Geographic
- Generally used by a firm selling national products
- On-line is not affected by geographic lines and to become a national company may be too expensive right now

B.   Product Management
- Used by firms producing and selling a variety of products and brands
- Usually used by another layer of management to correct any shortcomings of another management team

C.   Market Management
- Used by firms that sell a line of products to a diverse set of markets
- Good when customers fall into groups with distinct buying patters or product preferences

D.   Product/Market Management
- Large companies that produce many different products for many different people in many different areas
- Assures each function receives its share of management attention
- Can be costly and reduce management flexibility

Case #3   Don Seville Rum

1.   A

2.   D

3.   C

4.   A

5.   A

Case #4   Barth Enterprises

1.   The motorcycle/ATV dealership should be classified as a dog. It is a low growth, low market share business. It is marginally profitable and does not hold much promise to be a great source of cash.

Barth needs to determine what role the dealership should play in his business portfolio. Divesting himself of it may make sense from a financial standpoint. However, there may be other considerations such as family interests, which might lead Barth to allow it to remain.

The auto dealerships appear to be cash cows. The overall market is not expanding greatly. However, Barth controls a substantial share of the market. The dealerships produce a significant cash flow as indicated by the 18% profit margin. Barth may decide to build on his market share by investing even further in the industry. This may be achieved by acquiring additional dealerships and marketing program vehicles and/or by consolidating his operations into the now-popular auto superstore.

2.   Barth has adopted the marketing concept where customer interests determine (or at least influence) company plans. His product and service offerings as well as his growth and profitability can be attributed to philosophy or customer sovereignty and mutual gain.

Chapter 3

The Global Marketing Environment

Chapter Overview

Companies must constantly watch and adapt to the marketing environment in order to seek opportunities and ward off threats. The marketing environment comprises all the actors and forces influencing the company's ability to transact business effectively with its target markets. Companies are constrained by micro and macro forces, from suppliers to governments. Environmental forces change our lives daily, be it the news, the invention of new products, or corporate takeovers. Both consumers and businesses affect one another and in turn the marketing environment is affected by the world and the speed in which we live and the decisions we make to meet these daily changes.

Chapter Objectives

1. Describe the environmental forces that affect the company's ability to serve its customers.
2. Explain how changes in the demographic and economic environments affect marketing decisions.
3. Identify the major trends in the firm's natural and technological environments.
4. Explain the key changes in the political, ethical and cultural environments.
5. Know how to react to a changing marketing environment.

Chapter Topics

The Company's Microenvironment
- The Company
- Suppliers
- Marketing Intermediaries
- Customers
- Competitors
- Publics

The Company's Macroenvironment
- Demographic Environment
  - Changing Age Structure of the Canadian Population
  - The Changing Family
  - Geographic Shifts in Population

- A Better-Educated and More White-Collar Population
- Increasing Diversity
- Economic Environment
  - Changes in Income
  - Paradoxes of the New Economy
  - Changing Consumer Spending Patterns
- Natural Environment
  - Shortages of Raw Materials and Increased Pollution
- Technological Environment
  - Fast Pace of Technological Change
  - High R&D Budgets
- Political Environment
  - Legislation Regulating Business
- Cultural Environment
  - Persistence of Cultural Values
  - Shifts in Secondary Cultural Values

Responding to the Marketing Environment
- Changing Age Structure
- Changing Canadian Households
- Population Growth and Structure

Chapter Summary

1.   The environmental forces that affect the company's ability to serve its customers.

Companies are constrained by micro and macro environmental forces. Micro-environmental forces include company departments, suppliers, marketing intermediaries, customers, competitors, and various publics. Macroenvironmental forces include demographics, as well as economic, natural, technological, political, and cultural forces.

2.   The effect of changes in the demographic and economic environments on marketing management decisions affect a company's growth and international expansion.

Changes in the demographic environment that affect marketing decisions are the changing age structure of the Canadian population, the changing Canadian family, geographic shifts in population, a better-educated and more white-collar workforce, and increasing ethnic and racial diversity. Economic trends include changes in income and income distribution, and changes in consumer spending patterns. As Canada's major cities expand geographically and culturally new demands will be placed on marketers. Environment and ethics will be the driving factor of this century's growth mixed in with the changes of technology. The successful marketers will be diversified if they are to be prosperous.

3.	The major trends in the firm's natural and technological environments.

Trends in the natural environment include shortages of raw materials, increased cost of energy, increased pollution, and government intervention in natural resource management. Trends in the technological environment include the fast pace of technological change, high R & D budgets, concentration on minor improvements, increased regulation by government agencies, and meeting requirements for product differentation around the world because of different government regulations for each country.

4.	The key changes that occur in the political and cultural environments.

Changes in the political environment include legislation-regulating business, changing government agency enforcement, and the growth of public responsible actions. Changes in the cultural environment include the persistence of cultural values, shifts in secondary cultural values, and people's views of themselves, others, organizations, society, nature and the universe. As we continue to become more astute in the use of our resources more and more civilian pressure will come to bear on companies and what they produce and the by-products of their production.

5.	The significance of cultural values to marketers.

Marketers should remain alert to shifting cultural values in order to spot developing threats of opportunities and to help ensure that their marketing strategies reflect the relevant culture's values. Cultural values may be reflected in the political-legal environment and in the competitive environment. Firms that engage in international marketing may have to learn how to deal with completely different cultures. Ethical issues and production legislation is a new field for marketers to be involved in as laws and governments and culture put their own demand on products and their sources.

Key Terms

Baby boom	(pg. 109)	Marketing environment	(pg. 100)
Cultural environment	(pg. 130)	Marketing intermediaries	(pg. 101)
Demography	(pg. 107)	Microenvironment	(pg. 100)
Economic environment	(pg. 119)	Natural environment	(pg. 125)
Engel's laws	(pg. 93)	Political environment	(pg. 127)
Environmental mgmt perspective	(pg. 135)	Public	(pg. 105)
Macroenvironment	(pg. 100)	Technological environment	(pg. 126)

Multiple Choice Questions

3-1   Multiple

A very large towel supplier for Wal-Mart has just burned down; they have outstanding orders to fill, however, and Wal-Mart must find another supplier to fill them. This situation affects which of the following environments for Wal-Mart?

1.   Marketing environment
2.   Microenvironment
3.   Macroenvironment
4.   Customer environment
5.   Competitor environment

3-2   Multiple

Which of the following is not a marketing intermediary?

1.   Resellers
2.   Physical distribution firms
3.   Marketing services agencies
4.   Financial intermediaries
5.   Internet providers

3-3   Multiple

This group's image of the company really affects a company's buying patterns and behaviours.

1.   Financial publics
2.   Citizen action publics
3.   General public
4.   Government publics
5.   Internal publics

3-4   Multiple

The single most important demographic trend in Canada is:

1.   The changing age structure of the population
2.   The increasing amount of urban dwellers
3.   The increasing amount of immigration in the last few years
4.   The increasing amount of women in the workforce
5.   The increasing amount of divorces in the country

3-5   Multiple

Hong Kong is known as a(n) _____ and China is known as a(n) _____.

1.   economic environment, agricultural environment
2.   subsistence economy, self-sustaining economy
3.   industrial economy, self-sustaining economy
4.   industrial economy, subsistence economy
5.   first world economy, second world economy

3-6   Multiple

In the early 1990s Canada was faced with a recession. The carefree spending days of the late 80s were non-existent, as people became very conscious of how they spent their money. Marketers had to change the focus of their advertising to:

1.   Price sensitive marketing
2.   Value marketing
3.   Quality marketing
4.   Performance marketing
5.   Prestige marketing

3-7   Multiple

Ernst Engel studied how people shifted their spending as their incomes rose. Even though this research was done over a century ago, others have confirmed his findings. Which of the following is not a change in spending patterns despite an increase in income?

1.   Percentage spent on food declines
2.   Percentage spent on housing remains the same
3.   Percentage spent on savings increases
4.   Percentage spent on leisure activities increases
5.   Percentage spent on food increases

3-8   Multiple

Which of the following is not considered a trend in the natural environment?

1.   Shortages of raw materials
2.   Increased cost of energy
3.   Increased pollution
4.   Government intervention in resource management
5.   All are considered a trend in the natural environment

3-9   Multiple

Business practices have been enacted for many reasons. Which of the following is not one of those reasons?

1.   To protect the economic interest of the government of Canada
2.   To protect companies from each other
3.   To protect the consumers from unfair business practices
4.   To protect the interests of society against unrestrained business behaviour
5.   All of the above are good, viable reasons

3-10   Multiple

The past decade marked a change in the way society defines success, with achievements such as a happy family life and service to one's community replacing money as the measure of worth. This statement is a belief about:

1.   People's views of themselves
2.   People's views of the universe
3.   People's views of others
4.   People's views of society
5.   People's views of nature

3-11   Multiple

The adoption and adherence to professional codes of ethics among businesses reflects which trend in the political environment?

1.   Legislation regulating business
2.   The persistence of cultural values
3.   Changing government agency enforcement of existing laws regulating business
4.   The increased emphasis on ethics and socially responsible actions
5.   Societal pressures to do so

3-12   Multiple

In most economies this is the largest single market.

1.   Industrial market
2.   Consumer market
3.   Reseller market
4.   Government market
5.   Retail market

3-13   Multiple

Shareholders would be considered part of which of the following?

1.   Internal public
2.   Local public
3.   Financial public
4.   Media public
5.   General public

3-14   Multiple

The set of laws and regulations that guide commerce and that limit business for the good of society as a whole is called:

1.   Public policy
2.   Consumer protection
3.   Public interest group action
4.   Social responsibility
5.   Legislation

3-15   Multiple

The marketing environment is comprised of which of the following factors?

1.   A company's ability to serve its customers
2.   How changes in economic/demographic environments affect changes
3.   The ability to identify trends
4.   Explain changes in political and cultural environments
5.   All of the above

3-16   Multiple

Vansco Electronics recently introduced a global positioning system for use in tractors so that agricultural producers know their location within 10 meters. The idea behind this innovation is to help producers apply fertilizer and other chemicals more efficiently. Vansco is involved in the:

1.   Demographic environment
2.   Economic environment
3.   Technological environment
4.   Natural environment
5.   Agricultural environment

3-17   Multiple

Bell Canada's monthly newsletter meets the needs of which of the following publics?

1.   Financial
2.   Media
3.   Citizen-action
4.   Internal
5.   General

3-18   Multiple

Which of the following offers the most potential for consumer growth?

1.   Mexico
2.   Japan
3.   Hong Kong
4.   China
5.   Canada

3-19   Multiple

Which of the following countries has the highest GNP per capita?

1.   Australia
2.   Japan
3.   Hong Kong
4.   Canada
5.   USA

3-20   Multiple

The Canadian province with the highest percentage increase in population from 1991–94 was:

1.   Ontario
2.   Quebec
3.   British Columbia
4.   Yukon & Northwest Territories
5.   Alberta

3-21   Multiple

Which of the following would not be classified as a regional difference with respect to product usage patterns?

1.   Newfoundlanders think they are the hardest working Canadians
2.   British Columbians express the greatest love for reading
3.   Quebecers are less likely to use no-name products
4.   Montrealers eat more deep brown beans than other Canadians
5.   All of the above would classify as regional differences

3-22   Multiple

Imperial Oil teamed with the Toronto Hospital for Sick Children to sponsor a campaign to reduce preventable children's accidents, which is the leading killer of children. This act is considered:

1.   Cause-related marketing
2.   Charitable donations
3.   Tax reduction incentive
4.   Good-will marketing
5.   None of the above

3-23   Multiple

What would be considered the third largest industry in Canada?

1.   Forestry
2.   Fishery
3.   Car manufacturing
4.   Agriculture
5.   None of the above

3-24   Multiple

Which of the following statements about the marketing environment is (are) true?

1.   The marketing environment offers the company opportunities
2.   The marketing environment contains threats to the company
3.   The marketing environment requires the company to conduct research and use intelligence systems to monitor changes
4.   1 and 2
5.   All of the above

3-25   Multiple

A new "Burger Heaven" wants to open up in rural Ontario. Before this can happen, the management must establish all the marketing intermediaries they will require. Which of the following is not considered one?

1.   Suppliers
2.   Physical distribution firms
3.   Financial intermediaries
4.   Marketing service firms
5.   All of the above are considered marketing intermediaries

3-26   Multiple

The Manitoba Steel Association (MSA) purchases old cars and metal parts from auto wrecking lots from across Canada. They melt this metal down and make steel to use in casing. MSA is an example of the:

1.   Consumer market
2.   Business market
3.   Industrial market
4.   Supplier market
5.   Reseller market

3-27   Multiple

Shifts in secondary cultural values, such as the belief you should get married at an early age, can be expressed through which of the following?

1.   People's views of themselves
2.   People's views of others
3.   People's views of organizations
4.   All of the above
5.   None of the above

3-28   Multiple

McDonalds's construction of "Ronald McDonald Houses" for families to stay in while their children are in the hospital shows support for which public?

1.   Media
2.   Citizen-action
3.   Local
4.   General
5.   Internal

3-29   Multiple

Canadian Tire uses many of its employees as models for their television and print ads. This type of tactic is used to appeal to which type of public?

1.   Local
2.   Internal
3.   General
4.   Citizen-action
5.   Media

3-30   Multiple

If we were to make up a village of 1,000 people who would represent the entire population of the world and its characteristics, which of the following would NOT be true?

1.   There would be 520 women and 480 men
2.   About 1/3 of our people would have access to clean, safe drinking water
3.   The woodlands would be decreasing rapidly and the wastelands would be increasing rapidly
4.   Only 500 of the 1,000 people would control 75% of the village's wealth
5.   All the above are true

True/False Questions

3-1   True/False

Demographics, economics, and natural, technological, political and cultural factors affect the marketing environment.

3-2   True/False

Top management is part of the company's internal environment and can be grouped in with all other functional areas of a company.

3-3   True/False

Reseller organizations frequently have enough power to dictate terms or even shut the manufacturer out of large markets.

3-4   True/False

Companies need not adapt to the needs of target consumers as long as sales are up.

3-5   True/False

Seniors value information in advertising materials and claims based on impulse.

3-6   True/False

The United Nations reported Toronto to be the world's most multicultural city.

3-7   True/False

Depending on the cost of luxury products, the upper class will vary their spending patterns.

3-8   True/False

Many companies are investing a large amount of their R & D budget on new innovations, to develop new technologies and products to be profitable in the future.

3-9   True/False

Even the most liberal advocates of free-market economies agree the system works best with at least some regulation.

3-10   True/False

Marketers, through good, effective advertisement, have a good chance of changing core beliefs and even a better chance of changing secondary beliefs.

3-11   True/False

Companies who hire lobbyists to influence legislation affecting their industries and stage media events to gain favourable press coverage are taking an environmental management perspective to their business.

3-12   True/False

Consumer organizations and environmental groups are considered part of the company's general public.

3-13   True/False

The "baby boom" refers to the growth in population that occurred between World War I and World War II.

3-14   True/False

An ethical market place is one of the strongest forces shaping the market place.

3-15   True/False

A growing population means growing human needs to satisfy which definitely means growing market opportunities.

3-16   True/False

Today, people in charge of new product development always consider the opinions of ethnic groups when developing their product concepts.

3-17   True/False

For decades, many analysts predicted advances in technology would create a leisure generation. Their predictions have come true as people do have more time on their hands to use for leisure.

3-18   True/False

Instead of opposing regulations, marketers should help develop solutions to the material and energy problems facing the world.

3-19   True/False

One of the major potential problems with cause-related marketing is charitable corporate donation support will shift towards visible, popular, and low-risk charities—those with more substantial market appeal.

3-20   True/False

Neighbourhood residents and community organizations belong to the general public.

Applying Terms and Concepts

To determine how well you understand the materials in this chapter, read each of the following brief cases and then respond to the questions that follow. Answers are given at the end of this chapter.

Case #1   Barnes Coal Company[1]

The Barnes Coal Company has been in operation since 1872 and is the second largest producer of anthracite coal within the United States. The majority of its holdings are in northeastern Pennsylvania with major production in the Williamsport, Scranton, and Hazleton areas. The bulk of Barnes's production is sold to out-of-state buyers and moves through the Philadelphia and Erie ports. The Lehigh Valley and Pennsylvania Central Railroads are the prime movers of the coal to these ports of entry.

This year Scott Barnes, President of Barnes Coal Company, fought passage of the state law, which required all mining companies in Pennsylvania to reclaim mine land. All land according to the bill must be covered with no less than six inches of topsoil, whether or not the topsoil was evident prior to mining. Enforcement of this law was to be by the Pennsylvania Soil and Water Conservation Commission.

Barnes attributed passage of the bill to pressure put on the state legislators in Harrisburg by the Pennsylvanian Beautification Society (PBS). The PBS is a private group interested in promoting tourism and preserving wildlife throughout the beautification and reforestation of Pennsylvania.

Barnes expects the price of coal to increase by 8% if the costs associated with compliance are passed onto buyers. Production would likely decrease as buyers shift their purchasing to mines from Ohio, Kentucky, Illinois and West Virginia.

1. The Lehigh Valley and Pennsylvania Central Railroads are examples of what type of marketing intermediaries? What is their responsibility?

_____

_____

_____

_____

2. What are the implications of coal being a non-renewable resource for Barnes Coal Company with respect to the marketing environment?

_____

_____

_____

_____

---

[1] *Principles of Marketing*, 3rd Edition, Kotler, Armstrong, Warren (Prentice Hall) – pg. 49.

3.   What type of public is the Pennsylvanian Beautification Society? How do they
      have their voices heard with respect to their issues?

      _____

      _____

      _____

      _____

4.   How can they best pay for this service? Should the consumers really pay for it?

      _____

      _____

      _____

      _____

5.   What would be the effect if the government fails to intervene or if the government
      does not enact legislation to protect society from unrestrained business behaviour?

      _____

      _____

      _____

      _____

Case #2   Borden Eagle Brand

Eagle Brand SCM was developed in the mid-1800s as a result of many babies dying from
drinking the milk of diseased cows. In response to this, Mr. Borden developed a process
to preserve milk that was patented in 1956.

Eagle Brand SCM was first sold as baby formula door-to-door on milk trucks. During the
Civil War, Eagle Brand provided troops with the much-needed supply of milk, and
during WWII, women started using this milk as a sweetener for their coffee as well as in
baking products. Now the Eagle Brand SCM is commonly used in many desserts.

Borden is one of the largest and most successful food marketers in the US. Sales
increased from $5 billion in 1986 to $7.2 billion in 1988. Borden, like any other
company, is fighting hard to compete in the very competitive market. The challenge with
this product is that Eagle Brand SCM is not consumed on its own, rather it is used to
make other products. For this reason, Borden has advertised its products in many
women's magazines. Often recipes for delicious desserts are seen in the ad with slogans
such as "Easy to make, hard to resist."

Unfortunately for Borden, the amount of "from-scratch" baking has decreased dramatically in the last few years. Also the turn to a healthy lifestyle has caused many people to cut out many of the delicious desserts which Eagle Brand SCM makes. There has also been intense competition from Carnation, which has introduced a very similar product.

These circumstances have caused Borden to conduct a review of the current product strategy for Eagle Brand SCM and to explore new strategies for it. The goal is to continue the brand as a major, profitable product in the portfolio of Borden products, In other words, the issue is how to increase sales of a product that may be maturing in the product life cycle and is facing new competition on a price basis.

1. How can consumer awareness of the product and its benefits be increased?

   _____
   _____
   _____
   _____

2. How can repeat use be increased and sustained?

   _____
   _____
   _____
   _____

3. What form and sources of information should be used?

   _____
   _____
   _____
   _____

4. What promotional tools and strategies will be most effective?

   _____
   _____
   _____
   _____

Case #3   The Anther's Drug Co.

Anthers Drug Co. has been in business internationally for the past twenty years with plants in four countries. Since the creation of their new tanning drug—SURE SUN—environmental groups and ethical organizations have been putting pressure on them, because of their research techniques involving animals, and charges have been laid in England linked to possible bribery charges. They now face both legal and ethical problems that will result in the loss of sales or closing of their British operation.

1.   The drug company is tied up in a(n) _____ and _____dilemma.
2.   Laws that protect morals as detailed in this case are part of the _____ environment.
3.   Because of the closing of the British plant corporate profits will be down; in this case this is part of the _____ environment.
4.   Seeing that workers are still investing heavily in Anthers is a _____ belief and not easily changed.

Case #4   Martin Marietta[2]

Martin Marietta—the company that was big in the aerospace and defence industries and which became even bigger after its merger with Lockheed—is also big into aggregate. That's rocks, gravel and sand to the uninitiated. What is one of the nation's largest defence and space contractors doing in the aggregate business? Making money!

The market for aggregate is enormous. The amount used each year equates to approximately nine tons per American citizen. That is 50 pounds of aggregate needed per person per day. And just as the demand for aggregate is likely to increase, so is the price.

Aggregate is used for roads, driveways, concrete foundations and cement blocks. It is used in roofing and gardens. It is a decorative material replacing lawns in desert communities and as walkways and borders around shrubs. It is used in poultry feed and as a scrubbing agent in coal fired power plants. The list of uses of sand, gravel and rock is almost endless.

Make no mistake, aggregate is not rare. In fact, it is found just about everywhere. What makes aggregate increasingly valuable is the lack of government permission to expand existing pits or to open new pits. As existing pits run low on reserves (supply) local state and federal permits to expand become difficult to obtain. Environmentalists, as well as local residents, have blocked hundreds of proposed pits and some are seeking to close existing pits. The blasting vibration, dust, noise, danger and damage to local roads as well as the general unsightliness of the pits make them unpopular.

---

[2] Sources: "Business is Boring: Some Companies Really Dig Aggregate," *Wall Street Journal*, March 1, 1995, M. Charles, p. 1.

People don't want gravel pits and mines in their neighbourhood. Therefore, aggregate has to be brought in by truck, by rail and even by ship to coastal communities. This adds significantly to the cost. So while the actual cost of the material is quite low at the mine, the delivered cost can be quite high. By one estimate the cost of aggregate doubles for every 30 miles it must be transported by truck.

It is difficult to obtain a permit and those firms that do receive them have virtually a monopoly in the immediate area. One pit in an area may be bad—two is decidedly worse. This plays into the hands of major producers who have the financial resources needed to ensure the years it may take to obtain the needed permits. After several recent acquisitions, Martin Marietta became the nation's second largest aggregate producer just behind Vulcan Materials Co. of Birmingham, Alabama.

1.   Identify the major elements in Martin Marietta's microenvironment and explain how they might impact the company.

_____

_____

_____

_____

2.   Identify the major elements in Martin Marietta's macroenvironment and explain how they might impact the company.

_____

_____

_____

_____

Multiple Choice Answers

1. Correct Answer: 2   Reference: pg.100
2. Correct Answer: 5   Reference: pg. 119
3. Correct Answer: 3   Reference: pg. 105
4. Correct Answer: 1   Reference: pg. 107
5. Correct Answer: 4   Reference: pg. 119
6. Correct Answer: 2   Reference: pg. 100
7. Correct Answer: 5   Reference: pg. 100
8. Correct Answer: 5   Reference: pg. 125
9. Correct Answer: 1   Reference: pg. 100
10. Correct Answer: 2   Reference: pg. 105
11. Correct Answer: 4   Reference: pg. 130
12. Correct Answer: 2   Reference: pg. 124
13. Correct Answer: 3   Reference: pg. 119
14. Correct Answer: 1   Reference: pg. 105
15. Correct Answer: 5   Reference: pg. 134
16. Correct Answer: 3   Reference: pg. 126
17. Correct Answer: 4   Reference: pg. 105
18. Correct Answer: 4   Reference: pg. 108
19. Correct Answer: 2   Reference: pg. 108 (Table 3-1)
20. Correct Answer: 4   Reference: pg. 110
21. Correct Answer: 5   Reference: pg. 130
22. Correct Answer: 1   Reference: pg. 130

23.	Correct Answer:	5	Reference:	pg. 119
24.	Correct Answer:	5	Reference:	pg. 100
25.	Correct Answer:	1	Reference:	pg. 119
26.	Correct Answer:	2	Reference:	pg. 101
27.	Correct Answer:	4	Reference:	pg. 131
28.	Correct Answer:	3	Reference:	pg. 131
29.	Correct Answer:	2	Reference:	pg. 106
30.	Correct Answer:	4	Reference:	pg. 108

True/False Answers

1.	FALSE	Reference:	pg. 98	Topic:	Chapter Introduction
2.	TRUE	Reference:	pg. 100	Topic:	Figure 3-1
3.	TRUE	Reference:	pg. 101	Topic:	Marketing Intermediaries
4.	FALSE	Reference:	pg 102	Topic:	Competitors
5.	FALSE	Reference:	pg. 110	Topic:	Changing Age Structure Of the Canadian Population
6.	TRUE	Reference:	pg.116	Topic:	Increasing Diversity
7.	FALSE	Reference:	pg.122	Topic:	Paradoxes of the New Economy
8.	FALSE	Reference:	pg. 122	Topic:	High R&D Budgets
9.	TRUE	Reference:	pg. 128	Topic:	Legislation Regulating Business
10.	FALSE	Reference:	pg. 131	Topic:	Persistence of Cultural Values
11.	TRUE	Reference:	pg. 135	Topic:	Responding to the Marketing Environment
12.	FALSE	Reference:	pg. 110	Topic:	Publics

13.	FALSE	Reference:	pg. 110	Topic:	Changing Age Structure of The Canadian Population
14.	TRUE	Reference:	pg. 126	Topic:	Technological Environment
15.	FALSE	Reference:	pg. 107	Topic:	Demographic Environment
16.	TRUE	Reference:	pg. 118	Topic:	Marketing Highlight 3-3
17.	FALSE	Reference:	pg. 122	Topic:	Paradoxes of the New Economy
18.	TRUE	Reference:	pg. 125	Topic:	Shortages of Raw Materials and Increased Pollution
19.	TRUE	Reference:	pg. 132	Topic:	Marketing Highlight 3-5
20.	FALSE	Reference:	pg. 105	Topic:	Publics

Applying Terms and Concept Answers

Case #1   Barnes Coal Company

Question #1
- They are considered physical distribution firms who are responsible to transport the manufacturer's product to the retailers or the customers

Question #2
- Because coal is a non-renewable resource, it is a sought-after product
- Marketing efforts are minimal as usually the demand exceeds the supply; therefore, consumers come to you looking for products, instead of you looking for consumers for your products

Question #3
- The PBS is a citizen action public
- They lobby the government and educate the public on different issues
- By lobbying the government and pressing them to pass legislation, they get their voices heard and their concerns are addressed
- They work because there is safety in numbers; the more voices that are heard, the better the chance of action

Question #4
- Barnes can fund this project in a number of different ways: dip into the company's savings, take out a bank loan, cut costs to be able to pay for it, or charge consumers more for the product

- Because it is a non-renewable resource, it would not be unheard of if the price of coal went up
- Consumers may switch suppliers for a while, but because demand exceeds supply, Barnes will not have to worry about selling their product

Question #5
- Legislation intervenes on behalf of society to ensure that businesses do not take advantage of their position because they have the capital to do it
- If there were no legislation, then the waters would all be polluted, many species would be extinct, we all would be breathing bad air, etc.
- Businesses like many humans like to get away with all they can. Legislation is there to protect the silent minorities, the people

Case #2   Borden Eagle Brand

Question #1
- Increase advertising using different mediums like television, newspaper and radio
- Have samples available at supermarkets of products made with Eagle Brand so people can realize how good it is
- Provide free recipes with a purchase of Eagle Brand so people can try it

Question #2
- Once people use Eagle Brand and enjoy it, they will be looking for more exciting benefits
- Have an Eagle Brand cookbook published and either people have to send in 15 Eagle Brand wrappers to get it, or they can pay for it
- Perhaps send out new recipe books every few years to keep people interested in the product and wanting to try new recipes.

Question #3
- Television
- Newspapers
- Magazines
- In-store displays
- Billboards

Question #4
- Coupons will entice people to try it the first time
- Group purchasing will encourage people to buy more than one can at a time
- Provide a small recipe book (i.e., 5) with the purchase of 2 or more cans etc.

Question #5
- Older people are our target market as they have more time to start from scratch
- If our product works and are really easy, then anyone who likes to keep healthy will use them.

Case # 3   Anthers Drug Co.

     1.   legal and ethical

     2.   natural/political

     3.   economic

     4.   core

Case #4   Martin Marietta

1.

The Company –	Officials within the Martin Marietta organization are enthusiastically pursuing new sources of supply. This commitment, along with an expanding market, should allow the company to pursue its marketing strategy while generating profits.
Suppliers and Marketing Intermediaries –	Martin Marietta must work with their various suppliers of equipment and materials as well as their marketing intermediaries including resellers, physical distribution firms, marketing services agencies and financial intermediaries to ensure a profitable operation. Proper selection of suppliers and marketing intermediaries becomes increasingly important as competition and public concerns increase.
Customers –	The company needs to monitor its customer markets closely. Consumer, business, reseller and government markets all present an opportunity. Martin Marietta must study the markets closely to understand the needs of each market and then decide how best to satisfy them.
Competitors –	The marketing concept states that to be successful, a company must provide greater customer value and satisfaction than its competitors. Thus marketers must do more than simply adapt to the needs of target consumers. They also must gain strategic advantage by positioning their offerings against competitors' offerings in the minds of customers.
Publics –	There are seven different types of publics that have an actual or potential interest in or impact on an organization's ability to achieve its objectives. Anticipating and reacting to the financial, media,

government, citizen action, local, general and internal publics becomes increasingly important when there is opposition to the operation of the gravel pits. Strategies need to be developed which address and alleviate concerns thereby allowing the company to more effectively implement its marketing strategy to be met by being open for extended hours in special location.

2.

The Demographic Environment –

Given the geographic shifts in population, Martin Marietta needs to anticipate where growth will take place and work to secure the permits necessary to expand or open the aggregate pits necessary to supply the required materials.

The Natural Environment –

Concerns of environmentalists need to be considered for their potential impact on the firm and its ability to serve its customers. Land reclamation and beautification programs are expensive but increasingly important considerations in obtaining needed permits. Firms must be ready for this involvement whether it comes in the form of media pressure or government legislation. The key will be to have alternate plans available.

The Political Environment –

The political environment consists of laws, government agencies and pressure groups that influence and limit organizations and individuals within society. The fact that it may take years to obtain the needed permits and appease the various publics indicates that Martin Marietta must be cognizant of the various groups and their concerns. They must also be willing to work with the elements of the political environment to promote understanding and ultimately mutually beneficial relations regardless of which political power is in office.

Chapter 4

Marketing Research and Information Systems

Chapter Overview

In today's complex and rapidly changing environment, marketing managers need quality information to make effective and timely decisions. Fortunately, the explosion of information and the technologies for supplying information has matched this greater need for information. The common use of the Internet in business, research, test papers and for personal use are a few of the benefits of this ever changing technology. The Internet, and a host of other advances, now permits companies to handle great quantities of information—sometimes even too much. Yet marketers often complain they lack enough of the right kind of information, or have an excess of the wrong kind. The role of the marketer is changing at even a greater pace than before. Marketers are now experts not only in gathering information but also in the various ways and technologies available to gather information and the tools available to decipher this quickly. In response, many companies are now studying their managers' information needs and then designing information systems to satisfy those needs.

Chapter Objectives

1. Explain the importance of information to the company.
2. Define the marketing information system and discuss its parts.
3. Outline the four steps in the marketing research process.
4. Compare the advantages and disadvantages of various methods of collecting information.
5. Discuss the special issues some marketing researchers face, including public policy and ethics issues.

Chapter Topics

The Marketing Information System
- Assessing Information Needs
- Developing Information
  - Internal Data
  - Marketing Intelligence
  - Marketing Research
  - Information Analysis
- Distributing Information

The Marketing Research Process
- Defining the Problem and Research Objectives
- Developing the Research Plan
  - Determining Specific Information Needs
  - Gathering Secondary Information
  - Planning Primary Data Collection
  - Presenting the Research Plan
- Implementing the Research Plan
- Interpreting and Reporting the Findings
- Other Marketing Research Considerations
  - Marketing Research in Small Business and Non-Profit Organizations
  - International Marketing Research
  - Public Policy and Ethics in Marketing
  - Follow-up

Chapter Summary

1.   The importance of information to the company.

Marketing managers need timely, reliable, and relevant information in order to make decisions that will enhance the company's ability to compete successfully in the marketplace and increase customer value relative to the competition. Information is important but must be balanced between manager needs and what is feasible to offer. Too much information can overwhelm managers just as too little information can lead to poor decisions.

2.   The marketing information system and its parts.

A marketing information system (MIS) consists of people, equipment, and procedures to gather, sort, analyse, and distribute needed, timely, and accurate information to marketing decision makers. Its four parts consist of developing information components, information system components, marketing managers, and the marketing environment. The MIS links all elements in a useable form.

3.   The four steps in the marketing research process.

The four steps in the marketing research process are defining the problem and the research objectives; developing the research plan; implementing the research plan; and interpreting and reporting the findings.

4.   The different kinds of information a company might use.

A company might use secondary data information or primary data information. Secondary data consists of information that already exists somewhere, having been collected for another purpose. Primary data consists of information collected for the specific purpose at hand.

5.   Comparing the advantages and disadvantages of various methods of collecting information.

Advantages: Mail questionnaires—collect large amounts of information, low cost, more homes, and no interview bias. Telephone—best for quick collection, flexibility, sample control, and response rates. Personal—individual or group, flexible, focus. Disadvantages: Mail—not flexible, low response rates. Telephone—higher cost, interview bias. Personal—costs and sampling problems.

Key Terms

Casual research	(pg. 160)	Marketing research	(pg. 158)
Descriptive research	(pg. 160)	Observational research	(pg. 165)
Experimental research	(pg. 166)	On-line databases	(pg. 161)
Exploratory research	(pg. 160)	Primary data	(pg. 161)
Focus-group interviewing	(pg. 169)	Sample	(pg. 172)
Internal databases	(pg. 153)	Secondary data	(pg. 161)
Marketing information systems (MIS)	(pg. 152)	Single-source data systems	(pg. 166)
		Survey research	(pg. 166)
Marketing intelligence	(pg. 154)		

Multiple Choice Questions

4-1   Multiple

Which of the following is not a step in the MIS process?

1.   Develop needed information
2.   Provide necessary recommendations
3.   Analyze information
4.   Assess information needed
5.   Distribute information

4-2   Multiple

A database has been designed for a small hardware store for its customers. This database contains information on customer demographics, psychographics and buying behaviour. This database tool is classified as a(n) _____ type of information development.

1.   Marketing intelligence
2.   Marketing research
3.   Information analysis
4.   Internal data
5.   Marketing environment

4-3   Multiple Choice

_____ is a system used to gather, analyze and distribute information about a company's competitive, technological, customer, economic, social, political and regulatory environments.

1.   Marketing intelligence
2.   Marketing research
3.   Information analysis
4.   Internal data
5.   Marketing environment

4-4   Multiple Choice

Which of the following steps is the most difficult in the research process?

1.   Implementing the research plan and collecting and analyzing the data
2.   Interpreting and reporting the findings
3.   Defining the problem and research objectives
4.   Developing the research plan for collecting information
5.   All the above are equally difficult

4-5   Multiple

CCM hockey sticks have developed a new stick. Sales of the new product are up 22%. Marketing is curious what will happen if they drop the price of their original CCM by 15%. The sale of the new product continues to rise. This type of research would be classified as:

1.   Exploratory research
2.   Casual research
3.   Descriptive research
4.   Cause-and-effect research
5.   Market research

4-6   Multiple

Which of the following is not considered a source of secondary data?

1.   Government publications
2.   Periodicals and books
3.   On-line data
4.   Commercial data obtained from another company
5.   Telephone survey data conducted by your company

4-7   Multiple

Wal-Mart is very interested to know the effect floor greeters have on their customers. In the US the greeters are seen very positively, as the tiles leading to the greeters are very worn down. They will conduct the same test here in Canada to see how we perceive the greeters. This type if primary data collecting is known as:

1.   Single-source data research
2.   Survey research
3.   Experimental research
4.   Observational research
5.   Marketing research

4-8   Multiple

Which of the following types of primary data collection tries to gather information of cause-and-effect relationships?

1.   Single-source data research
2.   Survey research
3.   Experimental research
4.   Observational research
5.   Marketing research

4-9   Multiple

Which of the following contact methods is the quickest, provides flexibility, has fairly high response rates, and allows for a greater amount of sample control?

1.   Mail questionnaires
2.   Telephone interviews
3.   Personal interviewing
4.   Individual interviewing
5.   Group interviewing

4-10   Multiple

Which contact methods can be higher in cost than some, be time consuming because the respondents may want to get off topic and it is difficult to get back on track, exhibit interviewer bias, and allow the interviewer to skip some questions and fill the answers in themselves?

1.   Mail questionnaires
2.   Telephone interviews
3.   Personal interviewing
4.   Individual interviewing
5.   Group interviewing

4-11   Multiple

Which of the following questions is NOT part of designing a sample group?

1.   Where should the survey be conducted?
2.   Who should be chosen?
3.   How many people should be surveyed?
4.   How should the people in the survey be chosen?
5.   All the above are part of designing a sample group

4-12   Multiple

Open-end questions are especially useful in what type of research?

1.   Observational research
2.   Survey research
3.   Experimental research
4.   Marketing research
5.   Exploratory research

4-13   Multiple

Researchers are responsible to provide many services to management. Which of the following does management not appreciate?

1.   Providing complex numbers and statistical analysis of findings
2.   Interpreting findings
3.   Drawing conclusions
4.   Reporting findings to management
5.   All the above are appreciated by management

4-14   Multiple

International research presents many problems or difficulties for companies. These difficulties include all the following except:

1.   Markets often vary greatly in their levels of economic development, cultures, customs, and buying patterns
2.   In many foreign markets, the international researcher has a difficult time finding good secondary data
3.   It is often very difficult to collect primary data as some tools available in North America are lacking in other countries
4.   People in other countries are not as intelligent and sophisticated as those in North America; therefore, questionnaires and research methods used here would not be appropriate in other parts of the world
5.   It is often very difficult to reach people in order to collect data as many countries' systems of distribution are not as sophisticated as those of North America

4-15   Multiple

Internal data can be used for all the following except:

1.   Targeting segments of existing customers for special product and service offers
2.   Providing on-the-spot answers to customer questions
3.   Obtaining information on market share
4.   Analyzing daily sales performance

4-16   Multiple

Choosing between doing survey research and experimental research is decided at which step in the marketing research process?

1.   Defining the problem
2.   Setting the research objectives
3.   Developing the research plan
4.   Implementing the research plan
5.   None of the above

4-17   Multiple

Sara works for Quality Specialty Products in Toronto. Each day she downloads the previous day's sales figures to decide which products to keep and which to drop. By downloading daily sales figures staff can decide on what products to keep and which to drop. Staff is engaged in what area of MIS?

1. Internal records
2. Information analysis
3. Marketing intelligence
4. Marketing research
5. Providing recommendations

4-18   Multiple

Raphael's job is to make sure the people interviewed during a survey meet a certain profile. He is involved in which area of primary data collection planning?

1. Sampling plans
2. Screening process
3. Research approaches
4. Contact methods
5. Research instruments

4-19   Multiple

Shania finds the best secondary data information on foreign markets is available from *The Economist's Country Reports*. These reports are published annually and cost up to $5,000 per country. This is an example of what type of secondary data?

1. Internal sources
2. Government publications
3. On-line sources
4. Periodicals and books
5. Commercial data

4-20   Multiple

Information found in a company's internal database would include which of the following?

1. The accounting department's records on financial statements
2. The manufacturing department's records on production schedules
3. The marketing department's records on customer demographics and buying behaviour
4. The customer service department's records on customer satisfaction
5. All of the above could be found in a database

4-21   Multiple

US Industrial Outlook provides projections of industrial activity by industry and includes data on production, sales, shipments and employment. This type of data source is considered:

1.   Internal
2.   Commercial
3.   International
4.   Governmental
5.   Internet

4-22   Multiple

There have been many studies done to determine a basic characteristic of Internet users. Which of the following characteristics of Internet users was NOT found to be common:

1.   Are better educated
2.   Are on average younger than the average consumer
3.   Are usually male
4.   Are on average single or recently married
5.   Are more affluent

4-23   Multiple

When every member of a population has a known and equal chance of being selected for a study, this is known as a _____ type of sample.

1.   Simple random sample
2.   Stratified random sample
3.   Convenience sample
4.   Judgement sample
5.   Probable random sample

4-24   Multiple

A scale that rates some attributes from "poor" to "excellent" is known as a(n) _____ type of closed-ended question.

1.   Dichotomous
2.   Likert scale
3.   Rating scale
4.   Semantic differential
5.   Intention-to-buy scale

4-25   Multiple

"What is your opinion of Canadian Airlines?" is an example of a(n) _____ type of open-ended question.

1.   Word association
2.   Sentence completion
3.   Picture completion
4.   Completely unstructured
5.   Story completion

4-26   Multiple

Which of the following is a common problem facing marketers when using information gathered from internal data?

1.   It may be out of date
2.   It is too ordinary to be of much use
3.   It may be incomplete or in the wrong form for marketing needs
4.   It is too easily accessible to other areas of the company
5.   All the above are common problems

4-27   Multiple

Which, if any, of the following is NOT a typical source of marketing intelligence?

1.   Company executives
2.   Competitors
3.   Purchasing agents
4.   Consumers
5.   All the above are sources

4-28   Multiple

A simple definition of _____ is that it is the function linking the consumer, customer, and public to the marketer through information.

1.   Marketing intelligence
2.   Marketing research
3.   The marketing information system
4.   Marketing control
5.   Marketing segmentation

4-29   Multiple

Marcel has noticed fewer customers are stopping at his store in the mall. He has a hunch about the reason but thinks he needs a little preliminary information before acting. Which type of research should Marcel use?

1.   Exploratory research
2.   Investigative research
3.   Descriptive research
4.   Correlational research
5.   Observational research

True/False Questions

4-1   True/False

Marketing Information Systems begin with marketing managers and end with a joint effort of all managers in all functional areas.

4-2   True/False

The MIS must watch the marketing environment to provide decision-makers with information they should have in order to make key marketing decisions.

4-3   True/False

The database information can come from more than one source, including financial statements, sales costs and cash flow.

4-4   True/False

Internal records can be accessed more quickly than other information sources, but because of all the people involved are more expensive than other information sources.

4-5   True/False

A radio station wants to know what type of people listen to their station, how many people, how long they listen each day, and where they listen, in order to decide what their target market is. This type of information would be classified as marketing research.

4-6   True/False

Marketers cannot rely only on information that is available to the public and therefore often require specific studies related to specific situations.

4-7   True/False

When research, either primary or secondary, is gathered by companies, it must be translated into specific information needs.

4-8   True/False

The University of Manitoba wants to know how many potential students it can expect to enroll in Year 1 for the upcoming year. They decide to look at the number of graduating students in all of Manitoba for this year, obtained from the Manitoba High School Association's database. They will then use a pre-assigned number to decide how many will attend a post-secondary institution, obtained from a recently published article in the Winnipeg Free Press. Of this number, they have calculated about 58% will attend the U of M, which is based on a yearly average of the past 10 years. This type of data is known as primary research.

4-9   True/False

Experimental research is the approach best suited for gathering descriptive information.

4-10   True/False

Observational research is gathering primary data by observing relevant people, actions and situations.

4-11   True/False

"What is your income to the nearest hundred dollars?" is an example of a closed-ended question.

4-12   True/False

A written proposal is especially important when the research project is large and complex, or when many different departments inside the firm carry it out.

4-13   True/False

The data-collection phase of the marketing research process is generally the most expensive and the most subject to error.

4-14   True/False

The marketing research techniques discussed in this chapter are only appropriate for large companies with large budgets. Small businesses and non-profit organizations are not able to perform marketing research because of lack of resources.

4-15   True/False

In practice, a good MIS system can fulfil all the information manager's requests.

4-16   True/False

Descriptive research gathers preliminary information that will help define the problem and suggest a research hypothesis.

4-17   True/False

The main drawbacks of personal interviewing are costs and sampling problems.

4-18   True/False

Key customers are not a source for keeping companies informed about their competitors and their products.

4-19   True/False

The internet provides quick and inexpensive access to a rich assortment of intelligence information.

4-20   True/False

When multiple-source data systems are properly used, they can provide marketers with fast and detailed information about how their products are selling, who is buying them, and what factors affect purchases.

Applying Terms and Concepts

To determine how well you understand the materials in this chapter, read each of the following brief cases and then respond to the questions that follow. Answers are given at the end of this chapter.

Case #1   Hogan's Shoe Store[1]

Robert Hogan is the founder of Hogan's Shoe Store located in the business district of Brandon, Manitoba. Hogan's has been in business since 1952, and its past success has been attributable to personalized service combined with quality leather footwear offered at reasonable prices. Richard Hogan, the owner's son, assumed control of the store when his father retired two years ago. Richard immediately implemented several changes, including a shift in the store's promotion, a decision to favour radio advertising, and an increase in the store's inventory by 10%.

Sales at Hogan's have increased by an average of 5% in each of the past 2 years; however, net profit has decreased slightly. According to industry data, shoe stores similar to Hogan's experienced an average increase in sales of 12% and an average increase in net profit of 8% during the same period.

After causally speaking with the store manager, salesperson, and several customers, Hogan concluded that the declining profits could be attributed to the low inventory turnover resulting from the prices charged.

In an effort to increase the store's profitability, Hogan contacted Mary Collin, a distributor for the Hozelton brand of footwear. Although the Hozelton line is constructed of man-made materials, it has a good reputation in the business. Collins assured Hogan that Hozelton quality was comparable to his existing line and that the retail prices would be lower than of his current merchandise. Collins also stated that Hozelton would be willing to grant advertising allowances equal to 10% of Hogan's advertising budget to a maximum of $400, whichever was lower.

Hogan is seriously considering Collin's proposal; however, he in unsure how his customers will react if he begins to substitute Hozelton for his established line.

1.   List the type of internal reports which might prove useful to Hogan in this situation.

   _____

   _____

   _____

   _____

---

[1] *Principles of Marketing*, 3rd Edition, Kotler, Armstrong, Warren (Prentice Hall) – pg. 69.

2. List some possible external secondary sources of information which might prove useful to Hogan.

_____

_____

_____

_____

3. Since Hogan is unsure of his exact problem, which type of research would you recommend?

_____

_____

_____

_____

4. Do you feel Hogan needs to collect additional secondary data before he makes a decision?

_____

_____

_____

_____

5. List possible reasons for the decrease in the store's profitability during the past 2 years.

_____

_____

_____

_____

Case #2   Angus Reid Group[2]

Angus Reid Group is a marketing research group that conducts and analyzes results for many different companies around the world. They perform research on many different products in a variety of industries. An example of this is the food and beverage division.

---

[2] Information taken from the Angus Reid Web Site.

Packaged food and beverage is one of the most dynamic categories in Canada. The emergence of large volume retailers, endless product choices and the inroads of store brands have also made it one of the most competitive. The marketers who succeed will be armed with an accurate understanding of the motivations and commitments of consumers.

Marketing research performed by Angus Reid Group touches every stage of the product cycle: New Product Development, Product Marketing Strategies and Product Evaluation. Here are a few examples of their research.

- A North American beverage manufacturer was interested in new market niche opportunities. A US segmentation study revealed two largely ignored consumer segments.
- A large package dairy products manufacturer had to make a decision: from a number of alternative concepts, which new product combination would have had the most favourable market impact? Result: a new brand of cheese.
- A national manufacturer was faced with three alternative packaging options. Angus Reid research helped choose the winning design.

1.   What type of research models and techniques would you use for new product development?

_____

_____

_____

_____

2.   What type of research models and techniques would you use for product marketing strategies?

_____

_____

_____

_____

3.   What type of research models and techniques would you use for product evaluation?

_____

_____

_____

_____

4.   Do you believe it is beneficial for large companies to outsource their marketing
      research to companies like Angus Reid?

_____

_____

_____

_____

5.   What other companies or industries might benefit from this service?

_____

_____

_____

_____

Case #3   Margaret Gorman

Margaret Gorman was reading the *Wall Street Journal* when she came upon an article
with the headline "TV Networks Turning to Comedies as They Frantically Search for
Hits." The article went on to say that fluffy comic programming was being "shipped" up
after last season's flings with gumshoes, doctors, lawyers, and oil-drenched soap operas
produced one of the most dismal 23 weeks in television history. "All they want now is
sitcoms," said a veteran TV writer. The networks were depending on the old, reliable
laugh to produce some new hits and reverse the decline in share of viewers during prime
time.

Gorman had just formed her own TV company to produce TV programs for the networks
and independent stations. After reading this article, Gorman was convinced that this was
an excellent opportunity to produce a nonviolent, nonsexual adventure series for TV. She
believed that something different from standard fare would stand a good chance of
getting high ratings. Gorman planned to dramatize important historical events, and at the
beginning, middle, and end of each program a group of history professors would discuss
causes and effects of the event. To verify her belief that this kind of program would have
broad appeal, she had developed a plan for a survey of the university community in
which she lived. She wanted to do a good job of her research so that she could use the
results to help convince network and station executives that the new program would
capture the mass market, which she believed was now saturated with comedy; without
using violence or sex as an alternative.

Gorman spent a considerable amount of money to secure a computer-generated random
sample of telephone numbers of both professors and students—making sure she had
proportionate representation from both groups. She designed a questionnaire (shown
below) and hired twenty students to do the telephone interviewing at $2 per completed
interview. Each interviewer was given a batch of questionnaires and telephone numbers

and told to go home and start at the top of the list of numbers. Calls were to be made between 9 a.m. and 4 p.m. If contact could not be established on the first call, the interviewer was to make up to nine more calls to the same number at different times between 9 a.m. and 5 p.m. in an effort to reach the originally selected respondent. If the respondent could not be reached or refused to cooperate, the interviewer was to move on to the next name on the list and continue in this fashion until twenty questionnaires had been completed.

After two days of interviewing, Gorman was not sure how to evaluate the situation. Mary and Bill, two interviewers, completed twenty calls the first day, but all the others were having difficulty—they had many refusals, partially completed interviews, not-at-home respondents, busy numbers, changed or not working numbers, and so on. They seemed to be confused, and their questionnaires were often improperly filled out or unusable. Gorman was considering assigning to Mary and Bill some of the numbers given to other interviewers.

Gorman's Questionnaire

1. What is your income? _____

2. What is your sex? Male _____   Female _____   Bisexual _____

3. What is your age? _____

4. What kind of education do you have?_____

5. Is your race white or other?   W _____   O _____

6. Are you religious?   Yes _____   No _____

7. Most people feel that TV is bad and are watching less. Do you agree?
    Yes _____   No _____

8. Do you watch a lot of TV?   Yes _____   No _____   Sometimes _____

9. Do you think we should encourage criminal depravity by showing a lot of violence and sex on TV?   Yes _____   No _____

10. Do you agree with most people that most TV programs are not intellectually stimulating?   Yes _____   No _____

11. Do you think we can have interesting and intellectually stimulating programs without a lot of violence and sex?   Yes _____   No _____

---

12.   What is the least popular television program among your friends?

_____

13.   What's your general opinion of TV programming—that is, what do you dislike
       about it, and how can it be improved?

_____

_____

1.   What are the fundamental weaknesses in Gorman's marketing research plan?

_____

_____

_____

_____

2.   What should be done to improve Gorman's marketing research plan?

_____

_____

_____

_____

Case #4   Avion Bookstores

As an old established bookstore Avion has had a successful growth pattern in Ontario for
the past five years. They are now thinking of entering the broad and profitable American
market. With knowledge of the American market being their major stumbling block they
are concerned about entry into this market but are prepared to take the leap. They have
contacted International Research to assist them. Ron Hellier, the owner, is committed to
the idea of expansion and his management team agrees. Going into their meetings with
International Research there are many issues that must be discussed and resolved. As part
of Avion's management team, how do you see dealing with the following research issues
as both companies meet to delve into this research project? Avion has had a strong
reputation for quality and producing old established Canadian writers. New writers have
been signed and with these Avion hopes to break away from their mold as being a
Canadian company that produces Canadian books for a limited market. The American
book market has been growing in total sales by 12% for the last ten years and Ron Hellier

feels that the time is right and is looking to International Research for the proof he needs that now is the time to grow.

1. What is secondary data and what are the relative advantages and disadvantages of its review as part of a research project?

    _____

    _____

    _____

    _____

2   After gathering data how will Avion best interpret and implement this research?

    _____

    _____

    _____

    _____

Multiple Choice Answers

1.	Correct Answer:	2	Reference:	pg. 152
2.	Correct Answer:	4	Reference:	pg. 153
3.	Correct Answer:	1	Reference:	pg. 154
4.	Correct Answer:	3	Reference:	pg. 152
5.	Correct Answer:	2	Reference:	pg. 160
6.	Correct Answer:	5	Reference:	pg. 161
7.	Correct Answer:	4	Reference:	pg. 165
8.	Correct Answer:	3	Reference:	pg. 166
9	Correct Answer:	2	Reference:	pg. 172
10.	Correct Answer:	2	Reference:	pg. 172
11.	Correct Answer:	1	Reference:	pg. 172
12.	Correct Answer:	5	Reference:	pg. 160

13.	Correct Answer:	1	Reference:	pg. 175
14.	Correct Answer:	4	Reference:	pg. 175
15.	Correct Answer:	3	Reference:	pg. 153
16.	Correct Answer:	3	Reference:	pg. 165
17.	Correct Answer:	2	Reference:	pg. 154
18.	Correct Answer:	1	Reference:	pg. 172
19.	Correct Answer:	5	Reference:	pg. 176
20.	Correct Answer:	5	Reference:	pg. 161
21.	Correct Answer:	3	Reference:	pg. 162
22.	Correct Answer:	4	Reference:	pg. 163
23.	Correct Answer:	1	Reference:	pg. 172 (Table 4-5)
24.	Correct Answer:	3	Reference:	pg. 175
25.	Correct Answer:	4	Reference:	pg. 166
26.	Correct Answer:	3	Reference:	pg. 153
27.	Correct Answer:	5	Reference:	pg. 154
28.	Correct Answer:	2	Reference:	pg. 158
29.	Correct Answer:	1	Reference:	pg. 160

True/False Answers

1.	FALSE	Reference:	pg. 152	Topic: The Marketing Information System
2.	TRUE	Reference:	pg. 152	Topic: Assessing Information Needs
3.	TRUE	Reference:	pg. 152	Topic: Assessing Information Needs
4.	FALSE	Reference:	pg. 153	Topic: Internal Records

5.	TRUE	Reference:	pg. 158	Topic: Marketing Research
6.	FALSE	Reference:	pg. 158	Topic: Information Analysis
7.	TRUE	Reference:	pg. 161	Topic: Specific Information Needs
8.	FALSE	Reference:	pg. 161	Topic: Gathering Secondary Information
9.	FALSE	Reference:	pg. 165	Topic: Planning Primary Data Collection
10.	TRUE	Reference:	pg. 165	Topic: Primary Data Research
11.	FALSE	Reference:	pg. 172	Topic: Research Instruments
12.	FALSE	Reference:	pg. 175	Topic: Presenting the Research Plan
13.	TRUE	Reference:	pg. 175	Topic: Implementing the Research Plan
14.	FALSE	Reference:	pg. 176	Topic: Marketing Research in Small Businesses and Non-Profit Organizations
15.	FALSE	Reference:	pg. 180	Topic: Assessing Information Needs
16.	FALSE	Reference:	pg. 160	Topic: Defining the Problem and Research Objectives
17.	TRUE	Reference:	pg. 131	Topic: Contact Methods
18.	FALSE	Reference:	pg. 153	Topic: Marketing Highlight 4-1
19.	TRUE	Reference:	pg. 153	Topic: Marketing Highlight 4-1
20.	FALSE	Reference:	pg. 165	Topic: Marketing Highlight 4-3

Applying Term and Concepts Answers

Case #1   Hogan's Shoe Store

Question #1
- Operating and sales expenses
- Sales reports

- Inventory records
- Invoices
- Accounts receivable
- Balance sheets
- Profit and loss statements

Question #2
- Industry surveys
- Government publications
- Business periodicals
- Trade association information

Question #3
- Exploratory research
- This is marketing research which gathers preliminary information that will help better define problems and suggest hypotheses

Question #4
- Yes—the information collected is inadequate and unreliable
- His sample was far too small
- He spoke to these people in a casual manor, not a scientific one
- There was no patterning to his questions

Question #5
- Change in advertising medium
- Change in population characteristics
- Increased competition
- Increased operating expenses
- Change in salespeople
- Change in product price
- Downturn in local economy

Case #2   Angus Reid Group

Question #1
- Brand maps based on lifestyle and segmentation models
- Identify potential gaps in the market
- Future niches for new entries
- Idea generation sessions
- Concept tests to help refine product strategies, packaging and brand names

Question #2
- Models ranging from quasi-experimental customer tests to in-home placement
- Examine impact of alternative marketing
- Packaging and pricing scenarios for a broad range of packaged goods

Question #3
- Tracking studies to help evaluate product performance in the marketplace
- Plot changes in consumer perceptions
- Information useful in targeting further product enhancements

Question #4
- Unbiased research and interpretation of results
- May be cheaper as in-house resources are not being used
- They are specialists, therefore information may be more accurate
- Can focus on the implementation plan if the results are favourable

Question #5
- Drug stores
- Hardware stores
- Clothing and shoe stores
- Grocery stores
- Etc.

Case #3   Margaret Gorman

1.   There was an inadequate review of secondary data related to the research project.

The respondents who made up the sample may not be representative of the intended target market. Gorman stated she wanted the programming to have broad appeal; yet her sample was very narrowly defined—students and professors with telephones who were available between 9 a.m. and 5 p.m.

The questionnaire was poorly designed. There were too few questions used to gather data on which to draw conclusions and make decisions. The sequencing of the questions was wrong. Some questions were too vague and others were very leading. The questions were biased and would undoubtedly result in answers and opinions that support Gorman's beliefs.

The interviewers were inadequately trained and supervised. There is the potential for interviewer bias. There was no verification of interviews conducted by Mary and Bill—their results should be suspect given their high completion rate relative to the other interviewers.

2.   Gorman needs to have a better understanding of the situation she faces and therefore needs a better review of the secondary data. This will assist her in defining the "problem" and setting her research objective.

The sampling plan needs to be carefully analyzed. Gorman needs an appropriate sample unit and sample size. She needs to use an appropriate sampling procedure. There is some question as to whether her current sample plan is appropriate.

The current questionnaire needs to be discarded and a new one constructed. Questions should be placed in the proper sequence. That is, the demographic and biographic questions should be placed at the end of the questionnaire. A variety of open-end questions seeking the respondent's opinions should be meshed with the closed-end questions. The questions should not be vague or leading. The questionnaire should also be pretested to identify and correct problems which may skew the results.

The interviewers need to be properly trained and monitored as they gather data. This would help to minimize interviewer bias and help ensure the collection of reliable and accurate data.

Gorman may also wish to conduct personal interviews and/or group interviews (focus-group interviews) to complement the telephone interviews. Personal interviewing has several drawbacks, but the advantages may very well offset those disadvantages and yield very significant information.

Case #4   Avion Bookstores

1.   Secondary data consists of information that already exists, having been collected for another purpose. It is typically reviewed in a research project, because it helps the researcher understand better the situation to be studied. Its relative advantages are that it usually can be obtained more quickly and at lower cost than primary data. In many cases primary data is not needed and should be looked at in this case as unnecessary considering the amount of data available for this type of store. Secondary data provide a good starting point for research and often help to define problems and research objectives. In most cases, however, the company must also collect primary data.

2.   The first step in the marketing research process is often the hardest step. It is defining the problem and research objective. It must then be determined if the research meets the company's corporate objective. Are the plans for growth consistent with the research provided? How does it fit into the MIS? Can the marketing team develop strategies to meet their needs?

Chapter 5

Consumer Markets and Consumer Buying Behaviour

Chapter Overview

The Canadian Consumer Market consists of about 29 million people who consume billions of dollars worth of goods and services each year, making it one of the most attractive consumer markets in the world. As our world grows it continually changes along with its buying patterns and behaviour. The world consumer market consists of more than 5 billion people. Consumers around the world vary greatly in age, income, education level, and tastes. Marketing companies, no matter how small, must look to and comprehend the international market.

How consumers decide, when they decide, and who makes the final purchase decision are all questions that the marketer must face. The buyer's decision process and how a consumer makes a product their own through adoption are key components of this chapter. Understanding how these differences affect consumer buying behaviour is one of the biggest challenges marketers face.

Chapter Objectives

1. Define the consumer market and construct a simple model of consumer buyer behaviour.
2. Name the four major factors influencing consumer buyer behaviour.
3. List and understand the stages in the buyer decision process.
4. Describe the adoption and diffusion process for new products.

Chapter Topics

Model of Consumer Behaviour

Characteristics Affecting Consumer Behaviour
- Cultural Factors
  - Culture
  - Subculture
  - Social Classes
- Social Factors
  - Groups
  - Family
  - Roles and Status
- Personal Factors
  - Age and Life-Cycle Stage
  - Occupation
  - Economic Situation

- Lifestyle
- Personality and Self-Concept
- Psychological Factors
  - Motivation
  - Perception
  - Learning
  - Beliefs and Attitudes

Consumer Buying Roles

Types of Buying Decision Behaviours
- Complex Buying Behaviour
- Dissonance-Reducing Buying Behaviour
- Habitual Buying Behaviour
- Variety Seeking Buying Behaviour

The Buyer Decision Process
- Need Recognition
- Information Search
- Evaluation of Alternatives
- Purchase Decision
- Postpurchase Behaviour

The Buyer Decision Process for New Products
- Stages in the Adoption Process
- Individual Differences in Innovativeness
- Influence of Product Characteristics on Rate of Adoption

Consumer Behaviour Across International Borders

Chapter Summary

1.   The consumer market and the elements of a simple model of buying behaviour as identified in the text.

The consumer market is made up of all the final consumers of products and services combined. A simple model of consumer behaviour consists of the 4 Ps (Product, Place, Price, Promotion), Environmental Forces, the Buyer's Black Box (buyer characteristics, buyer decision processes), and Observable Choices (product, brand, dealer, purchase timing, and purchase amount).

2.	The major social factors that influence consumer buying behaviour.

Social factors include small groups, family, and social roles and status. Groups can be membership (primary, secondary) or reference or inspirational. Opinion leaders exert influence within reference groups.

Family or lifestyle also influence buying behaviour. Roles are expected activities and status is the esteem granted by society to the person performing roles.

3.	The four major psychological factors that affect the buying process.

Psychological factors include motivation, perception, learning, and beliefs and attitudes. A motive is a drive sufficiently pressing to direct the person to seek satisfaction. Perception is influence by selective retention, attention, and distortion. Learning arises from changes in behaviour due to experience and occurs through the interplay of drives, stimuli, cues, responses, and reinforcement. Beliefs are descriptive attitudes that endure.

4.	The stages in the consumer adoption process for new products.

New product adoption stages include awareness, interest, evaluation, trial and adoption.

5.	The four types of behaviour associated with different types of buying situations.

Four types of buying behaviour include complex buying behaviour, dissonance-buying behaviour, variety-seeking buying behaviour, and habitual-buying behaviour.

Key Terms

Multiple Choice Questions

5-1   Multiple

Which of the following does not comprise the marketing and other stimuli section of the Model for Buying Behaviour?

1.   Product
2.   Price
3.   Promotion
4.   Politics
5.   All of the above

5-2   Multiple

Cristina has been looking for a new VCR for a long time. She is interested in purchasing a fairly high-tech VCR as she has a top of the line television. The great salesman at Future Shop has convinced her the Zenith DVD 500 is the best value for her dollar. Cristina decides to go with this VCR and makes the purchase. Cristina used all the steps in the buyer's response except:

1.   Product choice
2.   Brand choice
3.   Purchase amount
4.   Dealer choice
5.   All of the above

5-3   Multiple

Canadians live in a very time-poor society. To help Canadians increase their leisure time, all the following are convenience goods and services, except _____, which help them accomplish this goal.

1.   Microwave ovens
2.   Fast food
3.   Catalogue industry
4.   Gas lawn mowers
5.   Automatic tellers

5-4   Multiple

Canada is a very multicultural country with very distinctive and significant ethnic markets. Which of the following does not belong to the three largest ethnic Canadian markets?

1.   Ukrainian
2.   Italian
3.   German
4.   Chinese
5.   All of the above do not belong to the top three

5-5   Multiple

The Canadian market is maturing, which is a very important issue marketers must address. Which of the following is (are) characteristic of the age group comprising people currently aged 50 and older?

1.   Possess 2/3 of the country's disposable income
2.   Represent 25% of the population
3.   Comprise 1/3 of the heads of households
4.   Possess 3/5 of the country's disposable income
5.   1,2,3

5-6   Multiple

As our market ages, seniors take over with money in their pockets and an urge to spend. With so much time and money available to them companies are scrambling to get their market share. Which of the following would not be profitable if marketed to seniors?

1.   Exotic travel
2.   Home physical-fitness products
3.   Financial services
4.   Health foods
5.   All of the above

5-7   Multiple

Which of the following class structure meets these criteria: They tend to be active in social and civic affairs and buy for themselves and their children symbols of status, such as expensive homes, swimming pools and cars.

1.   Upper Uppers
2.   Lower Uppers
3.   Upper Middles
4.   Middle Class
5.   Working Class

5-8   Multiple

Which of the following class structures meets these criteria: They perform unskilled work but they manage to present a picture of self-discipline and maintain some effort of cleanliness.

1.   Lower Lowers
2.   Upper Lowers
3.   Working Class
4.   Middle Class
5.   Upper Middles

5-9   Multiple

Social classes have always shown brand preference as part of their position and wealth for that class. Which of the following does not fall into that area?

1.   Clothing choices
2.   Home furnishings
3.   Food choices
4.   Leisure activities
5.   Automobiles

5-10   Multiple

All new and old engineers must belong to the Engineering Association of each province. This type of group would be considered a(n):

1.   Aspirational group
2.   Reference group
3.   Primary membership group
4.   Secondary membership group
5.   Membership group

5-11   Multiple

The importance of group influence varies across products and brands. However, group influence tends to be the strongest in which of the following situations?

1.   The product is visible to others
2.   The products are bought and used privately
3.   The product could be a reflection of your profession
4.   The products are bought publicly but used privately
5.   None of the above

5-12   Multiple

Which of the following would not be considered a group in the middle-aged stage of the life cycle?

1.   Single
2.   Married without children
3.   Single with children
4.   Married with children
5.   Divorced without children

5-13   Multiple

The VALS2 is a tool used to classify people into different lifestyles. Which category would include Stephan, a 25 year-old male who buys goods and services based on his views of the world, and is very content with minimal resources?

1.   Fulfilleds
2.   Achievers
3.   Strugglers
4.   Strivers
5.   Believers

5-14   Multiple

Various psychological factors play specific roles in our buying patterns. Of the following which is not considered a psychological factor?

1.   Motivation
2.   Self-concept
3.   Perception
4.   Learning
5.   Beliefs and attitudes

5-15   Multiple

Maslow's hierarchy of needs encompasses five distinct needs. The need for a sense of belonging and love falls under which category?

1.   Physiological needs
2.   Safety needs
3.   Social needs
4.   Esteem needs
5.   Self-actualization needs

5-16   Multiple

Many people perceive situations differently. This is a very difficult challenge for marketers. Paula is watching television and has probably seen 50 different ads. Currently she is not in the market for anything so when she sees the commercials, none of them really sink in. In this situation, marketers must really try to differentiate their ads from others in order to combat _____.

1.   Selective distortion
2.   Selective retention
3.   Selective perception
4.   Selective attention
5.   Selective recording

5-17   Multiple

Margaret is fourteen years of age and is buying a new dress for her graduation. Her mother takes her shopping and lets her pick a new outfit within the child's budget. When Margaret arrives home she has three outfits and shows her mother. After a long discussion the mother convinces the child which one is more appropriate. Which step was the mother not a part of?

1.   Influencer
2.   Decider
3.   Buyer
4.   She contributed to all of these roles

5-18   Multiple

Hen Wee does the grocery shopping for her family every week. She usually purchases Dad's oatmeal cookies but this time, she decided to buy the new Duncan Heinz oatmeal cookies for a change. This purchase does not require too much involvement, as there are few differences between brands. She is practicing this type of buying behaviour.

1.   Complex buying behaviour
2.   Dissonance-reducing buying behaviour
3.   Habitual buying behaviour
4.   Variety-seeking buying behaviour
5.   New product buying behaviour

5-19   Multiple

After saving enough money for his first car John buys a ten-year-old Honda Civic. After 6 months he has incurred over $800 in repairs. He now vows he will never purchase a used car again. At what stage in the buyer decision process is John?
1.   Information search
2.   Evaluation of alternatives
3.   Need recognition
4.   Purchase decisions
5.   None of the above

5-20   Multiple

Evaluation of alternatives is a very important step in the buyer decision process. Which of the following is not a consideration at this step?

1.   Product attributes
2.   Degrees of importance
3.   Brand attitudes
4.   Total product satisfaction
5.   All of the above

5-21   Multiple

Rachel has heard about a new hand-held computerized agenda from a friend of hers who bought one three months earlier. She is always losing her pens and therefore misses appointments because she cannot write them down. This new product would solve many of her problems. She decided to go to the corner computer store in the mall and talk to a sales agent there. She is sold right away on one of the three different choices, and takes one home and starts inputting all her data into this new agenda that afternoon. Which of the stages in the adoption process, if any, did Rachel miss?

1.   Adoption
2.   Trial
3.   Evaluation
4.   Awareness
5.   None of the above

5-22   Multiple

In the above example, Rachel would be considered a:

1.   Laggard
2.   Late Majority
3.   Early Majority
4.   Early adopter
5.   Innovator

5-23   Multiple

The new hand-held computerized agenda is considered a new product. Many characteristics will determine the rate of its adoption into today's society. These new agendas are easily portable and can be shown to many different people with ease. This characteristic is known as:

1.   Communicability
2.   Divisibility
3.   Complexity
4.   Compatibility
5.   Relative Advantage

5-24   Multiple

The type of purchase for which group influence is strongest is:

1.   Convenience purchases
2.   Consumptive purchases
3.   Conspicuous purchases
4.   Conventional purchases
5.   Collective purchases

5-25   Multiple

Hank relies on his parents for advice on all his major purchases and to help pay his bills. His father is the breadwinner in the family and his mom stays at home to care for his 2 younger sisters. Hank belongs to which social class?

1.   Middle class
2.   Lower uppers
3.   Upper lowers
4.   Lower lowers
5.   Working class

5-26   Multiple

Brand image, for example Guess Jeans, is formed from which of the following concepts associated with alternative evaluation?

1.   Product attributes
2.   Degrees of importance
3.   Brand beliefs
4.   Utility function
5.   Brand attitudes

5-27   Multiple

Regarding customer satisfaction, which of the following statements is true?

1.   Dissatisfied customers tend to behave much like satisfied customers
2.   Bad word of mouth travels farther and faster than good word of mouth
3.   Dissatisfied customers tell fewer people about their experiences than do satisfied customers
4.   Dissatisfied customers complain to the company in large numbers
5.   Satisfied customers will always come back and tell their friends

5-28   Multiple

Robert and his friends are tired of the same old nightclubs. A series of ads catches their eyes for a new entertainment arcade being opened up by Sega. In the new product adoption process what stage are Robert and his friends at?

1.   Awareness
2.   Interest
3.   Evaluation
4.   Trial
5.   Adoption

5-29   Multiple

Janiqua got to test-drive a new fuel-efficient car that ran on propane. Janiqua's trial qualifies as which of the following characteristics?

1.   Relative advantage
2.   Communicability
3.   Compatibility
4.   Divisibility
5.   Complexity

5-30   Multiple

After weeks of being begged by his son to purchase a new style suit for an upcoming wedding, Jack's father relented and went shopping at a trendy clothing store. What group does he belong to?
1.   Innovators
2.   Early Majority
3.   Late Majority
4.   Late Adopters
5.   Laggards

True/False Questions

5-1   True/False

The company who really understands how consumers will respond to different product features, prices, and advertising has only a moderate advantage over its competitors.

5-2   True/False

Cultural factors have the broadest and deepest influence on consumer behaviour.

5-3   True/False

Throughout their lives people learn from doing and seeing, which develop attitudes and beliefs. When added together these influence the buying behaviour of the consumer.

5-4   True/False

Despite the increasing number of immigrants to Canada in the last few years, consumers from ethnic groups still represent one of the slowest-growing markets in Canada.

5-5   True/False

Seniors are a growing market segment in Canada. Most of them are healthy and will therefore have many of the same wants as young consumers.

5-6   True/False

In recent years, marketers have adjusted to the fact that the Net is a means of one-way communication between the consumer and a vendor, much the same as traditional advertising.

5-7   True/False

Multiculturalism in Canada has had no effect on marketers and the buying behaviour of the consumers.

5-8   True/False

Manufacturers of products and brands subject to strong group influence must determine how to reach the opinion leaders in the relevant reference group instead of marketing to the general public.

5-9   True/False

Alternative evaluation is how the consumers process information in making their choice of a product.

5-10   True/False

The basic self-concept premise is that people's possessions contribute to their identities, but do not reflect them.

5-11   True/False

Learning, arising from experience, changes an individual's behaviour. The following make up and contribute to the entire learning process: needs, stimuli, cues and responses.

5-12   True/False

Habitual buying behaviour in purchasers occurs when they purchase products of little difference on a regular basis. Marketers are interested in the beliefs people formulate about specific products and services, because these beliefs comprise product and brand images that affect buying behaviour.

5-13   True/False

The buying decision process is a very thorough and complete process to purchasing value-added products. Despite this fact, in more routine purchases, consumers often skip or reverse some of these stages.

5-14   True/False

Generally the consumer receives the most information about a product from public sources, those controlled by the marketer.

5-15   True/False

Consumers will vary as to the attributes they consider relevant and they will pay the most attention to those attributes connected with their needs.

5-16   True/False

Two factors can come between the intention to buy and the purchase decision. These two factors are attitudes of others and expected situational factors.

5-17   True/False

In international situations, marketers must decide the degree to which they will adapt their marketing to various cultures and their needs, but the products can be homogeneous.

5-18   True/False

Middle class people serve as a reference group for others to the extent that their consumption decisions are imitated by other classes.

5-19   True/False

Firms with new concepts in technology must direct their research towards Early Adaptors and not the Laggards even though they may buy the product in the distant future.

5-20   True/False

Motivation research is based upon Freudian psychological principles.

Applying Terms and Concepts

To determine how well you understand the materials in this chapter, read each of the following brief cases and then respond to the questions that follow. Answers are given at the end of this chapter.

Case #1   Line-Haul Jeans[1]

Mike Ianari is a Line Haul (long-distance) truck driver for Richards Express, based in Thompson, Manitoba. Ianari recently saw an advertisement in *Overdrive Magazine* about a new type of blue jeans called "Line-Haul." "Line-Hauls" are made of stretch denim, cut wider in the seat and thighs and have oversized back pockets. The advertisement indicated unlike tighter fitting designer jeans, Line Hauls, at $39.95, were loose fitting, had plenty of stretch, and felt comfortable the first time worn. At 6'4" and 245 pounds Ianari reasoned that these prewashed, preshrunk jeans would be ideal.

Ianari, remembering the advertisement, was determined to buy a pair of these jeans on his next trip through Winnipeg, the city where STOP 55 Truck Stops, which sold them exclusively, were located. Ianari was even more determined to buy a pair of these jeans after he began noticing that the "Line-Haul" label was acquiring quite a following among his fellow drivers. Many truckers

---

[1] *Principles of Marketing*, 3rd Edition, Kotler, Armstrong, Warren (Prentice Hall) – pg. 97.

are now wearing "Line-Haul" caps, T-shirts, vests and belt buckles featuring the brand's "Tractor with Cab Over" emblem.

1.   Which marketing stimuli can be identified in the case?

   _____
   _____
   _____
   _____

2.   Which reference group would Ianari most likely be influenced by to purchase "Line-Haul" jeans?

   _____
   _____
   _____
   _____

3.   Ianari's purchasing of the jeans would satisfy which need or needs according to Maslow's theory of motivation?

   _____
   _____
   _____
   _____

4.   Which selective perceptual process was evident when Ianari remembered that information which supported his attitude and beliefs about "Line-Haul" jeans?

   _____
   _____
   _____
   _____

5.   Ianari just loves these new jeans and has decided he will never wear any other type of jeans. Which psychological factor most likely accounts for this change in his behaviour?

   _____
   _____
   _____
   _____

Case #2   Alfredo's Fine Cuisine

After ten years of working as a chef Vivian Edwards has decided to open up her own Italian cuisine restaurant. Making her decision on opening a restaurant was easy compared to the marketing questions she was now faced with. She decided on Toronto as a location and to move into the trendy area of King Street in the heart of the theatre district. Toronto's population is the most diverse in the world and the area depends not only on local traffic but on bus tours coming into the area as well. Would culture be the main concern as she looked at her multicultural market? Or should she be studying the tourist market coming into town from a radius of 150 km which gave her a market of over 3 million residents both Canadian and American? These are issues she had to deal with.

In marketing we often forget the proximity of many sites to international borders and who our customers may in fact be. Often we see ourselves serving a community and forgetting the vast market that may be walking right by our door. Marketers are individuals that can take primary and secondary research and utilize it to its maximum potential in making intelligent, profitable decisions.

1.   How does public opinion play a role in Vivian's restaurant? How does product placement help with the need recognition stage of the buyer decision process (BDP)?

_____

_____

_____

_____

2.   How does product placement help with the information search stage of consumers?

_____

_____

_____

3.   How does ad placement deal with the lifestyle of her customers?

_____

_____

_____

4.   Do you believe that this restaurant, being in a tourist area, should limit itself to tourists as a market?

_____

_____

_____

_____

Case #3   The Dawsons

Jeff and Margaret Dawson, after 15 years of marriage and two children, decided this past winter to purchase a power boat. Their income had increased to the point where a $16,000 to $21,000 expenditure was within reason. This boat was a lifelong dream for them. Their only previous experience with boats was a 14-ft Starcraft fishing boat with a 15 hp Mercury outboard motor. Their next purchase was to be in the 20- to 24-ft range with an inboard motor. The prime uses of this boat were to be for water-skiing, fishing, and leisurely motoring on the Finger Lakes of central New York where they lived.

The Dawsons wanted to stay with a Starcraft/Mercury combination if possible. They were disappointed to find, upon attending the Northeast Boat Show at the New York State Fairgrounds in Syracuse, that Starcraft did not produce a boat which suited them. Mercury engines, however, were available in a variety of sizes and price ranges.

Mr. Dawson's reason for wishing to stay with a Mercury engine was his past experience with his outboard motor. In the 14 years he had owned the motor he had had virtually no problems with it. Dawson's fishing friends who owned Johnson and Evinrude motors, however, seemed to experience an abnormally high (compared to Mercury) number of problems, several of which involved major expenditures.

The Dawsons collected literature from exhibitors at the boat show as they viewed a wide variety of boat and motor combinations.

At the boat show, Mercury was introducing a new 210 hp V8 engine. Mercury promoted its new engine as unique because it was the only engine on the market rated at 210 hp, and it introduced V8 cylinder design instead of the more traditional V4 and V6 designs. Dawson was impressed by the information in the literature on this new engine. Fuel consumption, speed, and ease of maintenance were reasonable. Mercury's price, however, was several hundred dollars more than the competition's.

Later, in speaking with his friends about what he had seen at the show, Dawson's friends cautioned him about the potential danger of buying an engine the first year it was produced. They felt it would take a year or two to work the bugs out of the new engine. Although an 8 cylinder engine was common in offshore racing boats, it was still unusual in this horsepower range and motor style for the sport market.

After reviewing the literature from the boat show and visiting several marinas where they spoke with sales representatives and took boats out for a "test drive," the Dawsons decided on a 22-ft craft made by Invader Industries. The boat could be equipped with either a 200 hp Volvo engine or the new 210 hp Mercury. Without hesitation, Dawson ordered the boat with the Mercury. Although they had spent more than they had planned, the Dawsons felt their purchase would be a source of considerable pride and enjoyment.

_____1. Identify the major cultural theme that played a role in the Dawsons' decision to purchase a power boat.
     A.   leisure time
     B.   health
     C.   youthfulness
     D.   informality
     E.   social

_____2. Dawson's fishing friends are an example of a(n) _____ group.
     A.   primary
     B.   secondary
     C.   aspirational
     D.   dissociative
     E.   normal

_____3. Which need or needs, according to Maslow's theory of motivation, would be satisfied by the Dawsons' purchase of the 22-ft Invader power boat?
     A.   social
     B.   esteem
     C.   self-actualization
     D.   only (A) and (B)
     E.   all of the above

_____4. Which selective process was evident when Dawson remembered information about Mercury motors which supported his attitudes and beliefs?
     A.   selective attention
     B.   selective distortion
     C.   selective retention
     D.   selective regression
     E.   selective intention

Multiple Choice Answers

1. Correct Answer: 5   Reference: pg. 218
2. Correct Answer: 3   Reference: pg. 225
3. Correct Answer: 4   Reference: pg. 207
4. Correct Answer: 1   Reference: pg. 198
5. Correct Answer: 5   Reference: pg. 203
6. Correct Answer: 5   Reference: pg. 207
7. Correct Answer: 2   Reference: pg. 203
8. Correct Answer: 2   Reference: pg. 203
9. Correct Answer: 3   Reference: pg. 203
10. Correct Answer: 4   Reference: pg. 198
11. Correct Answer: 1   Reference: pg. 203
12. Correct Answer: 3   Reference: pg. 204
13. Correct Answer: 5   Reference: pg. 207
14. Correct Answer: 2   Reference: pg. 211
15. Correct Answer: 3   Reference: pg. 212
16. Correct Answer: 4   Reference: pg. 215
17. Correct Answer: 2   Reference: pg. 216
18. Correct Answer: 4   Reference: pg. 218
19. Correct Answer: 1   Reference: pg. 220
20. Correct Answer: 3   Reference: pg. 222
21. Correct Answer: 2   Reference: pg. 226
22. Correct Answer: 4   Reference: pg. 226

23.	Correct Answer:	1	Reference:	pg. 226
24.	Correct Answer:	3	Reference:	pg. 195
25.	Correct Answer:	5	Reference:	pg. 203
26.	Correct Answer:	3	Reference:	pg. 226
27.	Correct Answer:	2	Reference:	pg. 223
28.	Correct Answer:	1	Reference:	pg. 225
29.	Correct Answer:	3	Reference:	pg. 227
30.	Correct Answer:	5	Reference:	pg. 227

True/False Answers

1.	FALSE	Reference:	pg. 195	Topic: Model of Consumer Behaviour
2.	TRUE	Reference:	pg. 196	Topic: Cultural Factors
3.	TRUE	Reference:	pg. 215	Topic: Beliefs and Attitudes
4.	FALSE	Reference:	pg. 198	Topic: Subculture
5.	TRUE	Reference:	pg. 199	Topic: Subculture
6.	FALSE	Reference:	pg. 199	Topic: Subculture
7.	TRUE	Reference:	pg. 200	Topic: Culture
8.	TRUE	Reference:	pg. 203	Topic: Groups
9	FALSE	Reference:	pg. 222	Topic: Evaluation of Alternatives
10.	FALSE	Reference:	pg. 211	Topic: Personality and Self-Concept
11.	TRUE	Reference:	pg. 218	Topic: Habitual Buying
12.	TRUE	Reference:	pg. 215	Topic: Beliefs and Attitudes
13.	TRUE	Reference:	pg. 217	Topic: The Buyer Decision

14.	FALSE	Reference:	pg. 220	Topic: Information Search
15.	TRUE	Reference:	pg. 222	Topic: Evaluation of Alternatives
16.	FALSE	Reference:	pg. 223	Topic: Purchase Decision
17.	FALSE	Reference:	pg. 227	Topic: Consumer Behaviour Across International Borders
18.	FALSE	Reference:	pg. 226	Topic: Individual Differences
19.	TRUE	Reference:	pg. 207	Topic: Lifestyle
20.	TRUE	Reference:	pg. 211	Topic: Motivation

Applying Terms and Concepts Answers

Case #1   Line Haul Jeans

Question #1
- Product   -   The jeans
- Place   -   STOP 55 Truck Stops where they are sold
- Price   - $39.95
- Promotion -   The advertisement in *Overdrive Magazine*

Question #2
- Primary Group

Question #3
- Physiological need for comfort and social need for belongingness and the need to identify with his fellow truckers

Question #4
- Selective retention

Question #5
- Learning
- Changes in an individual's behaviour arising from experience

Case #2   Alfredo's Fine Cuisine

Question #1
- Tourists or locals have planned a trip and decide to have dinner before the play and must eat.
- References from friends on the quality of the play will undoubtedly turn to the subject of a good restaurant in the area. If the play is favourable the dinner will be seen as part of a good night out.

Question #2
- The proximity of the restaurant to the theatre district.
- The restaurant ads may be in the brochures in the theatre and seen as part of the cultural experience.

Question #3
- If they see the ad in their theatre brochure, or earlier in their home town or Toronto newspapers, it will act as an automatic cultural link
- Seen as a step in the Buyer Decision Process.

Question #4
- No, it should not.
- Large cities depending on touristry also have a home market and in this case, 3 million people within its city boundaries.
- For residents it acts as Variety Seeking Behaviour even if it is or is not a night at the theatre.
- Habitual buying behaviour in this case is added onto a night out.

Case #3   The Dawsons

1.   A

2.   A

3.   E

4.   C

Chapter 6

Business Markets and Business Buyer Behaviour

Chapter Overview

Business markets and consumer markets are alike in some key ways. For example, both include people in buying roles who make purchase decisions to satisfy needs. Business markets, however, differ in many ways from consumer markets. For one thing, the business market is enormous, and individual corporate purchases can be in the millions, far larger than the consumer market. College students must learn to look at the job market that is available to them in the business market. Most will work in this area and therefore require an understanding of this, to them a new market, and must not limit themselves to solely the consumer market. All one has to do is look around their office or home and see the endless stream of business products. Within Canada alone, the business market includes more than one million organizations that annually purchase billions of dollars worth of goods and services.

Chapter Objectives

1. Define the business market and explain how business markets differ from consumer markets.
2. Identify the major factors that influence business buyer behaviour.
3. List and define the steps in the business buying-decision process
4. Compare the institutional and government markets and explain how institutional and government buyers make their buying decisions.

Chapter Topics

Business Markets
- Characteristics of Business Markets
  - Market Structure and Demand
  - Nature of the Buying Unit
  - Types of Decisions and the Decision Process
- Model of Business Buyer Behaviour

Business Buyer Behaviour
- Major Types of Buying Situations
- Participants in the Business Buying Process
- Major Influences on Business Buyers
  - Environmental Factors
  - Organizational Factors
  - Interpersonal Factors
  - Individual Factors
- The Business Buying Process
  - Problem Recognition
  - General Need Description
  - Product Specification
  - Supplier Search
  - Proposal Solicitation
  - Supplier Selection
  - Order-Routine Specification
  - Performance Review

Institutional and Government Markets
- Institutional Markets
- Government Markets

Chapter Summary

1.   How business markets differ from consumer markets.

Main differences include market structure and demand, nature of the buying unity, and types of decisions and decision processes. Business markets are geographically concentrated and have derived, inelastic, and fluctuating demand. Buying is more professional and involves more people. Decisions are more complex, more formalized, and the buyer and seller are more dependent upon one another.

2.   The major factors that influence business buyer behaviour.

There are four major influences. Environmental elements are level of primary demand, economic outlook, and cost of money, supply conditions, technological change, political/regulatory change, and competitive developments. Organizational elements are authority, status, empathy, and persuasiveness. Individual elements are age, education, job position, personality, and risk attitudes.

3.   The stages in the business buying decision process, and their definitions.

Stages include problem recognition, general need description, product specification, supplier search, proposal solicitation, supplier selection, order routine specification, and performance review.

4.   The three major types of buying situations.

Straight rebuy is a reorder without any modifications. A modified rebuy involves some changes in product specifications, prices, terms, and suppliers. New task buying occurs when a company buys a product or service for the first time. In such cases, greater risk or cost will lead to a larger number of decision participants and a greater information search effort.

5.   The unique aspects of how institutional and government buyers make their buying decisions.

Institutional buyers are schools, hospitals, prisons and other organizations. Many institutions have low budgets and captive patrons. Government buying may be coordinated by a special agency and the buying process may be scrutinized by various publics. Governments may be influenced by non-economic decision criteria. Government buying practices can be complex and can have too much paperwork, bureaucracy, regulation, low prices, and other factors.

Key Terms

Business buying	(pg. 243)	Order-routine specification	(pg. 258)
Business markets	(pg. 243)	Performance review	(pg. 258)
Buyers	(pg. 250)	Problem recognition	(pg. 255)
Buying center	(pg. 249)	Product specification	(pg. 256)
Deciders	(pg. 250)	Proposal solicitation	(pg. 257)
Derived demand	(pg. 244)	Straight rebuy	(pg. 248)
Gatekeepers	(pg. 250)	Supplier search	(pg. 257)
General need description	(pg. 256)	Supplier selection	(pg. 258)
Government market	(pg. 262)	Systems buying	(pg. 249)
Influencers	(pg. 250)	Users	(pg. 250)
Institutional market	(pg. 262)	Value Analysis	(pg. 256)
Modified rebuy	(pg. 249)		
New task	(pg. 249)		

Multiple Choice Questions

6-1   Multiple

Business buying involves a more professional purchasing effort in which of the following areas?

1.   Marketing structure and demand
2.   Nature of the buying unit
3.   Types of decisions
4.   The decision process
5.   None of the above

6-2   Multiple

A drop in the price of leather will not cause shoe manufacturers to buy more leather. This is considered what type of demand structure?

1.   Inelastic
2.   Elastic
3.   Fluctuating
4.   Stagnating
5.   Indifferent

6-3   Multiple

The business buying process tends to be more formal than the consumer buying process. Large business purchases require all the following except:

1.   Detailed product specification
2.   Written purchase orders
3.   Careful supplier searches
4.   Formal approval
5.   All of the above

6-4   Multiple

Buying centres and buying decisions in a business are influenced by the following forces except:

1.   Internal organizational
2.   Interpersonal
3.   Intrapersonal
4.   Individual
5.   External environment

6-5   Multiple

There are four major questions in the business buyer behaviour model. These questions include all the following except:

1.   What buying decisions do business buyers make?
2.   Who participates in the buying process?
3.   What are the major influences on buyers?
4.   Who are the buyers responsible to in the buying process?
5.   How do business buyers make their buying decisions?

6-6   Multiple

In which of the following do the "In" suppliers try to maintain product and service quality?

1.   Straight rebuy
2.   Modified rebuy
3.   New task buying
4.   Systems buying
5.   All of the above

6-7   Multiple

In a new task-buying situation, a buyer must concentrate on all the following issues except:

1.   Product specifications
2.   Price limits
3.   Payment terms
4.   Order quantities
5.   All of the above

6-8   Multiple

Teresa works at a cross stitching shop where she provides her patrons with the specifications on different patterns and gives out information to help her customers evaluate alternatives. Teresa is considered a(n):

1.   User
2.   Influencer
3.   Buyer
4.   Decider
5.   Gatekeeper

6-9   Multiple

Many international companies participate in business buying. In a recent study _____ was found to have the highest amount of team buying, where more than one person was involved in each purchase decision.

1.   United States
2.   Canada
3.   France
4.   Sweden
5.   Germany

6-10   Multiple

Economic factors play a key role in decisions by buyers in the business community. Which of the following does not belong?

1.   Level of primary demand
2.   Economic outlook
3.   Level of secondary demand
4.   The cost of money
5.   All of the above

6-11   Multiple

More and more companies are merging both in name and in joining their purchasing power. Companies that dealt with a number of companies are now finding that there are fewer and fewer, but these buyers are at a much higher management level. It can be said that these companies are moving towards a_____ system.

1.   Centralized buying
2.   Upgraded purchasing
3.   National account sales force
4.   Electronic data interchange
5.   Long-term contract

6-12   Multiple

Just-in-time production has grown in recent years as companies realize the great effects it has on profitability. Just-in-time production encompasses all the following concepts except:

1.   Vendor-managed inventory systems
2.   Value analysis
3.   Total quality management
4.   Flexible manufacturing
5.   Employee self-management

6-13   Multiple

Jacinta has worked for Maple Rock Foods for over a year. Maple Rock Foods has had a bad year and they need a change. The CEO has suggested the purchasing department either streamlines its activities or looks to new solutions. All the following would be stages of the buying process for Jacinta in this new task buy except:

1.   General need description
2.   Supplier search
3.   Proposal solicitation
4.   Order routine specification
5.   All of the above

6-14   Multiple

Che Lau has operated his own potting business for the last 5 years. He has established very good relations with a major supplier of peat moss and potting soil. There are relatively few changes in his orders as this purchase is considered a straight rebuy. From the following, which stage must Che Lau perform every time?

1.   Product specification
2.   Problem recognition
3.   Proposal solicitation
4.   General need description
5.   None of the above

6-15   Multiple

Choosing a supplier is a long and tedious process, however, finding the right supplier provides tremendous benefits. There are many important characteristics to look for in a supplier. Which of the following is NOT considered to be among these characteristics?

1.   Quality products and service
2.   Reasonable prices
3.   On-time delivery
4.   Ethical corporate behaviour
5.   Honest communication

6-16   Multiple

When Robert's Farming Products went looking for a new supplier, Robert looked at primary factors to make his decision. Secondary factors play just as an important role as the primary factors in helping a company choose new suppliers. Which of the following characteristics is not an important secondary factor?

1.   Repair and servicing capabilities
2.   Technical aid and advice
3.   Presence of an EDI system
4.   Performance history
5.   All of the above are important

6-17   Multiple

Institutional markets are different from business and consumer markets in many ways. All the following are considered institutional markets except:

1.   Schools
2.   Hospitals
3.   Prisons
4.   Recreational facilities
5.   Nursing homes

6-18   Multiple

Dealing with the government can be a long drawn-out process. There are many people involved, and the business must remember all but which of the following to be successful?

1.   Be able to locate the key decision makers
2.   Identify the factors that affect buying behaviour
3.   Know someone in the government who can help build a relationship with the buyers
4.   Understand the buying decision process
5.   All of the above are helpful and necessary

6-19   Multiple

Governments require companies to submit bids for their proposals and projects, and then select the lowest bidder. However, governments sometimes buy on a negotiated contract basis if all the following are true except:

1.   Major R&D costs are involved
2.   There is high risk
3.   It is a case where little competition exists
4.   It is a straight rebuy situation
5.   All of the above would qualify for a negotiated contract

6-20   Multiple

Although the government is quite a different business entity than "private" business, their buyers are affected by the same factors as consumer and business buyers. These factors include all the following except:

1.   Political
2.   Environmental
3.   Organizational
4.   Interpersonal
5.   Individual

6-21   Multiple

As stated before, government is usually different from "private" companies. Examples of issues businesses have in dealing with the government include all the following except:

1.   Bureaucracy
2.   Regulations
3.   Rapid decision making
4.   Frequent shifts in procurement personnel
5.   All of the above

6-22   Multiple

Sellers and buyers can use _____ as a tool to help secure a new contract.

1.   General need description
2.   Product specification
3.   Value analysis
4.   Product analysis
5.   None of the above

6-23   Multiple

Terrence and Phillip have worked as Wal-Mart buyers for the past 2 years. They graduated from university together and underwent their company training together. They are both good friends and accomplished buyers. Their style of buying is slightly different however. Terrence is very in-depth in his analysis of proposals, while Phillip is more interested in the relationship aspect of the proposal. These differences can be attributed to:

1.   Interpersonal factors
2.   Organizational factors
3.   Environmental factors
4.   Individual factors
5.   None of the above

6-24   Multiple

The buying centre is a fundamental part of the business buying process. One role not found in the buying centre is:

1.   Users
2.   Gatekeepers
3.   Influencers
4.   Buyers
5.   All roles are found in the buying centre

6-25   Multiple

All the following are differences in market structure and demand between consumer and business markets except:

1.   Business markets are more geographically concentrated
2.   Business markets have fewer buyers
3.   Business markets have derived demand
4.   Business markets have more elastic demand
5.   All of the above are true

6-26   Multiple

When consumer demand increases slightly, but leads to a large increase in business market demand, we can say that the business market is experiencing:

1.   Fluctuating demand
2.   Geographic demand
3.   Elastic demand
4.   Inelastic demand
5.   Offsetting demand

6-27   Multiple

Which of the following statements about buying centres is/are true?

1.   The buying centre is not a fixed and formally identified unit within the buying organization
2.   Buying centre roles can be assumed by different people for different purchases
3.   In some cases, one person may assume all the buying centre roles
4.   Only 1 and 2
5.   All of the above

6-28   Multiple

Factors such as supplier reputation for repair and servicing capabilities are important criteria for evaluation at which stage in the business buying decision process?

1.   Problem recognition
2.   Supplier selection
3.   Product specification
4.   Value analysis
5.   Proposal solicitation

6-29   Multiple

From your knowledge of buying situations, which two stages of the business buying process can always be expected to be completed for new task, modified rebuy, and straight rebuy?

1.   Problem recognition and product specification
2.   General need description and proposal solicitation
3.   Product specification and performance review
4.   General need description and supplier selection
5.   Problem recognition and supplier selection

6-30   Multiple

Gina is the Executive Assistant to Ang Lee, Vice President of Purchasing for Radenko Industries. Gina fills which buying centre role?

1.   Gatekeeper
2.   Influencer
3.   Buyer
4.   Decider
5.   User

True/False Questions

6-1   True/False

Business markets are much larger than consumer markets.

6-2   True/False

Business demand is desired demand.

6-3   True/False

Business marketers may roll up their sleeves and work closely with their customers during all stages of the buying process.

6-4   True/False

The greater the cost or risk, the fewer the number of participants involved in the decision process.

6-5   True/False

Systems selling is a key business marketing strategy for holding accounts, but it is not successful for winning accounts.

6-6   True/False

Purchasing agents often have the authority to prevent salespersons from seeing users or deciders.

6-7   True/False

The buying centre is a fixed and formally identified unit within the buying organization.

6-8   True/False

A buying centre is only composed of people from one firm.

6-9   True/False

Business buyers actually respond to both economic and personal factors.

6-10   True/False

When competing products differ greatly, business buyers are more accountable for their choices and pay more attention to economic factors.

6-11   True/False

Business buyers are increasingly seeking short-term contracts with suppliers.

6-12   True/False

In advertising to business customers, marketers often alert customers to potential problems, and show how their products provide solutions.

6-13   True/False

A supplier's primary task is to get listed in major buying directories, and a secondary task is to build a good reputation in the marketplace.

6-14   True/False

Many buyers prefer to limit their numbers of suppliers to ensure high quality and reliable service. They are reluctant to increase suppliers because the risks outweigh the benefits.

6-15   True/False

Blanket contracting leads to more single-source buying and to buying more items from that source.

6-16   True/False

Low budgets and captive patrons characterize many institutional markets.

6-17   True/False

Although institutional marketers have special needs, many marketers use the same divisions to meet the special characteristics and needs of institutional buyers.

6-18   True/False

Government organizations are not concerned with the issue of domestic or foreign suppliers. Their major concern is the lowest bid.

6-19   True/False

On an open-bid basis, advertising and personal selling makes no difference in winning a bid.

6-20   True/False

By showing buyers a better way to make an object, outside sellers can turn a straight rebuy situation into a new task situation.

Applying Terms and Concepts

To determine how well you understand the materials in this chapter, read each of the following brief cases and then respond to the questions that follow. Answers are given at the end of this chapter.

Case #1   Replating Car Bumpers

Bill Majors has been supplying the province of Alberta's repair shop for over twenty years by replating old chrome bumpers and replacing new cars with plastic bumpers.

In an auto-based society accidents are a way of life and Bill has been capitalizing on insuring accidents profitably for years. As cars developed and advanced in the components that made them up, Bill found a niche and stuck to it. He has built up a steady market of over 300 shops that regularly use his service. His prices have been reasonable, and he has few complaints and virtually no competition.

But in the last five years he has seen a new type of competitor moving into his area of expertise. And that has been foreign products being dumped into Canada at a fraction of the price that he can do repairs for or even buy product from his usual supplier.

As environmental laws have become more and more strict, Bill has found himself investing more and more money into legislative safety for his workers in the handling of the chemicals needed in his business and proper storage and disposal of this material. Because of this he has had to extend his line of credit at the bank as interest rates creep upwards.

1. How does the economic outlook and the high cost of money affect his business?

   _____

   _____

   _____

   _____

2. What supply conditions are affecting his business, and what types of new businesses are available to Bill?

   _____

   _____

   _____

   _____

3. What is the effect of the price of money on international growth?

   _____

   _____

   _____

   _____

4. What are the steps in the buying decision process that would mostly influence his customers? What steps would you expect to be affected by competition in the eyes of Bill's customers? Which steps of the business buying process would you expect a tradeshow to influence?

   _____

   _____

   _____

   _____

5. What role do government and environmental restrictions play in his future?

   _____

   _____

   _____

   _____

Case #2   Buffalo Express[1]

Darin Cosentino, executive vice-president of Buffalo Express, recently completed negotiations with the Black Eagle Paper Company of Montreal, Quebec, to be the exclusive transportation company moving Black Eagle newsprint roll paper into the United States.

Buffalo could easily handle the projected annual volume of 50,000 tonnes with its current fleet of trailers; however, Cosentino believed a special trailer might better haul this high-density, high-weight freight. He authorized Eric Moore, director of operations, to organize a committee to investigate the problem.

Moore's committee posed the problem to representatives of the major trailer manufacturers, including Fruehauf, Intercontinental Truck Body, Great Dane, and Trailmobile. Buffalo has purchased hundreds of trailers from each of these manufacturers in building its fleet of 1,500 trailers, but this was the first time it wanted a manufacturer to modify its product specification to meet the needs of a single shipper.

Each manufacturer supplied a written proposal for the project, with most simply offering their standard trailer with a reinforced frame to handle the weight. Intercontinental, however, sent a sales representative who presented information on a unique trailer design called the Wedge. The Wedge was similar to a standard trailer, with two important differences: first, the front of the trailer was 20 cm lower than the rear; and second, instead of traditional rectangular shape, the sides of the trailer in the front were slightly tapered to form a less blunt front end—hence the name Wedge.

The trailer was in compliance with Transport Canada Regulations, specifying a length of no more than 15 metres and a width not exceeding 3 metres. The Wedge, with a reinforced frame, could easily carry the 20,000–22,000 kg load without difficulty. Additionally, the aerodynamics of the Wedge were projected to decrease fuel consumption by 1 litre per 100 km.

Moore's committee reviewed each manufacturer's proposal regarding trailer design, capacity, price, delivery date, warranty, and construction. After some deliberation, the contract for 25 trailers was awarded to Intercontinental.

1.   What type of buying situation did Buffalo create with Intercontinental and why?

_____

_____

_____

_____

[1] *Principles of Marketing*, 3rd Edition, Kotler, Armstrong, Warren (Prentice Hall) – pg. 115.

2. The demand for trailers was based on the demand for roll paper, which in turn was based on the consumer demand for newspapers. What type of demand is exemplified by the demand for trailers and roll paper and why?

_____

_____

_____

_____

3. What is the main type of influence on business buying illustrated in Buffalo's business decision to haul Black Eagle's paper? Why?

_____

_____

_____

_____

4. What other types of influences or factors did the buying committee respond to?

_____

_____

_____

_____

5. Why was personal selling important in this case?

_____

_____

_____

_____

Case #3   Fort McMurray Community College

Fort McMurray Community College is one of seven community colleges in Alberta. Located in the city of Fort McMurray, it is a two-year school which offers degrees in a variety of programs including business administration, engineering science, mathematics, liberal arts, the natural sciences, and telecommunications. The college also offers certificates in the occupational trades of industrial electricity, automotive mechanics, industrial machining, and drafting.

Carl Palmer, the coordinator of occupational education at the college, was faced with the need to acquire two additional vertical milling machines for the industrial machining program in which there had been a substantial increase in enrollment in recent years. After consulting with Vincent Barone, the dean of instruction, the administration decided that the college would apply for a provincial grant, which if received, would allow the college to purchase the machine tools.

Since the college had not purchased such equipment since 1989, an ad hoc committee was formed to gather the appropriate information and write the grant proposal. The committee was composed of Palmer, Michael Whyte, an instructor of industrial machining, and Lisa Klein, the college's assistant business manager. In gathering information the committee met with the department's advisory council, made up of area employers, to learn their opinions as to which makes and models of machine tools were used in their machine shops and which might meet the college's needs. The committee also attended the Northwestern Tool Show held in Seattle, Washington, where members spoke with manufacturers' representatives and also gathered brochures on various pieces of equipment.

The committee learned that a general price increase of 10 percent was expected by most manufacturers on February 1. The committee realized it would not receive final notification of the grant until April 1, but decided that the price increase would not affect the decision to purchase any equipment, even if additional funds had to come from the college.

The committee applied for the grant and also developed the set of specifications for the milling machine that would meet the school's needs. The specification sheets indicated that the firm awarded the contract must supply a machine equal to or better than a Bridgeport series one vertical mill, with the college reserving the right to reject any or all bids. The specification sheets, which also stipulated that the machines must be delivered and set up at the college by August 1, were then distributed to all interested parties that had responded to the invitation to bid notice placed in area newspapers.

Supplier	Manufacturer	Price per Machine (CDN)
Langley Brothers	Jet	$12,995
J and B Industrial Supply	Bridgeport	16,750
Belros Corporation	Enterprise	13,750
Yukon Supply	Bridgeport	16,250
U. T. A.	Savrin	14,950

After careful consideration, the committee rejected the Jet, Enterprise, and Savrin milling machines as not meeting specifications. The committee awarded the bid to Yukon Supply.

1.   Identify the type of demand faced by Fort McMurray Community College when it decided to place an order for the two milling machines after the price was scheduled to increase.
    A.   derived demand
    B.   inelastic demand
    C.   latent demand
    D.   full demand
    E.   elastic demand

2.   Identify the type of demand faced by Fort McMurray Community College when it made a decision to purchase two additional milling machines due to an increase in enrollment in the machine trades program.
    A.   derived demand
    B.   inelastic demand
    C.   latent demand
    D.   full demand
    E.   elastic demand

3.   The buying process used by Fort McMurray Community College is an example of _____ buying.
    A.   value analysis
    B.   negotiated contract
    C.   open bid
    D.   open-to-buy
    E.   top-down

4.   Identify the type of buying situation faced by Fort McMurray Community College. Provide justification for your answer.

Multiple Choice Answers

1.	Correct Answer:	2	Reference:	pg. 245
2.	Correct Answer:	1	Reference:	pg. 245
3.	Correct Answer:	5	Reference:	pg. 250
4.	Correct Answer:	3	Reference:	pg. 250
5.	Correct Answer:	4	Reference:	pg. 251
6.	Correct Answer:	1	Reference:	pg. 248
7.	Correct Answer:	5	Reference:	pg. 248
8.	Correct Answer:	2	Reference:	pg. 250
9.	Correct Answer:	4	Reference:	pg. 251
10.	Correct Answer:	3	Reference:	pg. 252
11.	Correct Answer:	1	Reference:	pg. 252
12.	Correct Answer:	5	Reference:	pg. 254
13.	Correct Answer:	5	Reference:	pg. 255 (Table 6-2)
14.	Correct Answer:	1	Reference:	pg. 255 (Table 6-2)
15.	Correct Answer:	2	Reference:	pg. 257
16.	Correct Answer:	5	Reference:	pg. 257
17.	Correct Answer:	4	Reference:	pg. 262
18.	Correct Answer:	3	Reference:	pg. 262
19.	Correct Answer:	4	Reference:	pg. 263
20.	Correct Answer:	1	Reference:	pg. 264
21.	Correct Answer:	3	Reference:	pg. 264
22.	Correct Answer:	3	Reference:	pg. 256

23.	Correct Answer:	4	Reference:	pg. 255
24.	Correct Answer:	5	Reference:	pg. 250
25.	Correct Answer:	4	Reference:	pg. 245
26.	Correct Answer:	1	Reference:	pg. 245
27.	Correct Answer:	5	Reference:	pg. 250
28.	Correct Answer:	2	Reference:	pg. 257
29.	Correct Answer:	3	Reference:	pg. 256
30.	Correct Answer:	1	Reference:	pg. 250

True/False Answers

1.	TRUE	Reference:	pg. 243	Topic:	Business Markets
2.	FALSE	Reference:	pg. 244	Topic:	Market Structure and Demand
3.	TRUE	Reference:	pg. 246	Topic:	Types of Decisions and the Decision Process
4.	FALSE	Reference:	pg. 248	Topic:	Major Types of Buying Situations
5.	FALSE	Reference:	pg. 248	Topic:	Major Types of Buying Situations
6.	TRUE	Reference:	pg. 249	Topic:	Participants in the Business Buying Process
7.	FALSE	Reference:	pg. 250	Topic:	Participants in the Business Buying Process
8.	FALSE	Reference:	pg. 250	Topic:	Participants in the Business Buying Process
9.	TRUE	Reference:	pg. 251	Topic:	Major Influences on Business Buyers
10.	TRUE	Reference:	pg. 251	Topic:	Major Influences on Business Buyers

11.	FALSE	Reference:	pg. 254	Topic: Organizational Factors
12.	TRUE	Reference:	pg. 256	Topic: Problem Recognition
13.	FALSE	Reference:	pg. 257	Topic: Supplier Search
14.	FALSE	Reference:	pg. 258	Topic: Supplier Selection
15.	TRUE	Reference:	pg. 258	Topic: Order-Routine Specification
16.	TRUE	Reference:	pg. 262	Topic: Institutional Markets
17.	FALSE	Reference:	pg. 262	Topic: Institutional Markets
18.	FALSE	Reference:	pg. 262	Topic: Government Markets
19.	TRUE	Reference:	pg. 262	Topic: Government Markets
20.	TRUE	Reference:	pg. 256	Topic: Product Specification

Applying Terms and Concepts Answers

Case #1   Replating Car Bumpers

Question #1
- The high cost of money will result in additional costs to his product.
- Loss of business to cheaper importers.
- Business customers are geographically separated from his customers, resulting in high transportation costs.
- Business purchasing involves more buyers, because of the constant increase in car sales, both new and old
- Business buyers because of increased costs often buy directly from producers.

Question #2
- Importing costs and shipping to his warehouse
- Modified products being shipped directly to his customers rebuy
- A new business that he may look into is a distribution company, and import product directly to his shop or directly to his customers
- Another business would be the manufacturing of new bumpers, rather than just repairs, and buying them from manufacturers
- System buying

Question #3

- If he stays in Canada for funding he may not be able to compete in other countries
- Influencers such as other manufacturers may set up alliances with overseas production houses
- Buyers may find it easier to bypass him and go right to the Internet (manufacturers)
- Deciders
- Being able to meet orders quickly in relationship to importers

Question #4

- Problem recognition
- Product specification
- Supplier search
- Supplier selection
- Order-routine specification

Question #5

- Government restrictions will result in higher manufacturing costs.
- Environmental laws and their restrictions will result in new equipment purchase and additional storing and handling costs.

Case #2   Buffalo Express

Question #1

- Buffalo created a modified rebuy situation because they wanted to modify product specifications before their purchase.

Question #2

- Derived demand is exemplified as the business demand ultimately comes from the demand for consumer goods.
- Consumer purchases drive the need to produce and/or deliver the product.

Question #3

- The organizational influence on business buying is illustrated because Buffalo's decision to contract with Intercontinental was based on their client's needs as well as their supplier's capacities.
- The buying committee had their own organizational objectives to fulfil.

Question #4

- Economic
- Environmental (regulations and laws)

Question #5

- Personal selling was imperative in this case because it was what distinguished Intercontinental from its competitors.
- The Wedge product along with personal selling persuaded the buying committee that the Wedge was the trailer best suited for their purposes.

Case #3   Fort McMurray Community College

1.   B

2.   A

3.   C

4.   The administrative and instructional staff of Fort McMurray Community College faced a purchasing decision that involved the gathering of considerable information from a variety of sources. This information included machine manufacturers' distributors, machine specification and capabilities, delivery dates, prices, machine setup, and so on. The buying process was conducted over several months. Also, the college had not purchased such a machine in some years and was unlikely to purchase additional machinery in the near future. Therefore, although this approximated the new-task buying process used by business firms, technically, Fort McMurray Community College used the open bid buying process.

Chapter 7

Market Segmentation, Targeting, and Positioning for Competitive Advantage

Chapter Overview

Organizations selling to consumer and business markets recognize that they cannot appeal to all buyers in those markets or at least not to all buyers in the same way. Buyers are too numerous, too widely scattered and too varied in their needs and buying practices. Marketers now pick their markets, zoom in on them and position themselves for competitive advantage. By deciding on various market strategies marketers are able to meet the requirements of various specific groups and design products for their specific wants and needs. The idea of selling the same product to all markets, the same way, is an idea of the past. With the proper research we can segment our market to meet the needs of our company. Therefore, most companies are moving away from mass marketing. Instead they practice target marketing—identifying market segments, selecting one or more of them, and developing products and marketing mixes tailored to each. In this way, sellers can develop the right product for each target market and adjust their prices, distribution channels, and advertising to reach the target markets efficiently. From reaching mass markets to niche markets, market segmentation gives marketers the tools they need.

Chapter Objectives

1. Define the three steps of target marketing: market segmentation, market targeting, and market positioning.
2. List and discuss the major levels of market segmentation and bases for segmenting consumer and business markets.
3. Explain how companies identify attractive market segments and choose a market-coverage strategy.
4. Explain how companies can position their products for maximum competitive advantage in the marketplace.

Chapter Topics

Markets

Market Segmentation
- Levels of Market Segmentation
  - Mass Marketing
  - Segment Marketing
  - Niche Marketing
  - Micromarketing
- Bases for Segmenting Consumer Markets
  - Geographic Segmentation
  - Demographic Segmentation
    - Age and Life-Cycle Stage
    - Gender
    - Income
  - Psychographic Segmentation
    - Social Class
    - Lifestyle
    - Personality
  - Behavioural Segmentation
    - Occasions
    - Benefits Sought
    - User Status
    - Usage Rate
    - Loyalty Status
  - Using Multiple Segmentation Bases
- Segmenting Business Markets
- Segmenting International Markets
- Requirements for Effective Segmentation

Market Targeting
- Evaluating Market Segments
  - Segment Size and Growth
  - Segment Structural Attractiveness
  - Company Objectives and Resources
- Selecting Market Segments
  - Undifferentiated Marketing
  - Differentiated Marketing
  - Concentrated Marketing
  - Choosing a Market-Coverage Strategy

Positioning for Competitive Advantage
- Positioning Strategies
- Choosing a Positioning Strategy
  - Identifying Possible Competitive Advantages
    - Product Differentiation
    - Services Differentiation
    - Personnel Differentiation
    - Image Differentiation
  - Selecting the Right Competitive Advantages
    - How Many Differences to Promote
    - Which Differences to Promote
  - Selecting an Overall Position Strategy
    - More for More
    - More for the Same
    - The Same for Less
    - Less for Much Less

Chapter Summary

1.   The definitions of market segmentation, market targeting, and market positioning.

Market segmentation is the process of dividing a market into distinct groups of buyers with different needs, characteristics, or behaviour who might require separate products or marketing mixes. Market targeting is evaluating each segment's attractiveness and deciding which segments to enter. Market positioning is the setting of the competitive position and creating a detailed marketing mix.

2.   The major bases for segmenting consumer and business markets.

The major bases for segmenting consumer markets are geographic, demographic, psychographic, and behavioural. The major bases for segmenting business markets are demographics, operating variables, purchasing approaches, situational factors, and personal characteristics.

3.   How companies identify attractive market segments and choose a market-coverage strategy.

Segment attractiveness depends upon desirable segment size and growth, current and potential competitors, threat of substitutes, power of buyers, and the power of suppliers. Market-coverage can include undifferentiated, differentiated, and concentrated strategies.

150

4.   The four characteristics of effective market segmentation.

Market segments must have measurability (in terms of size, purchasing power, and clear profiles), accessibility (can be effectively reached and served), substantiality (large or profitable enough), and accountability (can design programs for attracting customers effectively).

5.   How companies can position their products for maximum competitive advantages in the marketplace.

Competitive advantage (Porter) offers consumers a superior value for the price. Differentiation is the key to competitive advantage. A product's position is the view customers have of its value. Positions can be differentiated by product attributes, services, or image characteristics.

Key Terms

Age and life-cycle segmentation	(pg. 282)	Local marketing	(pg. 278)
		Market positioning	(pg. 275)
Behavioural segmentation	(pg. 285)	Market segmentation	(pg. 275)
Benefit segmentation	(pg. 286)	Market targeting	(pg. 275)
Competitive advantage	(pg. 301)	Micromarketing	(pg. 278)
Concentrated marketing	(pg. 296)	Niche marketing	(pg. 276)
Demographic segmentation	(pg. 282)	Occasion segmentation	(pg. 285)
Differentiated marketing	(pg. 295)	Product position	(pg. 297)
Gender segmentation	(pg. 283)	Psychographic segmentation	(pg. 285)
Geographic segmentation	(pg. 282)	Segment marketing	(pg. 276)
Income segmentation	(pg. 284)	Target market	(pg. 294)
Individual marketing	(pg. 278)	Undifferentiated marketing	(pg. 294)
Intermarket segmentation	(pg. 291)	Value proposition	(pg. 306)

Multiple Choice Questions

7-1   Multiple

Sprite has begun a new marketing campaign to attract the world's youth to their product. They are focusing on being individual and drinking something because you want to drink it, not because somebody tells you to. Sprite is practicing:

1.   Market segmentation
2.   Market targeting
3.   Target marketing
4.   Market positioning
5.   Direct targeting

7-2   Multiple

Markets consist of many different buyers and these buyers differ in many different ways. Which of the following would not be considered a buyer difference?

1.   Needs
2.   Wants
3.   Locations
4.   Buying attitudes
5.   All of the above

7-3   Multiple

When Coca-Cola first came into the market, they tried to promote their drink to every one hoping it would be enough to gain reasonable market share. This type of promotional strategy is considered:

1.   Niche marketing
2.   Segment marketing
3.   Macromarketing
4.   Mass marketing
5.   Micromarketing

7-4   Multiple

Wal-Mart and Sears have similar merchandise in their stores; however, they do not sell or promote snowblowers in Texas and they do not sell lawn mowers in Canada in January. This type of marketing would be considered:

1.   Niche marketing
2.   Segmented marketing
3.   Macromarketing
4.   Mass marketing
5.   Micromarketing

7-5   Multiple

Mass customization is the ability to prepare on a mass basis individually designed products and communication to meet each customer's requirements. All the following help the progress of mass customization except:

1.   Detailed databases
2.   Call display
3.   Robotics production
4.   E-mail
5.   Internet

7-6   Multiple

Consumer markets can be segmented in various ways. The population density distribution of an area, urban, suburban or rural, is classified as which of the following?

1.   Geographic
2.   Demographic
3.   Psychographic
4.   Behavioural
5.   1 and 2

7-7   Multiple

Samia comes from a large family. She has 4 brothers and 2 sisters. It was quite difficult for her to really express herself in such an environment. Through her childhood she learned to fend for herself and to really push herself hard if she wanted something in life. Samia is an achiever and now, after completing her Bachelor of Commerce degree, she is a financial analyst for Procter & Gamble and very proud of her achievements. This characteristic of Samia is considered a:

1.   Geographic
2.   Demographic
3.   Psychographic
4.   Behavioural
5.   3 and 4

7-8   Multiple

All markets can be segmented into different user statuses. Which of the following would not be considered a user status?

1.   Non-user
2.   Post-user
3.   Ex-user
4.   Potential user
5.   First-time user

7-9   Multiple

Rodrigo loves Lays potato chips. Out of the last 10 times he visited the store he purchased Lays 9 times and he got Lays and Old Dutch once. This routine of always purchasing Lays is an example of which trait?

1.   Brand loyalty
2.   Indifference
3.   Low price
4.   Habit
5.   All of the above

7-10   Multiple

Marketers are using _____ in an effort to identify smaller, better defined target groups.

1. Behavioural segmentation
2. Psychographic segmentation
3. Demographic segmentation
4. Multiple segmentation
5. Geographic segmentation

7-11   Multiple

Many studies have been done indicating the affluent people of Quebec do not travel as much as affluent people from other provinces in Canada; however, when they do travel they prefer Latin America as their destination. This type of segmentation would be considered:

1.   Demographic
2.   Psychographic
3.   Geodemographic
4.   Geographic
5.   Psychodemographic

7-12   Multiple

Market segmentation for businesses is slightly different than that for consumer markets. The decision to focus on companies whose people and values are similar to your company would be considered a part of which of the following variables?

1.   Demographic
2.   Operating variables
3.   Purchasing approaches
4.   Situational factors
5.   Personal characteristics

7-13   Multiple

Business buying behaviour is very closely related to the benefits derived from a purchase.
Harold's cement business success is mostly due to his understanding of his competition's
pricing. He therefore is ready to change suppliers based on price even if their service may
falter. Harold's buying behaviour would be considered:

1.   Transaction buying
2.   Bargain hunting
3.   Relationship buying
4.   Programmed buying
5.   1 and 2

7-14   Multiple

G7 is a group of 7 countries from around the world. In segmenting the world market, the
most common way would be through economic factors. Which of the following countries
would not be considered part of this group?

1.   France
2.   Canada
3.   Japan
4.   Spain
5.   Germany

7-15   Multiple

There are many ways you can segment markets. Bush Pilots Inc. identified seven major
market segments, however its staff was too small to develop separate marketing programs
for each one. Bush Pilots Inc. has a problem with:

1.   Measurability
2.   Actionability
3.   Accessibility
4.   Substantiality
5.   All of the above

7-16   Multiple

Effective marketing plans are the result of evaluation done on markets that have been properly segmented. Segmenting markets is only useful if the evaluation of such segments leads to concrete marketing plans, and eventually, sales. In the process of evaluating these different segments companies must consider all of the following except:

1.   Segment size
2.   Segment growth
3.   Segment purchasing power
4.   Segment structural attractiveness
5.   Company objectives

7-17   Multiple

Which of the following business segments have knowledge of competitors' offerings, view packaging as moderately important, and receive a small discount?

1.   Programmed buyers
2.   Relationship buyers
3.   Transaction buyers
4.   Bargain hunters
5.   Price conscious buyers

7-18   Multiple

Dyson in a manufacturer of kitchen utensils. They researched their markets thoroughly and they segmented their markets according to certain characteristics. They found the market segment of DINKs (dual income no kids) was not only growing but was also large enough to help their company grow and prosper. However, over the last few months they have been having troubles. They know their planning and research was not the problem, so it must be all of the following except:

1.   Aggressive competitors
2.   Substitute products
3.   Power of sellers
4.   Powerful suppliers
5.   All of the above

7-19   Multiple

_____ marketing relies on mass distribution and advertising and aims to give the product a superior image in people's minds.

1.   Differentiated
2.   Concentrated
3.   Mass
4.   Undifferentiated
5.   Unilateral

7-20   Multiple

Russell Stover's is a growing chocolate shop with limited resources. It has a very unique product and the owners know they can be a profitable company with the right approach to marketing. Which marketing strategy would you recommend for them?

1.   Concentrated
2.   Differentiated
3.   Unilateral
4.   Undifferentiated
5.   Mass

7-21   Multiple

Market-coverage strategy depends on a number of components. Some of these factors include all the following except:

1.   Product variability
2.   Product's stage in the life cycle
3.   Supplier variability
4.   Market variability
5.   Competitors marketing strategy

7-22   Multiple

Competitive advantage is fundamental to the success of a company. Which of the following would not be a means by which a company or market can be fundamentally differentiated?

1.   Product
2.   Price
3.   Personnel
4.   Services
5.   Image

7-23   Multiple

TaiTai's is a new oriental cloth embroidery company that has experienced phenomenal growth in the last few years. They do have a distinct competitive advantage; however, they have failed to position the company well and therefore people are only vaguely familiar with their services or do not really know anything special about it. TaiTai's has performed which of the following positioning errors?

1.   Over-positioning
2.   Confused positioning
3.   Reluctant positioning
4.   Under-positioning
5.   2 and 4

7-24   Multiple

Product differentiation for the sake of differentiation is not a measure of success. Not all brand differences are worthwhile. Product differentiation should therefore include which of the following?

1.   Superior
2.   Distinctive
3.   Affordable
4.   Profitable
5.   All of the above

7-25   Multiple

Market segmentation by quality, service, or economy would be an example of behavioural segmentation by:

1.   Purchase occasion
2.   Benefits sought
3.   User status
4.   User rate
5.   Loyalty status

7-26   Multiple

Dividing markets by categories such as none, medium, strong, or absolute would be examples of which type of behavioural segmentation?

1.   User rate
2.   User status
3.   Loyalty status
4.   Purchase occasion
5.   Benefits sought

7-27   Multiple

In terms of the purchasing approach segmentation for business markets, focus on centralized organizations would be an example of which kind of segmentation?

1.   Power structure
2.   Nature of existing relationships
3.   General purchase policies
4.   Purchasing function
5.   Purchasing criteria

7-28   Multiple

A focus on the urgency for delivery or service as the basis for segmenting business markets is an example of segmentation by:

1.   Demographics
2.   Situational factors
3.   Operating variables
4.   Purchasing approaches
5.   Personal characteristics

7-29   Multiple

Consumers who enjoy skydiving, bungee jumping and white water rafting could all be grouped using this segmentation variable.

1.   Geographic
2.   Demographic
3.   Psychographic
4.   Behavioural
5.   Personal

7-30   Multiple

Punjabi is responsible for market targeting at Chapters Book Sellers. Chapters is looking at entering the Regina market within the next year. Punjabi is currently in Regina to visit current competitors and learn if Barnes and Noble is considering the Regina market. Punjabi's work at Chapters contributes to which area of marketing targeting?

1.   Assessing segment structural attractiveness
2.   Undifferentiated marketing strategy
3.   Differentiated marketing strategy
4.   Choosing a market coverage strategy
5.   Concentrated marketing

True/False Questions

7-1   True/False

Companies who scatter their marketing approach are practicing the "shotgun" approach, while those who focus on the buyer who has greater purchasing interest are practicing the "rifle" approach.

7-2   True/False

Because buyers have unique needs and wants, each buyer is potentially a separate market.

7-3   True/False

The proliferation of advertising and distribution channels has made it much easier to practice the "one-size-fits-all" marketing strategy.

7-4   True/False

Market segments are usually small identifiable groups within a market.

7-5   True/False

In Canada the beer industry has expanded into a few small microbreweries. These in turn are quite small and are seeking a relatively small market. Niches are becoming more common in today's society.

7-6   True/False

A marketer is only required to segment the market according to one variable to find the best view of the market structure.

7-7   True/False

Geographic variables are easier to measure than other variables.

7-8   True/False

Demographic segmentation means dividing the market into their geographic location and their attitude towards a product.

7-9   True/False

Young adults want ads to tell them about the company and the product, and then leave it up to them to decide whether or not they like the company and its product.

7-10   True/False

Many marketers believe that behaviour variables are the best starting point for building market segments.

7-11   True/False

Companies have not always practiced target marketing. They have also practiced mass production and mass distribution and promoting.

7-12   True/False

International geographic segmentation assumes that nations close to one another will have very different traits and behaviours.

7-13   True/False

Marketers regularly study consumers' lifestyles to segment markets, which in turn can result in profits.

7-14   True/False

There are many ways to segment markets, and they are all equally effective.

7-15   True/False

The largest, fastest-growing segments are always the most attractive ones for every company.

7-16   True/False

If a segment fits the company's objectives, then the company will seek the skills and resources needed to succeed in that segment.

7-17   True/False

Companies should enter segments only where it can offer superior value and help gain advantages over competitors.

7-18   True/False

One way smaller companies can segment world markets is by grouping countries by regions instead of by individual countries.

7-19   True/False

Consumers position products only with the help of marketers.

7-20   True/False

Positioning strategy can be achieved by image changing, by the sponsoring of sporting or theatrical events.

Applying Terms and Concepts

To determine how well you understand the materials in this chapter, read each of the following brief cases and respond to the questions that follow. Answers are given at the end of this chapter.

Case #1   Eldin Incorporated[1]

Marjorie Miele, a former vice-president of marketing at General Dynamics of England, was often dismayed at the clutter on her desk. The paperwork was bad enough, she reasoned, but the telephone, calculator, and rolodex file only contributed to the lack of order.

Miele informally researched the problem and found that she was not alone in her thoughts about the need to have a more organized desk. She left General Dynamics to start Eldin Incorporated. After engaging in a formal research project where she studied the office equipment needs of executives, Miele found a definite need for a desktop organizer. Her solution to the problem was the Mark 3 Execusystem.

The Mark 3 incorporated the more cumbersome office devices into a single unit. The system, which looked like a desk blotter, had a built-in digital clock with alarm and calendar. Other components of the Mark 3 included a radio, calculator, computerized file system, and a telephone with an automatic dialer. The telephone was a "hands-free" model with a "mute" button, ideal for those conference calls where occasional privacy was needed while conferring with other people in the office. The Mark 3 was 60 x 100 cm, weighed 6 kilograms, and was made of black leather with nickel trim.

The profile of potential customers included the following characteristics: college educated, married, male, age 35-49, title of vice president or director, and income over $100,000 a year.

---

[1] *Principles of Marketing*, 3rd Edition, Kotler, Armstrong, Warren (Prentice Hall) – pg. 154.

The selling price of the Mark 3 was $685.00 and she calculated her first year break-even point to be 425 units. The potential demand was many times this number as she planned to market the product using world-wide mail-order utilizing *The Globe and Mail* and *The Financial Post* to advertise. Competition at this level was nonexistent. While many companies produced executive desk products, not one had the features of the Mark 3.

1. Miele determined the market segment was large enough to be served at a profit. Which requirement does this market meet for effective market segmentation? Why?

    _____

    _____

    _____

    _____

2. The customer profile developed by Miele is made up of demographic characteristics. Define demographic segmentation.

    _____

    _____

    _____

    _____

3. Which market coverage strategy is Miele pursuing? Explain.

    _____

    _____

    _____

    _____

4. Miele had designed the Mark 3 to provide those benefits identified and desired by her intended target market. Which basic variable has she used in segmenting this market? Why?

_____

_____

_____

_____

5. There are several stages of marketing such as segmentation, or positioning. At which stage of marketing is Eldin Incorporated operating? Explain.

_____

_____

_____

_____

Case #2   Crew Toothpaste

Michel Joudrey, a chemist by trade, began mixing his own toothpaste three years ago after being bothered by sensitive teeth and sore gums. He had tried commercially available toothpastes specially formulated for sensitive teeth, but he found that even the most popular pastes—Sensodyne and Promise—were of little help. He began to neglect his dental hygiene and in time his teeth also became stained from coffee and tobacco.

As his teeth and gums became increasingly sensitive, Joudrey tried a number of folk remedies. He was surprised to find that aloe, a gel extracted form the aloe vera plant, was quite effective in reducing pain during brushing. Looking for a more convenient method of application, Joudrey formulated his own toothpaste by combining aloe with flavoring and most of the other ingredients found in regular toothpaste. Jedra also added a polishing agent to help his toothpaste brighten teeth.

Joudrey passed samples of his paste to friends who had similar dental complaints. Based upon their very favourable responses, Joudrey, at the age of 54, retired from his position at DuPont Research Laboratories to devote his energies to promoting his toothpaste, which he called "Crew."

After designing an attractive package, Joudrey ordered 400,000 tubes and cartons and hired a company to manufacture and pack the toothpaste. Without benefit of an advertising budget or the blessing of the Canadian Dental Association, Joudrey began to call on wholesalers who serviced drugstore chains and supermarkets. He also called on the health and beauty aid buyers of discount department stores. Distributors at first were hesitant to stock the product, but after reviewing the testimonials Joudrey produced, they agreed to handle Crew if he would advertise it and agree to buy back any unsold tubes.

Crew sells for $3.89 for a 150 ml tube, about twice as much as other "sensitive teeth" toothpastes. Crew is intended for those people who have sensitive teeth, canker sores, fever blisters, sensitive gums, or stained teeth.

To almost everyone's amazement, Crew is selling well. Crew is currently stocked in over 700 stores in Ontario and Quebec, including such well-known chains as Shoppers Drug Mart, Pharmasave and Jean Coutu.

Research conducted by Joudrey indicates that most customers prefer Crew over Sensodyne because of Crew's polishing agent, which brightens teeth without irritation. Customers do admit, however, that they do occasionally buy Sensodyne because of its lower cost.

Although Joudrey had recently begun to make a profit on his investment, he decided to spend the money on advertising. His new campaign will stress Crew's superiority to Sensodyne, the leader of the market.

_____1. Michel Joudrey was practicing which philosophy of marketing?
- A.   mass marketing
- B.   product-differentiated marketing
- C.   selling differentiated marketing
- D.   target marketing
- E.   market penetration

_____2. The loyalty status of Crew's customers may be used to segment the market. Loyalty status is an example of _____ segmentation.
- A.   behavioristic
- B.   psychographic
- C.   demographic
- D.   geographic
- E.   socialistic

_____3. The placement of Crew toothpaste in 700 stores indicates that which requirement for effective segmentation has been met?
- A.   substantiality
- B.   measurability
- C.   accessibility
- D.   actionability
- E.   marketability

_____4. Which market coverage alternative is Joudrey pursuing?

     A.   concentrated marketing

     B.   differentiated marketing

     C.   undifferentiated marketing

     D.   mass marketing

     E.   hybrid marketing

Case #3   Ron Anderson

Ron Anderson has a small Internet company and has been in operation for five years. His expertise is sports memorabilia and his company, run out of his home, puts buyers and sellers together—for a fee. As a new company in a small market he has the advantage of being in the lead and hopes to stay there. His major concern, in time, will be keeping ahead of the competition, finding his target market, and being able to reach them and expand into other memorabilia or antiques for different target markets.

_____1. At this point in his company what kind of marketing is he practising?

     A.   concentrated marketing

     B.   test marketing

     C.   differentiated marketing

     D.   undifferentiated marketing

     E.   hybrid marketing

_____2. Anderson's marketing has always been simple; the customer comes to him because he provides a service and a product that they are looking for at a price they can afford. Which of the following best reflects his buyer?

     A.   age

     B.   buyer readiness

     C.   benefits

     D.   social class

     E.   income

_____ 3. If Anderson keeps in mind that his main asset is product differentation in dealing only with products in a price range affordable to most people (especially 20-25 year olds), he can actually segment his market even more. If he decides to do this the segment will be beneficial to him in the future because it will have all of the following traits except:

A.   measurability
B.   actionability
C.   originality
D.   accessibility
E.   marketability

_____ 4. If Anderson were to limit his market and only sell sporting memorabilia and not enter the antique market he would be practicing:

A.   concentrated marketing
B.   differentiated marketing
C.   environmental marketing
D.   undifferentiated marketing
E.   hybrid marketing

Multiple Choice Answers

1.	Correct Answer:	3	Reference:	pg. 294
2.	Correct Answer:	1	Reference:	pg. 275
3.	Correct Answer:	4	Reference:	pg. 276
4.	Correct Answer:	5	Reference:	pg. 278
5.	Correct Answer:	2	Reference:	pg. 278
6.	Correct Answer:	1	Reference:	pg. 282 (Table 7-1)
7.	Correct Answer:	3	Reference:	pg. 282 (Table 7-1)
8.	Correct Answer:	2	Reference:	pg. 286
9.	Correct Answer:	5	Reference:	pg. 288
10.	Correct Answer:	4	Reference:	pg. 288
11.	Correct Answer:	3	Reference:	pg. 288
12.	Correct Answer:	5	Reference:	pg. 289 (Table 7-3)
13.	Correct Answer:	1	Reference:	pg. 290
14.	Correct Answer:	4	Reference:	pg. 290
15.	Correct Answer:	2	Reference:	pg. 292
16.	Correct Answer:	3	Reference:	pg. 292
17.	Correct Answer:	2	Reference:	pg. 278
18.	Correct Answer:	3	Reference:	pg. 294
19.	Correct Answer:	4	Reference:	pg. 294
20.	Correct Answer:	1	Reference:	pg. 296
21.	Correct Answer:	3	Reference:	pg. 297
22.	Correct Answer:	2	Reference:	pg. 298

23.	Correct Answer:	4	Reference:	pg. 304
24.	Correct Answer:	5	Reference:	pg. 304
25.	Correct Answer:	2	Reference:	pg. 306
26.	Correct Answer:	3	Reference:	pg. 285
27.	Correct Answer:	4	Reference:	pg. 289
28.	Correct Answer:	2	Reference:	pg. 289
29.	Correct Answer:	3	Reference:	pg. 285
30.	Correct Answer:	1	Reference:	pg. 304

True/False Answers

1.	TRUE	Reference:	pg. 274	Topic: Markets
2.	TRUE	Reference:	pg. 275	Topic: Levels of Segmentation
3.	FALSE	Reference:	pg. 276	Topic: Mass Marketing
4.	FALSE	Reference:	pg. 277	Topic: Niche Marketing
5.	TRUE	Reference:	pg. 277	Topic: Niche Marketing
6.	FALSE	Reference:	pg. 281	Topic: Bases for Segmenting Consumer Markets
7.	FALSE	Reference:	pg. 282	Topic: Demographic Segmentation
8.	FALSE	Reference:	pg. 282	Topic: Age and Life-Cycle Stage
9.	TRUE	Reference:	pg. 282	Topic: Age and Life-Cycle Stage
10.	TRUE	Reference:	pg. 285	Topic: Behavioural Segmentation
11.	TRUE	Reference:	pg. 286	Topic: User Status
12.	FALSE	Reference:	pg. 290	Topic: Segmentation of International Markets

13.	TRUE	Reference:	pg. 285	Topic: Psychographic Segmentation Markets
14.	FALSE	Reference:	pg. 291	Topic: Requirements for Effective Segmentation
15.	FALSE	Reference:	pg. 292	Topic: Segment Size and Growth
16.	FALSE	Reference:	pg. 292	Topic: Company Objectives and Resources
17.	TRUE	Reference:	pg. 292	Topic: Company Objectives and Resources
18.	TRUE	Reference:	pg. 290	Topic: International Markets
19.	FALSE	Reference:	pg. 297	Topic: Positioning for Competitive Advantage
20.	TRUE	Reference:	pg. 305	Topic: Positioning Strategy

Applying Terms and Concepts Answers

Case #1   Eldin Incorporated

Question #1
- This market meets the substantiality requirement for effective segmentation because the market is large and profitable enough to consider and serve.

Question #2
- Demographic segmentation consists of dividing the market into groups based on variables such as age, gender, family size, income, occupation, education, religion, race, and nationality.
- Demographic variables are often used because they are more easily measured than other variables.

Question #3
- Miele is pursuing a concentrated marketing strategy.
- Miele has chosen to pursue a large share of one or a few submarkets, instead of pursuing a small share of a large market.
- Concentrated marketing can help establish a strong market position (or a niche) because of its greater knowledge of the segments' needs and the special reputation it acquires.

Question #4
- Miele has isolated and satisfied the behavioural variable (needs) of her intended target market.
- This is evident, as she has satisfied such concerns as user status, usage rate, and benefits sought.

Question #5
- Eldin Incorporated is operating at the target marketing stage because Miele (the seller) is identifying market segments, selecting these segments, and developing products and marketing mixes to tailor the needs of her target market.

Case #2   Crew Toothpaste   Case #3   Ron Anderson

1.   D   1.   D

2.   A   2.   C

3.   C   3.   C

4.   A   4.   A

Chapter 8

Product and Services Strategies

Chapter Overview

When purchasing a product, be it as a business or as a consumer, it is more than an independent "thing." What are we buying when we buy a pair of Levis jeans or a Rolex? They are more than just a pair of jeans or a watch. A product is more than a set of tangible features. In fact, many marketing offers consist of combinations of both tangible goods and services. Offerings range from pure tangible goods at one extreme to pure services at the other. Products must be looked at in relationship to features, style design and branding. Each product or service offered to customers can be viewed on three levels. Strategies must look at multibranding, private brands, packaging concepts and product support services. As products travel the world, service and its offshoots that marketers must factor in include service inseparability, intangibility, perishability and variability. The core product consists of the problem-solving benefits consumers seek when they buy a product. The actual product exists around the core and includes the quality level, features, design, brand name, and packaging. Installation, warranty, free delivery, and availability all make up the product and augmented product. This service must be considered part of the product, for without them we have only a partial product.

Chapter Objectives

1.   Define the product and the major classifications of products and services.
2.   Describe the roles of product and service branding, packaging, labelling, and product support services.
3.   Explain the decisions that companies make when developing product lines and mixes.
4.   Identify the four characteristics that affect the marketing of a service.
5.   Discuss the additional marketing considerations that services require.

Chapter Topics

What is a Product?
- The Product-Service Continuum
- Levels of Product

Product Classifications
- Consumer Products
- Industrial Products
- Organizations, Persons, Places and Ideas

Individual Product Decisions
- Product Attributes
    - Product Quality
    - Product Features
    - Product Design
- Branding
    - Brand Equity
    - Brand Name Selection
    - Brand Sponsor
        - Manufacturers Brands vs. Private Brands
        - Licensing
        - Co-Branding
    - Brand Strategy
        - Line Extensions
        - Brand Extensions
        - Multibrands
        - New Brands
- Packaging
- Labelling
- Product Support Services

Product Line Decisions
- Stretching Downward
- Stretching Upward
- Stretching Both Ways
- Filling in the Product Line

Product Mix Decisions

Services Marketing
- Nature and Characteristics of a Service
  - Intangibility
- Marketing Strategies for Service Firms
- The Service-Profit Chain
  - Managing Service Differentiation
  - Managing Service Quality
  - Managing Productivity

International Product and Services Marketing

Chapter Summary

1.   The definition of product and the major classifications of consumer and industrial products.

A product is anything that can be offered to a market for attention, acquisition, use, or consumption and that might satisfy a want or need. Products can be classified as durable, non-durable, and services. Consumer classifications include convenience, shopping, speciality, and unsought. Industrial classifications are material and parts, capital items, and supplies and services.

2.   The roles of product packaging and labelling.

Packaging refers to the design and producing of a container or wrapper for the product. The packaging concept states what the package should be or do for the product. Packages at least protect and, hopefully, promote and distinguish the product. Labelling at least identifies and perhaps grades, describes, and promotes the product.

3.   Brand equity.

Powerful brands have equity. Brand equity combines high brand awareness with brand preference and loyalty to create value in and of itself. The credibility of brand equity becomes a marketable product commodity in itself. Over time, brand equity can be the enduring asset of a company as it reliably provides continuing customer equity.

4.   The definition of service and the four characteristics that affect the marketing of a service.

A service is any activity or benefit that one party can offer to another that is essentially intangible and does not result in the ownership of anything. The four characteristics of services are intangibility, inseparability, variability, and perishability.

5. How persons are marketed.

Person marketing consists of activities undertaken to create, maintain, or change attitudes or behaviour toward particular people. The objective of person marketing is to create a celebrity whose name generates attention, interest, and action. Key aspects of celebrity status are durability life-cycle patterns (standard, overnight, comeback, and meteor) and scope (the geographic range of their celebrity).

Key Terms

Actual product	(pg. 322)	Packaging concept	(pg. 346)
Augmented product	(pg. 324)	Private brand	(pg. 336)
Brand	(pg. 331)	Product	(pg. 321)
Brand equity	(pg. 332)	Product design	(pg. 330)
Brand extension	(pg. 342)	Product line	(pg. 348)
Capital items	(pg. 327)	Product mix	(pg. 350)
Co-branding	(pg. 340)	Product quality	(pg. 329)
Consumer products	(pg. 326)	Product support services	(pg. 349)
Convenience products	(pg. 226)	Service	(pg. 322)
Core product	(pg. 322)	Service inseparability	(pg. 353)
Industrial marketing	(pg. 327)	Service intangibility	(pg. 352)
Interactive marketing	(pg. 355)	Service perishability	(pg. 353)
Internal marketing	(pg. 355)	Service variability	(pg. 353)
Line extension	(pg. 341)	Shopping products	(pg. 327)
Manufacturers brand (or national)	(pg.336)	Slotting fees	(pg. 336)
Materials and parts	(pg. 327)	Social marketing	(pg. 329)
Multibranding	(pg. 342)	Specialty products	(pg. 327)
Packaging	(pg. 343)	Supplies and services	(pg. 328)
		Unsought products	(pg. 329)

176

Multiple Choice Questions

8-1   Multiple

Which of the following is not considered a product?

1.   A Sony CD Player
2.   A Terri Clark concert
3.   A GMC Truck
4.   Advice from an attorney
5.   All of the above are products

8-2   Multiple

Products include more than just tangible goods. Broadly defined products include everything except:

1.   Ideas
2.   Persons
3.   Thoughts
4.   Places
5.   Organizations

8-3   Multiple

Rhonda has just changed insurance companies. As part of the promotion to obtain business, Avion Insurance Co. ran a promotion that allowed drivers under the age of twenty-five such benefits as discount travel, a free portable CD player and air miles when paying premiums. This experience is considered:

1.   A service with accompanying goods
2.   A hybrid offer
3.   A tangible good with accompanying services
4.   An intangible good with accompanying services
5.   None of the above

8-4   Multiple

Which of the following five characteristics does an actual product not possess?

1.   Quality level
2.   Features
3.   Brand name
4.   Image
5.   Packaging

8-5   Multiple

Warranties on parts and service, free lessons, and quick repair services are all considered part of the _____.

1.   Core benefit
2.   Core service
3.   Augmented product
4.   Actual product
5.   Core product

8-6   Multiple

An umbrella purchased during a rainstorm is a(n):

1.   Staple product
2.   Impulse product
3.   Necessary product
4.   Emergency product
5.   2 and 4

8-7   Multiple

_____ products are bought less frequently and more consideration goes into each purchase.

1.   Consumer
2.   Shopping
3.   Convenience
4.   Specialty
5.   Unsought

8-8   Multiple

On a trip to Mexico John broke his arm and had to visit a doctor and was charged $200.00 for the service. This purchase is said to be what kind of product?

1.   Consumer
2.   Shopping
3.   Convenience
4.   Specialty
5.   Unsought

8-9   Multiple

In the car battery business which of the following is not considered a group of industrial products?

1.   Final consumer feedback
2.   Materials and parts
3.   Capital items
4.   Suppliers and services
5.   All of the above

8-10   Multiple

Fax machines, desks and garbage cans would be considered:

1.   Capital items
2.   Manufactured materials
3.   Accessory equipment
4.   Fixed equipment
5.   Supplies

8-11   Multiple

Small motors, small tires, and castings would be considered:

1.   Component materials
2.   Manufactured material
3.   Natural products
4.   Component parts
5.   Supplies

8-12   Multiple

In recent years, marketers have broadened the concept of a product to include all other "marketable entities" not already included. All the following except _____ have been added to the list, as they were not previously considered products.

1.   Services
2.   Organizations
3.   Persons
4.   Places
5.   Ideas

8-13   Multiple

Motor clubs, oil companies, hotels, and government agencies have all pitched in to help with:

1.   Social marketing
2.   Tourism marketing
3.   Place marketing
4.   Business site marketing
5.   All of the above

8-14   Multiple

Timex has always believed in its product and is committed to its staff and customers. Their customers and staff know that their products are both free from defect and reliable. This statement is based on:

1.   Product quality
2.   Performance quality
3.   Conformance quality
4.   Total quality management
5.   1 and 3

8-15   Multiple

All the following questions help a company identify new features and decide which ones to add to their product except:

1.   What is your frequency of use of our product?
2.   How do you like the product?
3.   Which specific features of the product do you like the most?
4.   Which features could we add to improve the product?
5.   All the above are useful

8-16   Multiple

Pietro is assigned the task of developing a design for P&G's new product that they will launch this fall. Pietro knows there are many benefits of a good design. These benefits include all the following except:

1.   It can attract attention
2.   It can improve product performance
3.   It can obtain better shelf space in retail outlets
4.   It can cut production costs
5.   It can give a product a strong competitive advantage in the target market

8-17   Multiple

Professional marketers have many distinctive skills. Among these skills is their ability to do everything except:

1.   Create brands
2.   Cannibalize competitors' brands
3.   Maintain brands
4.   Protect brands
5.   Enhance brands

8-18   Multiple

A consumer's view of a brand is very important to the future success of a company. Everything is considered part of the brand except:

1.   A name
2.   A term
3.   A symbol
4.   An idea
5.   A design

8-19   Multiple

Well engineered, well built, high resale value, durable, and high prestige are considered product _____.

1.   Attributes
2.   Benefits
3.   Values
4.   Personality
5.   None of the above

8-20   Multiple

Brands vary in the amount of power and value they have in the marketplace. P&G's Tide laundry detergent has a large amount of power in the marketplace because of everything except:

1.   Brand loyalty
2.   Name awareness
3.   Deep corporate pockets
4.   Perceived quality
5.   Channel relationships

8-21   Multiple

A high level of brand equity provides a company with many competitive advantages.
Which of the following is not considered to be one of these advantages?

1.   Brand awareness
2.   Bargaining leverage with resellers
3.   Brand loyalty
4.   Launch lines are easier to establish
5.   Economies of scale

8-22   Multiple

When General Mills and Hershey's joined forces to create Reese's Peanut Butter Puffs
cereal, they engaged in _____.

1.   Store branding
2.   Co-branding
3.   Licensed branding
4.   Distributor branding
5.   Private branding

8-23   Multiple

Store brands like Presidents Choice, Safeway Select and Our Compliments are becoming
very popular household items. Currently ____ % of Canadian households buy at least
some store brands.

1.   50
2.   80
3.   100
4.   75
5.   65

8-24   Multiple

_____ gives a new product instant recognition and faster acceptance.

1.   Line extension
2.   Multibranding
3.   New brands
4.   Brand extension
5.   Product extension

8-25   Multiple

The packaging of a container of shampoo includes everything but:

1.   The actual container holding the shampoo
2.   The plastic wrap covering the bottle of shampoo together with the conditioner
3.   The large cardboard box used to ship the shampoo from the manufacturer to the retailer
4.   The labelling on the bottle of shampoo
5.   All the above are considered part of packaging

8-26   Multiple

Mercedes-Benz realized the market for their luxury cars has been decreasing over the last few years. To counter this trend, they will introduce a new more affordable car, backed by their high quality guarantee, during the 2000 model year. This new car is a product line decision to:

1.   Stretch downward
2.   Stretch upward
3.   Stretch both ways
4.   Fill in the product line
5.   Grab more market share

8-27   Multiple

The quality of a service depends on who provides it as well as when, where and how the service is delivered. These issues are considered a(n) _____ characteristic of services.

1.   Intangible
2.   Inseparable
3.   Variable
4.   Perishable
5.   Personable

8-28   Multiple

The service-profit chain consists of five links. The first chain in that link is:

1.   Satisfied and loyal customers
2.   Healthy service profits and growth
3.   Greater service value
4.   Satisfied and productive service employees
5.   Internal service quality

8-29   Multiple

Interactive marketing is the marketing process between _____ and _____.

1.   Customers, companies
2.   Companies and employees
3.   Employees and employees
4.   Employees and customers
5.   Companies and companies

8-30   Multiple

Many people judge the quality of service on five different dimensions. Which of the following is not considered one of these?

1.   Credible
2.   Empathetic
3.   Reliable
4.   Responsive
5.   Valuable

True/False Questions

8-1   True/False

Services are a form of product that consists of activities, benefits and satisfaction.

8-2   True/False

A hybrid offer is one that consists of 75% goods and 25% service.

8-3   True/False

Product planners need to consider product on one level.

8-4   True/False

When buying specialty products and services, consumers spend considerable time and effort in gathering information and making comparisons.

8-5   True/False

Consumer products are those that are for personal use and are not intended for resale.

8-6   True/False

In the end, marketing is about an idea.

8-7   True/False

Product quality is two dimensional, consisting of both "level and consistency."

8-8   True/False

The ultimate goal of total quality is to improve consumer value.

8-9   True/False

Being one of the first producers to introduce a needed and valued new feature is one of the most effective ways to compete.

8-10   True/False

Features of little value to consumers in relation to cost should be added, as this is very profitable for the company.

8-11   True/False

A brand is identifiable to a consumer and a reflection of the quality of the product that the consumer has come to expect.

8-12   True/False

Since retailing is more concentrated in Canada than in the US, store brands are more powerful.

8-13   True/False

Brand equity is the power and prestige, both positive and negative, that a brand brings to the marketplace. A major drawback of brand extensions is each brand might obtain only a small market share, and none may be very profitable.

8-14   True/False

Some marketers have considered packaging as the fifth "P" along with place, price, promotion and product.

8-15   True/False

Companies keen on high, short-term profitability generally carry longer lines consisting of selected items.

8-16   True/False

The product mix dimensions of width, length, depth and quality provide the handles for defining a company's product strategy.

8-17   True/False

A service provider's task is to make the service tangible in one or more ways.

8-18   True/False

Apparel and accessories sellers pay licensing fees to companies like Gucci, Microsoft, Calvin Klein to use their names on their products.

8-19   True/False

To the extent that customers view the service of different providers as similar, they care less about the provider than the price.

8-20   True/False

The key is to exceed the customer's service-quality expectations in order to succeed as a service company.

Applying Terms and Concepts

To determine how well you understand the materials in this chapter, read each of the following brief cases and then respond to the questions that follow. Answers are given at the end of this chapter.

Case #1   Martha Hamel[1]

Martha Hamel was in her third year of high school when her father lost his job. His employer was closing the carpet manufacturing plant in Windsor where he worked as a weaver. Martha's father, George, had spent 29 years working at the plant and at the age of 53, was looking for a new job. His employer had moved south to Mexico with its cheaper labour and more favourable tax structure. George was offered an opportunity to move south with his employer, but family concerns made that option unworkable. George

---

[1] *Principles of Marketing*, 3rd Edition, Kotler, Armstrong, Warren (Prentice Hall) – pg. 174.

decided he would make the best of his situation, but without much of a formal education, and with other manufacturing plants in the area either closing or downsizing, his prospects were not promising.

Martha never forgot the effect the plant closing had on her father. This once proud and fiercely independent man was suddenly racked by self-doubt. His sense of self-worth was shaken and his ability to provide for his family uncertain. George shielded his family from most of the problems but the strain was evident. George ultimately did land a position with another firm, but Martha decided she would do what she could to take control over her life, so she would have greater flexibility than he had. Control for Martha meant a university education. Eight years later, Martha had earned a BComm (Accounting) from Laurier, an MBA in Marketing from Queen's and a Chartered Accountant designation.

1. A university degree is an example of what type of product?

    _____

    _____

    _____

    _____

2. When Martha chose to pursue an education, she ultimately realized the product she was buying existed on three levels. Explain how a university degree exists on each of the following levels.
    a. core product:

    _____

    _____

    _____

    _____

    b. actual product:

    _____

    _____

    _____

    _____

c. augmented product:

_____

_____

_____

_____

3.   Discuss the implications of your answer to the previous question from the perspective of university administrators.

_____

_____

_____

_____

Case #2   Woodstock '94[2]

Woodstock '94: three days of peace, love, and music, not to mention cash machines, metal detectors, corporate sponsor, the Eco Village, the Peace Patrol, mud, and 2,800 overflowing portable toilets. It wasn't quite the same as the original Woodstock held some 25 years earlier, but then it couldn't be.

For three days in August 1994, approximately a quarter of a million people descended on an 840 acre site in Saugerties, New York. The mainly white, middle class crowd came to the 25th anniversary of the Woodstock Music and Art Fair originally held in Bethel, New York. Such diverse groups as The Band, Red Hot Chili Peppers, Blind Melon, Salt-n-Pepa, Bob Dylan, Joe Cocker and the Cranberries were among the 50 bands invited to entertain the fair-goers. Corporate sponsors, such as Pepsi, Apple Computers and Häagen-Dazs were also there, promoting their wares and subsidizing the event.

The Eco Village—reportedly there to educate the masses about the environment—seemed more about making money than education. The private security force dubbed the "Peace Patrol" reinforced the 550 State Troopers enforcing the ban on alcohol and drugs, while maintaining order.

Where the original concert didn't even have an official T-shirt, Woodstock '94 seemed decidedly mainstream. Blatant commercialism caused some idealistic musicians to boycott the event. But most seemed genuinely glad to have been invited—besides, the better paid acts reportedly received $350,000 plus a share of the royalties. Promoters of Woodstock '94 reportedly filed a multi-million dollar lawsuit against rival promoters who wanted to stage an event called Bethel '94—a concert on the site of the original

---

[2] _Principles of Marketing_, 3rd Edition, Kotler, Armstrong, Warren (Prentice Hall) – pg. 422.

event. Two concerts, commemorating the same event in the same general area, at the same time, would be bad for business.

Some complained the event should have been called Greenstock, not Woodstock. But Woodstock '94 cost $42 million, more than ten times the cost of the original concert. It takes money to stage such a colossal event. This is not to suggest the organizers sold out completely. Other corporate sponsors including alcohol and tobacco companies were politely turned away, even though profits would have been higher, and ticket prices lower.

Apparently, the commercialism wasn't too much of a deterrent. Over 250,000 people paid the $190 ticket price (compared to the $25 price for the original event) for three days of music, camping, camaraderie, and parking. And by some estimates, that was a bargain.

Note: All figures are in Canadian dollars

1.   Briefly explain how the promotion of Woodstock '94 might deal with the following characteristics of their offerings.
   a. Intangibility:

   _____

   _____

   _____

   _____

   b. Inseparability:

   _____

   _____

   _____

   c. Variability:

   _____

   _____

   _____

   _____

d. Perishability:

_____

_____

_____

_____

2.   How does the experience of Woodstock '94 constitute a service?

_____

_____

_____

_____

Case #3   Ajax Supermarkets

Several Ajax supermarkets have been located in upper-class neighbourhoods throughout the Toronto area for over 35 years. Ajax enjoys an excellent reputation for a wide range of high-quality, high-priced, difficult-to-find food items, and it caters almost exclusively to the upper-income market segment. The number of supermarkets in the Toronto area has been increasing steadily, and Ajax has experienced a slowing in its growth trend. Dollar sales are up significantly, but unit volume is only slightly ahead of last year in most of the Ajax locations in established neighbourhoods, and profit margins have been squeezed.

Management is considering a number of alternatives as possible remedies. One of these is the establishment of the Ajax brand name on several product lines. Ajax has carried only the highest-quality national brands in the past, and there is some question in the minds of two members of the management committee about whether the use of a private label would be appropriate in Ajax's prestige stores. Another possibility under review is the addition of generic lines. During the last meeting of the management committee it was pointed out that the lower prices of generics have a strong appeal to consumers during inflationary times. The attraction is even stronger during recessions when there is high unemployment. Furthermore, profit margins on the generics could be expected to be about the same as the current average, with only slightly reduced quality that would be barely detectable by consumers.

_____1. The alternatives being considered deal with:
- A. brand repositioning.
- B. product line stretching.
- C. the depth of the product line.
- D. brand extension decisions.
- E. both (A) and (C)

_____2. If the generic labels are added, this would be a(n):
- A. augmentation of the core product.
- B. blanket family name.
- C. downward stretch in the product line.
- D. widening of the product line.
- E. none of the above

_____3. The decision to add or not to add generics concerns not only quality considerations, but also considerations regarding the:
- A. core product offered by Ajax.
- B. consistency of the product line.
- C. products that must be deleted to make room for the new line.
- D. classification of the generic line.
- E. breadth of the product line.

_____4. What is the proper decision for Ajax regarding the addition of generic products?
- A. Add them—this will broaden its market.
- B. Adding generics is a line-filling decision that will not broaden the market but will create an opportunity to sell more to the existing market.
- C. Generics should increase sales, but will not add much to profit margins.
- D. The addition of generics is a bad idea because it may damage the company's prestige reputation.
- E. none of the above

_____5. The addition of a private brand with the Ajax label would:
- A. damage the quality image Ajax has built over many years.
- B. offer the company an opportunity to capitalize on its reputation and widen profit margins.
- C. only reduce profit margins even further.
- D. attract another market segment.
- E. both (A) and (C)

Case #4   Irish Shoes

James O'Donovan is president of Irish Shoes, a Kelowna, BC distributor of specialty athletic shoes. Three years ago O'Donovan was a centre for the University of British Columbia Thunderbirds. He spent two seasons at that position until serious foot and ankle injuries ended his career. It seems that the constant running, jumping, and dead stops placed excessive pressure on his back, legs, and feet. This ultimately resulted in permanent damage which surgery could not correct.

In discussing his problems with Dr. H. N. Woofe, a prominent Canadian podiatrist, O'Donovan learned that the type of difficulty he suffered was quite common, although usually not so severe, in the athletic community. Collegiate tennis, basketball, and football players, in addition to track and field athletes, were very susceptible to the problem. Dr. Woofe also mentioned that amateur joggers were also coming to her complaining of foot and leg problems.

With Dr. Woofe and her two partners providing technical advice and financial backing, O'Donovan developed a unique athletic shoe. The sole of the shoe contains a polyurethane pad, partially filled with mineral oil. There is sufficient resilience within the pad to prevent it from bursting on impact from the foot as the wearer runs and jumps. The pads essentially act as shock absorbers, significantly reducing impact and so pressure on the legs, feet, and back.

O'Donovan called his creation the Irish Shoe. To further distinguish it from the inevitable competitors, he designed a symbol of an eagle in flight, and had it made as a blue rubber implant into the sole of the shoe.

The shoe sells for $140, about the price of other quality shoes; its acceptance has been phenomenal. In only six months, O'Donovan had nearly sold out his initial factory runs of 5,000 pairs. He has since placed another order for 2,000 pairs from his manufacturer in Italy. Irish Shoes are distributed throughout Canada—although on a very limited basis in all provinces—by independent shoe stores. Store managers indicate that it is not unusual for shoe store patrons to drive over 160 kilometres to a store which stocks the shoes and to ask for them by name.

Although the shoe was originally intended for athletes, distributors have noted that approximately 60 percent of sales have been to nonathletes. In fact, senior citizens are the most avid fans of the shoe. This has O'Donovan and the podiatrists working on designs for shoes more appropriate for work settings and leisure activities.

_____1. The comfort provided by the Irish Shoe is an example of a(n) _____ product.
     A.   core
     B.   augmented
     C.   tangible
     D.   intangible
     E.   actual

_____2. The shoe itself is an example of a(n) _____.
     A.   nondurable good
     B.   durable good
     C.   service
     D.   intangible
     E.   convenience

_____3. The fact that customers drive many kilometres to a store which carries the shoe and ask for it by name indicates that this shoe has achieved _____ status for those customers.
     A.   convenience goods
     B.   homogeneous shopping
     C.   heterogeneous shopping
     D.   specialty goods
     E.   unsought goods

_____4. The Blue Eagle implant, which has come to symbolize Irish Shoes, is an example of:
     A.   brand
     B.   brand name
     C.   brand mark
     D.   trademark
     E.   both (A) and (C)

_____5. Irish Shoes is an example of a _____ brand.
     A.   manufacturer
     B.   private
     C.   national
     D.   dealer brand
     E.   both (B) and (D)

Case #5   Madame Zorba

Madame Zorba, a former fortuneteller, has just opened Yellowknife's first complete occult science centre. Madame Zorba offers a complete line of paranormal services. In addition to palmistry, tarot readings, and crystal ball gazing, interested customers can have their aura analyzed, engage in seances, receive training in astral projection, test their powers of ESP, or sample any number of the more exotic occult practices.

Madame Zorba has invested in an unusually nice facility housing a large staff and supported by the best equipment. She expects to enjoy a brisk business, with clientele drawn from "widely diverse socio-economic strata." Like any other businessperson, she is concerned about how best to market her rather unusual "product."

1.   Briefly explain how Madame Zorba might deal with each of the following characteristics which will affect her marketing program:
   A.   Intangibility
   B.   Inseparability
   C.   Variability
   D.   Perishability

2.   Madame Zorba should be classified as providing a(n) _____-_____ service.

3.   Since the client's presence is necessary in the performance of this service, Madame Zorba is correct to invest in impressive facilities and equipment.

True/False

4.   Madame Zorba's clients are most likely to purchase the services to meet a(n) _____ need, although some clients will purchase for _____ reasons.

5.   At present, Madame Zorba has little or no competition. What will be the major concern of her marketing program after she opens her business?

Case #6   Jackson and Jackson Strawberry Farms

Jackson and Jackson is a strawberry farm that ships its products throughout North America. Jim, the owner, believes the success of his company is based on producing a quality product that is standard in size and quality and marketing his product to Canadian and American grocery stores: President's Choice, Sarran and Dominion stores. His staff consists of 20 full time workers and a farming staff that expands from 15 to 300 during prime picking season. He has always been able to keep his staff happy and his pickers are the same (within 5%) year in and year out. Constant slow growth has made him one of the top five producers of strawberries in Canada. Brand equity is new in the strawberry business and Jim hopes to take advantage of this by being the first to develop brand equity under his farm's name. His customers demand quality and reliability or else a price sensitive market will quickly leave. Because of economic success he is hoping to be able to expand greatly by licensing his name and taking advantage of the goodwill it has developed.

1.   How has Jim maintained brand equity?

       A.   Through producing a quality product

       B.   The amount of power through sheer quantity in the market place

2.   What would be the advantages of licensing for Jim's firm? The people interviewed and the behaviours observed on a given tour are unique and differ from one to another. This suggests the _____ of the tours associated with Soc. 365.

       A.   Name/brand recognition

       B.   Inseparability of product with corporate name

       C.   Discounts on quantity shipping

       D.   Opening up of national and international markets

       E.   Substantiality

Multiple Choice Answers

1. Correct Answer: 5   Reference: pg. 321

2. Correct Answer: 3   Reference: pg. 322

3. Correct Answer: 1   Reference: pg. 322

4. Correct Answer: 4   Reference: pg. 324

5. Correct Answer: 3   Reference: pg. 326

6. Correct Answer: 4   Reference: pg. 326

7. Correct Answer: 2   Reference: pg. 327

8. Correct Answer: 5   Reference: pg. 326

9. Correct Answer: 1   Reference: pg. 327

10. Correct Answer: 3   Reference: pg. 327

11. Correct Answer: 4   Reference: pg. 328

12. Correct Answer: 1   Reference: pg. 328

13. Correct Answer: 2   Reference: pg. 330

14. Correct Answer: 5   Reference: pg. 330

15. Correct Answer: 1   Reference: pg. 332

16. Correct Answer: 3   Reference: pg. 331

17. Correct Answer: 2   Reference: pg. 331

18. Correct Answer: 4   Reference: pg. 332

19. Correct Answer: 1   Reference: pg. 332

20. Correct Answer: 3   Reference: pg. 332

21. Correct Answer: 5   Reference: pg. 332

22. Correct Answer: 2   Reference: pg. 340

23.	Correct Answer:	3	Reference:	pg. 336
24.	Correct Answer:	4	Reference:	pg. 342
25.	Correct Answer:	5	Reference:	pg. 343
26.	Correct Answer:	1	Reference:	pg. 348
27.	Correct Answer:	3	Reference:	pg. 353
28.	Correct Answer:	2	Reference:	pg. 354
29.	Correct Answer:	4	Reference:	pg. 355
30.	Correct Answer:	5	Reference:	pg. 355

True/False Answers

1.	TRUE	Reference:	pg. 321	Topic:	What is a Product?
2.	FALSE	Reference:	pg. 322	Topic:	The Product-Service Continuum
3.	FALSE	Reference:	pg. 322	Topic:	Levels of Products
4.	FALSE	Reference:	pg. 326	Topic:	Consumer Products
5.	TRUE	Reference:	pg. 327	Topic:	Industrial Products
6.	TRUE	Reference:	pg. 326	Topic:	Consumer Products
7.	TRUE	Reference:	pg. 329	Topic:	Product Quality
8.	TRUE	Reference:	pg. 329	Topic:	Product Quality
9.	FALSE	Reference:	pg. 330	Topic:	Product Features
10.	FALSE	Reference:	pg. 330	Topic:	Product Features
11.	TRUE	Reference:	pg. 329	Topic:	Product Attributes
12.	TRUE	Reference:	pg. 336	Topic:	Brand Sponsor
13.	TRUE	Reference:	pg. 332	Topic:	Brand Equity

14.	TRUE	Reference:	pg. 343	Topic: Packaging
15.	FALSE	Reference:	pg. 348	Topic: Product Line Decisions
16.	FALSE	Reference:	pg. 350	Topic: Product Mix Decisions
17.	TRUE	Reference:	pg. 353	Topic: Intangibility
18.	FALSE	Reference:	pg. 338	Topic: Licensing
19.	TRUE	Reference:	pg. 355	Topic: Managing Service Differences
20.	TRUE	Reference:	pg. 355	Topic: Managing Service Quality

Applying Terms and Concepts Answers

Case #1   Martha Hamel

Question #1
- Specialty product

Question #2
a. The core product identifies what the customer is really buying. In this situation Martha is acquiring the means to control her professional life. Her education will give her the flexibility to pursue a variety of opportunities as she wishes. Her degrees will provide significant earning potential, and personal as well as professional satisfaction. Martha's education also provided her with specific technical skills, which have enhanced her decision making and communication skills. Her conceptual and human skills were also more developed as a result of her education. Martha might say the prestige associated with her graduation from the various universities is also part of the core product.

b. The actual product would be the degrees earned from each university. The university name and reputation and level of degree would further identify her accomplishment.

c. The augmented product would be the variety of services and activities provided by the colleges and universities, which enhanced her educational experience. These might have included counselling, financial aid, library, computer facilities, housing, placement, clubs and organizations, social and cultural events (concerts, speakers and sporting events). These services and activities add quality, texture and variety and are designed to enrich the educational experience.

Question #3

- University administrators must realize they are selling a product, just as their competition is doing.
- When students choose to attend a particular school, they are really buying a total product.
- The more administrators understand what students really need, want, and demand, the more they will be able to offer these prospective students and distinguish themselves from the competition.

Case #2   Woodstock '94

Question #1

a. *Intangibility* – means that the services cannot be seen, tasted, heard, felt or smelled before they are bought. Organizers gave festival-goers an idea of what to expect by announcing the preparations that had taken place. Preparations included offsite parking with shuttle buses, camping areas, a ban on drugs and alcohol, the list of performers and the number of portable toilets along with a host of others. References to the original gathering also gave attendees a sense of what to expect.

But neither organizers nor attendees knew exactly what to expect prior to the concert. Advanced preparations and the actual event would still be affected by external uncontrollables such as weather.

b. *Inseparability* – means that services cannot be separated from their providers. Because the customer is also present as the service is provided, the outcome is affected by both the provider and the customer.

This meant that to some extent, the success of the concert would be dependent on the behaviour of the concert-goers as well as that of the performers, vendors, security force and the organizers. So collectively they, along with other publics, created the event.

c. *Variability* – means that the quality of the service depends on who provides the service as well as when, where and how they are provided.

Concert organizers hoped to instill confidence in potential attendees by providing information about the concert and their preparations. The suggestion was that a less organized concert would be less enjoyable.

d. *Perishability* – means that services cannot be stored for later use. The point was that one had to be there to truly experience the event. Although there were numerous news broadcasts from Saugerties—MTV televised some of the festival, there was pay-per-view on cable, and there would be the inevitable CD and film—nothing compared to actually being present at the concert.

The sights, sounds, smells, and tastes cannot be totally captured or recreated during or after the event. Once the event is over, it is over—the experience cannot be recreated. Even another concert—Woodstock '94 compared to Woodstock '69—cannot recreate the events. Each becomes its own happening.

Question #2

- Woodstock '94 is an activity (or event) that is essentially intangible and does not result in the ownership of anything. The event is not tied to a physical product.

Case #3 Ajax Supermarkets

1. B
2. C
3. A
4. D
5. B

Case #4 Irish Shoes

1. A
2. B
3. D
4. E
5. E

Case #5   Madame Zorba

1. A. *Intangibility*—Madame Zorba should emphasize the benefits of her services. Testimonials from respected customers would be helpful.
    B. *Inseparability*—Madame Zorba should carefully select and personally train her staff. Their experiences, training, and credentials should be matched to their services and publicized.
    C. *Variability*—Madame Zorba should establish and enforce training and service standards to ensure as much uniformity of quality as possible.
    D. *Perishability*—Madame Zorba should consider reservation systems and increased customer participation.

2. people based

3. True

4. personal, business

5. To present an image of professionalism and credibility for both her services and her staff.

Case #6   Jackson and Jackson Strawberry Farms

1. B
2. A

Chapter 9

New-Product Development and Life-Cycle Strategies

Chapter Overview

Firms that produce only one product are doomed to extinction. These companies must extend product line and depth as well as improve products regularly or they will be as obsolete as their products. Marketers cannot afford to ride on the success of one sole product. As a product becomes successful it also starts to go out of style, and it also begins to be copied by other forms. Just look at the advances in technology in the last hundred years or closer at hand in the last two years.

The technology we thought was state-of-the-art last year is now nothing but an old out-of-date piece of equipment. Marketers continually act to extend the life cycle of their products and to get maximum use out of each one. Organizations must develop effective new products and service strategies. Their current products face limited life spans and must be replaced by newer products. But new products can fail—the risks of innovation are as great as the rewards. Understanding the market, the product, its life and new-product development methods are key components to marketing and the key to successful innovation. This, along with research and development, total-company effort, strong planning, and a systematic new-product development process, acts to give continual new life to products as they meet the needs and wants of the market.

Chapter Objectives

1. Explain how companies find and develop new-product ideas.
2. List and define the steps in the new-product development process.
3. Describe the stages of the product life cycle.
4. Describe how marketing strategies change during the product's life cycle.

Chapter Topics

New-Product Development Strategy
- The New-Product Development Process
- Idea Generation
- Idea Screening
- Concept Development and Testing
  - Concept Development
  - Concept Testing
- Marketing Strategy Development
- Business Analysis
- Product Development
- Test Marketing
  - Standard Test Markets
  - Controlled Test Markets
  - Simulated Test Markets

- Commercialization
- Speeding Up New-Product Development

Product Life-Cycle Strategies
- Introduction Stage
- Growth Stage
- Maturity Stage
- Decline Stage

Chapter Summary

1.   The steps in new-product development.

Steps include idea generation, idea screening, concept development and testing, marketing strategy development, business analysis, product development, test marketing, and commercialization. Products are run through standard, controlled, and simulated testing. As they are run through these, important decisions are made at each level as to changes and modifications. Meeting consumer needs and "to proceed or not to proceed" decisions become more and more important and decisive to the continuation of the product to completion.

2.   How companies find and develop new-product ideas.

Major sources of new-product ideas include internal sources (sales force, employees), customers, competitors, distributors and suppliers, and the general public or societal trends. With so many products failing to make it to maturity, it is no wonder that companies reach out to all sectors in an attempt to find new ideas. From Gillette to Texas Instruments the hunt for the next product is a mainstay in marketing.

3.   The stages of the product life cycle.

The product life cycle is made up of development, introduction, growth, maturity and decline. Each stage serves a purpose both for the product and for the future growth of the company. Marketers take advantage of each stage to ensure continued profits through the life of the product and to maximize each product's life.

4.   How the marketing strategy changes during a product's life cycle.

As products are prepared to be launched, marketers must choose the initial positioning carefully. Strategies must decide between short-term and long-term profits, especially in the case of market pioneers. During the introduction, strategy focuses on awareness and acceptance of the basic product. Growth attracts competitors and more features. In maturity, strategy looks to modify the market, product, or mix. Decline forces choices on dropping or continuing a weak product.

5.   Distinguishing between the sequential product development and simultaneous product development processes.

In sequential product development, each functional area of the company works on the new product and sends its complete work to the next division. In simultaneous product development, each functional area provides ongoing (or real-time or on-line) feedback that is incorporated into the design, production, and marketing planning stage. Simultaneous design is organizationally more complicated but reduces total development and improves quality.

Key Terms

Business analysis	(pg. 388)	Maturity stage	(pg. 398)
Commercialization	(pg. 391)	New-product development	(pg. 380)
Concept testing	(pg. 386)	Product concept	(pg. 385)
Decline stage	(pg. 401)	Product development	(pg. 388)
Fads	(pg. 397)	Product life cycle (PLC)	(pg. 395)
Fashion	(pg. 396)	Sequential product development	(pg. 391)
Growth stage	(pg. 397)		
Idea generation	(pg. 382)	Simultaneous product development	(pg. 393)
Idea screening	(pg. 384)		
Introduction stage	(pg. 397)	Style	(pg. 396)
Marketing strategy development	(pg. 387)	Test marketing	(pg. 389)

Multiple Choice Questions

9-1   Multiple

Given the rapid changes in all the following except _____ companies must develop a steady stream of new products and services.

1.   Consumer tastes
2.   Technology
3.   Competition
4.   Maturing markets
5.   All the above

9-2   Multiple

When companies talk about new products and services, they may be talking about all the following except:

1.   Original products
2.   Product revival
3.   Product improvements
4.   Product modifications
5.   New brands

9-3   Multiple

In business today, all company members, from salespeople to executives, have their opinions on why products fail, but none usually realizes the true reason for failure. To continue to exist companies must produce new products for survival. Which of the following would not be a reason for failure?

1.   The market size may have been overestimated
2.   The actual product was not designed as well as it should have been
3.   The product was incorrectly placed in the market
4.   The product was priced too high
5.   The product was over-advertised

9-4   Multiple

In a product's life cycle it may serve a number of different functions for a company. The many roles it plays could include:

1.   To help the company remain an innovator
2.   To defend the company's market share
3.   To cannibalize the competition
4.   Only 1 and 2
5.   All of the above

9-5   Multiple

The product life cycle is made up of:

1.   Development
2.   Growth
3.   Maturity
4.   Decline

9-6   Multiple

New-product ideas come from a variety of places. Which of the following does not fit into the top five major sources of new product ideas?

1.   Internal sources
2.   Trade magazines
3.   Competitors
4.   Suppliers
5.   Consumers

9-7   Multiple

The purpose of the final stages in the new-product development process is to _____ the number of products introduced.

1.   Reduce
2.   Increase
3.   Hold constant
4.   Improve
5.   1 and 4

9-8   Multiple

At the outset of a new product companies naturally ask for reports to show the planned product and future expectations. In this process there is basic information that is required for review by the firm's executives. Which of the following information is not required at this stage?

1.   Consumer perception
2.   Market size
3.   Development time and costs
4.   Manufacturing costs
5.   All of the above

9-9   Multiple

Once the committee receives all the proposals for new products, they would probably ask the following questions except:

1.   Is the product truly useful for consumers and society?
2.   Is it good for our particular company?
3.   Does it mesh well with company strategies and objectives?
4.   Is the competition developing something similar?
5.   Do we have the people, resources and skills to succeed?

9-10   Multiple

A _____ is a detailed version of the idea stated in meaningful consumer terms.

1.   Product development
2.   Concept testing
3.   Product concept
4.   Concept development
5.   Product test

9-11   Multiple

At what stage does the marketing strategy study potential sales, market share and profit share of the initial years of a product?

1.   First
2.   Second
3.   Third
4.   Fourth
5.   In all of the above

9-12   Multiple

The planned long-run sales goals, the profit goals and the marketing mix strategy are all described in the _____ stage of the marketing strategy statement.

1.   First
2.   Second
3.   Third
4.   Fourth
5.   In all of the above

9-13   Multiple

The business analysis stage of new-product development is a very crucial step. After preparing the sales forecast for the new product, management is able to estimate the costs and profits for all the following except:

1.   Marketing
2.   Competition
3.   R&D
4.   Accounting
5.   Manufacturing

9-14   Multiple

The product development stage of the new-product development process calls for a large investment of both time and money. Developing a successful prototype can take:

1.   Days
2.   Weeks
3.   Months
4.   Years
5.   All of the above

9-15   Multiple

When a product is at the _____ stage it enters a more realistic market situation before it moves onto the next stage in its life.

1.   Marketing program
2.   Commercialization
3.   Marketing strategy development
4.   Test marketing
5.   Concept development and testing

9-16   Multiple

Janice has been asked by her boss to develop a marketing plan for Campbell Soup's new baby formula soups. Which of the following would not be part of this marketing program?

1.   Positioning strategy
2.   Advertising
3.   Financing
4.   Distribution
5.   Branding

9-17   Multiple

In the following type of test marketing, the results are used to forecast national sales and profits, discover potential problems, and fine-tune the marketing program.

1.   Controlled
2.   Standard
3.   Simulated
4.   Multiple
5.   All of the above

9-18   Multiple

Controlled test marketing takes less time than standard test marketing and usually costs less. However, there are some downfalls in using this strategy. Which of the following would not be included?

1.   Companies are not able to control important variables in the testing
2.   The small cities used may not be representative of society as a whole
3.   The panel consumers may not be representative of society as a whole
4.   It allows the competitors to get a look at the new product
5.   All of the above

9-19   Multiple

Simulated test marketing is the fastest and easiest method of testing a new product. It is used widely and often used as _____.

1.   Post-test markets
2.   Multiple-test markets
3.   Preliminary markets
4.   Pre-test markets
5.   Joint-test markets

9-20   Multiple

Business markets and consumer markets vary in certain ways. It would be logical to
assume that the way a new product is test-marketed would also vary somewhat. All the
following are acceptable ways to test market business products except:

1.   Product-use tests
2.   Tradeshows
3.   Simulated test markets
4.   Standard test markets
5.   All of the above

9-21   Multiple

Suet Mai works for Nabisco. Their new bedtime snack has passed all the stages in the
new-product development process and is now at the commercialization stage. It is Suet
Mai's job to ensure this product passes this stage. When launching a new product, the
company must first decide on:

1.   Introduction timing
2.   Where to launch the new product
3.   The planned market roll-out for the product
4.   The financing required for the product
5.   The reception the new product will receive in the marketplace

9-22   Multiple

_____ product development is an easy and quick way for companies to
market their product efficiently.

1.   Sequential
2.   Simultaneous
3.   Congruent
4.   Concurrent
5.   Successive

Multiple

Teams of different departments are all pitching in to help new products progress along the new-product development process with greater speed. The different people involved in this process come from all the following departments except:

1.   Supplier
2.   Finance
3.   Manufacturing
4.   Legal
5.   All of the above

9-23   Multiple

In the product life cycle, the stage which is characterized as a period of rapid market acceptance and increasing profits is the _____ stage.

1.   Product development
2.   Introduction
3.   Growth
4.   Maturity
5.   Decline

9-24   Multiple

_____ have the longest life cycles as their products stay in the mature stages of the life cycle for a long time.

1.   Product forms
2.   Product classes
3.   Brand classes
4.   Fashions
5.   Fads

9-25   Multiple

Victorian homes, casual clothing and abstract art are all considered:

1.   Fashion
2.   Fad
3.   Product class
4.   Style
5.   None of the above

9-26   Multiple

Because the market is not ready for product refinements at the _____ stage, the company and its few competitors produce basic versions of the product.

1.   Introduction
2.   Product development
3.   Maturity
4.   Decline
5.   Growth

9-27   Multiple

At the _____ stage in the product life cycle, educating the market remains a goal, but now the company also needs to meet the competition.

1.   Introduction
2.   Product development
3.   Maturity
4.   Decline
5.   Growth

9-28   Multiple

At the maturity stage of the life cycle, the company has an opportunity to prolong the life of its products in many ways. When a company tries to _____, the company is trying to increase the consumption of the current product.

1.   Modify the product
2.   Modify the marketing mix
3.   Modify the line extensions
4.   Modify the market
5.   Modify the target market

9-29   Multiple

Carrying a weak product can be very costly to a firm. The following are all problems with carrying a weak product except:

1. A weak product may take too much manager's time
2. A weak product often requires frequent price adjustments
3. A weak product takes advertising and salesforce attention away from "healthy" products
4. A weak product may delay searching for new products
5. All of the above

True/False Questions

9-1   True/False

A key element of any successful company is its ability to innovate.

9-2   True/False

New products continue to fail at a disturbing rate. One recent study estimated new consumer packaged products fail at a rate of 60%.

9-3   True/False

One study found the number one success factor in new products is a unique, superior product: one with high quality, new features and a low price.

9-4   True/False

The search for new-product ideas should be systematic rather than haphazard.

9-5   True/False

Companies can watch competitors' ads and other communications for clues about their new products.

9-6   True/False

The purpose of idea-generation is to create a list of good, quantifiable ideas.

9-7   True/False

The product idea rating process promotes a more systematic product idea evaluation and basis for discussion; however, it is not designed to make the decision for management.

9-8   True/False

An attractive idea is already considered a product concept.

9-9   True/False

For concept tests, a word or picture description is not sufficient, physical presentation of the product must be used.

9-10   True/False

The launch of new products is decided by management through test marketing .

9-11   True/False

Once management has decided on its product concept, it can evaluate the business attractiveness of the proposal.

9-12   True/False

Prior to the product development stage, the product may have existed as only a word description, a drawing or perhaps a crude mockup.

9-13   True/False

In the growth stage the product is satisfying the need of the market.

9-14   True/False

The prototype must have the required functional features and also convey the intended physical characteristics of the proposed new product.

9-15   True/False

When the costs of developing and introducing the new product are low, or when management is already confident about the new product, the company may do little or no test marketing.

9-16   True/False

Competitors often do whatever they can to make test market results hard to read; for example, they will lower their prices in the test market area so consumers will buy their products, or they will purchase all the competitors' products to skew the results.

9-17   True/False

Modifying the product to attract new customers is done during the growth stage.

9-18   True/False

Test marketing gives management the information needed to make a final decision about whether to launch the new product.

9-19   True/False

In rapidly changing industries facing increasingly shorter product life cycles, the rewards of fast and flexible product development are minimized by the risks.

9-20   True/False

Using the product life-cycle concept to develop a marketing strategy can be difficult because strategy is both a cause and a result of the product's life cycle.

9-21   True/False

Sales decline because of technological advances, competition and shifts in consumers' taste.

Applying Terms and Concepts

To determine how well you understand the materials in this chapter, read each of the following brief cases and then respond to the questions that follow. Answers are given at the end of this chapter.

Case #1   Oat Bran[1]

Everyone seems to be selling it, and we've all heard over and over again that oat bran can lower cholesterol levels. But a study detailed in the *New England Journal of Medicine* says it's not necessarily so. This prompts the question: Is oat bran good for your health or not?

Judging by the number of new oat bran cereals introduced in the last few years, cereal manufacturers suggest the answer is yes. Kellogg's, with approximately 40 per cent of the ready-to-eat cereal market, recently introduced Heartwise, Common Sense Oatbran, S.W. Graham, Nut and Honey, Crunch Biscuits, Oatbake, and Golden Crunch Mueslix for health-conscious consumers. General Mills, holding a 27 per cent share of the market, introduced Benefit; Ralston Purina, with 5 per cent of the market, has put out Oatbran Options; Nabisco, with 6 per cent of the market, has introduced Wholesome and Harty, a hot breakfast cereal; and Quaker Oats Company, with 8 per cent of the market, has brought out a new ready-to-eat version of its Quaker Oatbran. (It should be noted that Heartwise and Benefit also contain an exotic grain called psyllium, which like oat bran, is being hailed as a cholesterol reducer, and that S.W. Graham is made from whole-wheat flour. Both ingredients are aimed at health-conscious consumers.)

---

[1] *Principles of Marketing*, 3rd Edition, Kotler, Armstrong, Warren (Prentice Hall) – pg. 192.

Consider the impact the oat bran mania has had on one cereal alone. General Mills' Cheerios is now the most popular cereal in the United States, having replaced Kellogg's Frosted Flakes. Cheerios gained just over 3 percentage points in market share (to 9.9 per cent), with each percentage point worth $66 million in revenues. General Mills has benefited enormously from the oat bran craze—more so than Kellogg, because only 20 per cent of Kellogg's cereals are made with oats, compared to 40 per cent of General Mills cereals.

Oat Bran is a manufacturer's dream come true. Consumers love it—not for the taste, but because research suggests they could eat it and reduce their cholesterol level and their chances of getting heart disease. Cereal makers love it for the profits to be made, and farmers love it because it increases the demand for their grain. The demand for oat bran increased by 800 percent in 1988 alone, and the growth has been sustained. In 1989, sales of all oat bran products totaled over $1 billion. It seems that high-fibre food is the hottest craze to hit supermarket shelves in years.

There is now some evidence that rice bran and corn bran have cholesterol-reducing properties. Although this evidence is preliminary and far from conclusive, it might stimulate the market for these grains as well.

But what of the oat bran study reported in the *New England Journal of Medicine*, which concluded that "Oat-bran has little cholesterol-lowering effect and that high-fiber and low-fiber dietary grain supplements reduce serum cholesterol levels about equally, probably because they replace dietary fats." Dr. Timothy Johnson of *ABC News* makes these points: (1) a low-fat diet is extremely important in lowering cholesterol, and the extent to which oat bran contributes to this is debatable; (2) despite the criticism raised by the *New England Journal of Medicine* study of some of the hype about oat bran, it is a nutritious food worth eating in moderation; (3) the benefit of grain fibre, both soluble and insoluble, on the gastrointestinal tract is considerable—perhaps decreasing the risk of several ailments, including colon cancer.

So the answer to the question posed appears to be if consumers substitute oat and oat bran products for cheese and eggs and other foods that are high in cholesterol, they will succeed in lowering their cholesterol level—but through the substitution effect rather than through any independent cholesterol-lowering benefit from oat bran.

1.   What typically happens during the market maturity stage of the product life cycle?

   _____

   _____

   _____

   _____

2. Explain how cereal manufacturers could modify the market, the product or the marketing mix to stimulate sales during the market maturity stage of the product life cycle.

a. The market:

_____

_____

_____

_____

b. The product:

_____

_____

_____

_____

c. The marketing mix:

_____

_____

_____

_____

3. If oat bran is found to have no unique ability to lower cholesterol levels, what is likely to happen to those products whose main attribute is oat bran?

_____

_____

_____

_____

Case #2   Scented Disc Player

The House of Butler, a perfume maker and subsidiary of the William Schwab Corporation, is selling a device it calls "The Newest Horizon in Home Entertainment." The device is called the Scented Disc Player.

The player, which costs about $25, is a box about the size of a portable radio (30 cm wide, 35 cm long, and 8 cm high). The discs are scented pads nearly identical in size to a 45 RPM record. When slipped into the player, a scent is given off as the disc is heated. Each "play" lasts about two minutes, but the aroma from the play may linger for as long as an hour.

The company currently offers 50 scents, including Spring Garden, Ocean Mist, Spruce, Locker Room, and Arousal. Butler believes that virtually any scent can be reproduced and plans to introduce many more as the market builds. A long-play disc can give up to 100 plays and cost approximately $7, while a short-play disc costs $2, but gives only 15 plays. Butler has been working on the device for three years. It acquired the rights to the player from an inventor who wishes to remain anonymous.

After significant development work in the laboratory, the device was introduced on a trial basis in June 1994 in three markets. Information was gathered from these markets in Winnipeg, St. John's and Sudbury, which led Butler to decide on the final selling price, promotional campaign, and distribution strategy. Information from these markets also led to development of the long-play disc.

The company is limiting distribution of the player to 300 stores this fall so it won't be treated as a fad. It is now in national distribution and is currently being sold in such stores as Eaton's and The Bay. Sales at this point are relatively low and profits are negligible as Butler builds its distribution system and heavily promotes the device. Competition is currently nonexistent and Butler expects to turn a profit in the upcoming Christmas selling season.

____1. The idea for the Scented Disc Player came from:
    A.   an internal source.
    B.   customers.
    C.   competition.
    D.   suppliers.
    E.   another source.

____2. The Scented Disc Player is currently in the _____ stage of its life cycle.
    A.   introduction
    B.   growth
    C.   maturity
    D.   decline
    E.   market modification

_____3. The Scented Disc Player is an example of a product _____. (class or form)

_____4. The introduction of the long-playing disc is an example of:
- A. product modification.
- B. market modification.
- C. commercialization.
- D. concept development.
- E. test marketing.

_____5. The introduction of the Scented Disc Player in the Idaho, Louisiana, and Georgia markets is an example of:
- A. commercialization.
- B. business analysis.
- C. product development.
- D. market testing.
- E. market penetration.

Case #3   Ace's Energy Bars

Ace's is a successful candy company with 40 national products. They recently decided to take advantage of their name and enter the health bar market. With their new product idea called Ace's Energy Bar they decided to enter the young adult market. They are at the idea stage and see their product as a successful addition to their product line. With a well-known name and an efficient distribution network they see a whole new line of serials to be launched in the future.

With the current boom in fitness Ace's feels confident. They have run test markets to test out the consumer market in Guelph, Ontario and Vancouver, British Columbia with strong positive results that were better than anticipated after initial surveys were done. With a strong market name, product line and relationships with grocery stores and variety stores, the Ace Corporation is looking forward to a banner year.

_____1. The testing that was done in this case is referred to as
- A. functional
- B. consumer
- C. market
- D. concept
- E. viability

_____2. When Ace's decided to proceed with production of their new product what step in the new product development were they entering?
    A.   market test
    B.   commercialization
    C.   product development
    D.   market strategy
    E.   market development

_____3. When Ace's Energy Bars were sold in Guelph and Vancouver they were involved in_____.
    A.   market testing
    B.   product development
    C.   consumer testing
    D.   package testing
    E.   idea screening

_____4. When the executives meet to go over projected sales, costs, and break-even and profit estimates they are said to be entering the _____phase of the new development process.
    A.   market strategy development
    B.   market analysis
    C.   concept analysis
    D.   business analysis
    E.   commercialization

_____5. This product is at what stage in the product development life cycle?
    A.   market modification
    B.   growth
    C.   introduction
    D.   product modification
    E.   marketing-mix modification

Multiple Choice Answers

1.	Correct Answer:	4	Reference:	pg. 380
2.	Correct Answer:	2	Reference:	pg. 381
3.	Correct Answer:	5	Reference:	pg. 382
4.	Correct Answer:	4	Reference:	pg. 384
5.	Correct Answer:	3	Reference:	pg. 383
6.	Correct Answer:	2	Reference:	pg. 384
7.	Correct Answer:	5	Reference:	pg. 384
8.	Correct Answer:	1	Reference:	pg. 385
9.	Correct Answer:	4	Reference:	pg. 386
10.	Correct Answer:	3	Reference:	pg. 385
11.	Correct Answer:	1	Reference:	pg. 387
12.	Correct Answer:	3	Reference:	pg. 387
13.	Correct Answer:	2	Reference:	pg. 388
14.	Correct Answer:	5	Reference:	pg. 388
15.	Correct Answer:	4	Reference:	pg. 389
16.	Correct Answer:	3	Reference:	pg. 389
17.	Correct Answer:	2	Reference:	pg. 389
18.	Correct Answer:	1	Reference:	pg. 390
19.	Correct Answer:	4	Reference:	pg. 390
20.	Correct Answer:	3	Reference:	pg. 390
21.	Correct Answer:	1	Reference:	pg. 391
22.	Correct Answer:	2	Reference:	pg. 391

23.	Correct Answer:	5	Reference:	pg. 394
24.	Correct Answer:	3	Reference:	pg. 395
25.	Correct Answer:	2	Reference:	pg. 395
26.	Correct Answer:	4	Reference:	pg. 395
27.	Correct Answer:	1	Reference:	pg. 397
28.	Correct Answer:	5	Reference:	pg. 397
29.	Correct Answer:	4	Reference:	pg. 397
30.	Correct Answer:	5	Reference:	pg. 401

True/False Answers

1.	TRUE	Reference:	pg. 380	Topic: New-Product Development Strategy
2.	FALSE	Reference:	pg. 380	Topic: New-Product Development Strategy
3.	FALSE	Reference:	pg. 380	Topic: New-Product Development Strategy
4.	TRUE	Reference:	pg. 382	Topic: Idea Generation
5.	TRUE	Reference:	pg. 382	Topic: Idea Generation
6.	FALSE	Reference:	pg. 384	Topic: Idea Screening
7.	TRUE	Reference:	pg. 384	Topic: Idea Screening
8.	FALSE	Reference:	pg. 385	Topic: Concept Development and Testing
10.	TRUE	Reference:	pg. 386	Topic: Concept Testing
11.	FALSE	Reference:	pg. 388	Topic: Business Analysis
12.	TRUE	Reference:	pg. 388	Topic: Product Development

13.	TRUE	Reference:	pg. 388	Topic: Product Development
14.	FALSE	Reference:	pg. 388	Topic: Product Development
15.	TRUE	Reference:	pg. 389	Topic: Test Marketing
16.	TRUE	Reference:	pg. 390	Topic: Standard Test Markets
17.	FALSE	Reference:	pg. 390	Topic: Standard Test Markets
18.	TRUE	Reference:	pg. 391	Topic: Commercialization
19.	FALSE	Reference:	pg. 391	Topic: Speeding Up New-Product Development
20.	TRUE	Reference:	pg. 395	Topic: Product Life-Cycle Strategy

Applying Terms and Concepts Answers

Case #1   Oat Bran

Question #1
- During the market maturity stage of the product life cycle, sales typically slow down because many producers are selling the product.
- Overcapacity leads to greater competition.
- Competitors begin marking down prices and increasing their advertising and sales promotions.
- They may also increase their research and development budgets to find better versions of the product.
- Usually, these steps lead to a drop in profits, and some of the weaker competitors withdraw.

Question #2
a. Through market modification, the manufacturer tries to increase the consumption of the product by looking for new users and market segments. The firm would also look for ways to increase usage among current customers, or it might reposition the brand to appeal to a larger or faster-growing market segment—in this case, health-conscious consumers.
b. Using product modification, the manufacturer could increase the amount of oat bran in its cereal to attract new users and more usage.
c. Marketing-mix modification means the manufacturer would try to improve sales by changing one or more marketing-mix elements. Prices could be cut to attract new users and competitors' customers. A new advertising campaign highlighting changes in the product and/or new research could be launched. Aggressive sales promotion—

trade deals, coupons, gifts, and contests—could be used. The company could also seek new distribution channels, such as mass merchandisers, to move the product.

Question #3
- It is likely that certain brands of cereal will quickly move through the growth and maturity stages of the product life cycle to the sales decline stage.
- Sales and profits will continue to decline; competition will be reduced as some firms pull their product from the market; and minimal amounts will be spent to promote the product, which will remain essentially unchanged.
- The strategic focus will be on improving productivity in view of a low cash flow.
- Eventually, many of the brands of cereal could be pulled from the market.

Case #2 Scented Disc Player	Case #3 Ace's Energy Bars
1. E	1. A
2. A	2. B
3. Form	3. A
4. A	4. A
5. D	5. C

Chapter 10

Pricing Strategies

Chapter Overview

Price can be defined narrowly as the amount of money charged for a product or service that the consumer is willing to pay for the use of the product. When both of these components reach a happy medium it can be said that we have a true price. When the manufacturer prices a product too high or the consumer deems the value they obtain from the product is not worth the selling price, then the product falters and adjustments to product or price must be attended to. For if there is no union between the asking price and a consumer's willingness to pay the price, then there is no price—just a product in search of a non-existent market.

Despite the increased role of non-price factors in the modern marketing process, price remains an important element in the marketing mix. It is the only element in the marketing mix that produces revenue; all other elements represent costs. Price is also one of the most flexible elements of the marketing mix. Unlike product features and channel commitments, price can be raised or lowered quickly.

As is evident in the text's Chapter 10 introduction, Kellogg's, like many companies, is not good at handling pricing—pricing decisions and price competition are major problems for many marketing executives. Pricing problems often arise because prices are too cost-oriented, not revised frequently enough to reflect the impact of consumer perceptions of price and value or the impact of market changes, not consistent with the rest of the marketing mix, or not varied enough for differing products, market segments, and purchase occasions. Therefore, because of the different types of situations that may arise, different pricing techniques must be implemented.

Chapter Objectives

1.   Identify and define the internal factors affecting a firm's pricing decisions.
2.   Identify and define the external factors affecting pricing decisions, including the impact of consumer perceptions of price and value.
3.   Contrast the three general approaches to setting prices
4.   Describe the major strategies for pricing new products and product lines.
5.   Discuss the key issues related to initiating and responding to price changes.

Chapter Topics

Factors to Consider when Setting Prices
- Internal Factors Affecting Pricing Decisions
  - Marketing Objectives
  - Marketing-Mix Strategy
  - Costs
    - Types of Costs
    - Costs at different levels of production
    - Costs as a function of production experience
  - Organizational Considerations
- External Factor Affecting Pricing Decisions
  - The Market and Demand
    - Pricing in different types of markets
    - Consumer perceptions of price and value
    - Analyzing the price-demand relationship
    - Price elasticity of demand
  - Competitors' Costs, Prices, and Offers
  - Other External Factors

General Pricing Approaches
- Cost-Based Pricing
  - Cost-Plus Pricing
  - Breakeven Analysis and Target Profit Pricing
- Value-Based Pricing
- Competition-Based Pricing
- Going-Rate Pricing
- Sealed-Bid Pricing
- Product-Line Pricing
- Product Pricing
- Product-Bundle Pricing

Price-Adjustment Strategies
- Discount and Allowance Pricing
- Segmented Pricing
- Psychological Pricing
- Promotional Pricing
- Geographical Pricing
- International Pricing

Price Changes
- Responding To Price Changes

Chapter Summary

1.   How marketing objectives affect pricing decisions.

Marketing objectives are among the internal company factors affecting price. Current profit maximization sets a high price to meet current financial outcomes rather than long-term performance. Market-share leadership seeks the dominant market share through low prices to gain low-cost advantages. Product quality leadership sets high prices for superior products and high R & D.

2.   How costs affect pricing decisions.

Costs set the floor for the price. Costs include variable costs that vary directly with the level of production and fixed costs that remain constant. Total costs are the sum of both. Costs can also be influenced by experience curves that lower costs as production becomes more efficient. Companies must estimate demand for each level of price considered and set the price that makes best use of the company's resources.

3.   Factors outside the company that affect pricing decisions.

Several external factors affect price. The nature of the market (pure competition, monopolistic, oligopolistic, pure monopoly) describes the number of buyers and sellers in a market. The competition and its resources also affect price. Demand elasticity and economic, social, and political factors must also be considered.

4.   The price-demand relationship and its effect on pricing decisions.

Each price a company might charge leads to a difficult level of demand expressed as the demand curve. Generally, the more a product costs, the lower its level of demand, although consumer perceptions of value for many premium goods are exceptions. Price elasticity can also affect price. If demand is inelastic, then changes in price won't affect demand. The less elastic the demand, the more it pays for the seller to raise the price.

5.   The three general pricing approaches.

Cost-plus pricing adds a standard mark-up to the cost of the product. Break-even analysis and target profit pricing are common cost-oriented methods. Buyer-based, or perceived-value, pricing uses buyers' perceptions of value, not the seller's cost, as the key to pricing. Competition-based pricing focuses on competitive prices over seller costs. Two forms are going-rate pricing, which matches the competition, and sealed-bid pricing which tries to anticipate their price.

6. Price changing and responding to price change.

Changes in price by competition, and changes because of market conditions, quite often result in companies changing their initial pricing. Complex problems now arise, from increasing pricing to the effect of pricing on competition. A firm must be able to take their price and be willing and able to respond to price changes. It must consider its own product's life cycle, consumer reactions, and possible moves by the competition.

Key Terms

Allowances	(pg. 438)	Product line pricing	(pg. 437)
Break-even pricing	(pg. 430)	Promotional pricing	(pg. 440)
Captive-product pricing	(pg. 437)	Psychological pricing	(pg. 441)
Cash discount	(pg. 438)	Pure competition	(pg. 424)
Cost-plus pricing	(pg. 429)	Pure monopoly	(pg. 424)
Demand curve	(pg. 427)	Quantity discounts	(pg. 440)
Experience curve	(pg. 422)	Reference prices	(pg. 440)
Fixed cost	(pg. 421)	Sealed-bid pricing	(pg. 434)
F.O.B. origin pricing	(pg. 441)	Segmented pricing	(pg. 488)
Going-rate pricing	(pg. 433)	Total costs	(pg. 421)
Market penetration pricing	(pg. 436)	Uniform delivered pricing	(pg. 441)
Market skimming pricing	(pg. 435)	Value-based pricing	(pg. 432)
Monopolistic competition	(pg. 424)	Value pricing	(pg. 433)
Oligopolistic competition	(pg. 424)	Variable costs	(pg. 423)
Price	(pg. 415)	Zone pricing	(pg. 441)
Price elasticity	(pg. 427)		
Product bundle	(pg. 438)		

Multiple Choice Questions

10-1   Multiple

Internal factors affecting pricing include all of the following except:

1.   Marketing objectives
2.   Marketing-mix strategy
3.   Costs
4.   Organization
5.   All of the above

10-2   Multiple

Companies set _____ as their major objective if they are troubled by too much capacity, heavy competition, or changing consumer wants.

1.   Survival
2.   Current profit maximization
3.   Market-share leadership
4.   Product-quality leadership
5.   Price leadership

10-3   Multiple

Companies interested in _____ set their prices as low as possible.

1.   Survival
2.   Current profit maximization
3.   Market-share leadership
4.   Product-quality leadership
5.   Price leadership

10-4   Multiple

If a product is positioned on non-price factors, which of the following will not affect price?

1.   Quality
2.   Promotion
3.   Distribution
4.   Value
5.   All of the above

10-5   Multiple

Rent, heat and interest costs are considered what type of cost?

1.   Fixed
2.   Variable
3.   Total
4.   Expendable
5.   Predictable

10-6   Multiple

Management must decide who within the organization sets prices. Which of the following groups of people would set prices in an organization?

1.   Top management
2.   Division managers
3.   Product line managers
4.   Salespeople
5.   All of the above

10-7   Multiple

Not everybody in an organization actually sets the prices; however, many people influence the pricing strategies used. Who among the following would not have any influence in setting a pricing strategy?

1.   Sales managers
2.   Production managers
3.   Packaging managers
4.   Finance managers
5.   Accountants

10-8   Multiple

There are many external factors affecting a pricing strategy. Which of the following does not influence the pricing strategy?

1.   Nature of the market
2.   Demand
3.   Competition
4.   Supply
5.   Environmental elements

10-9   Multiple

Whereas costs set the lower limit of prices, the _____ and _____ set the upper limit.

1.   Market, demand
2.   Market, supply
3.   Consumers, market
4.   Consumers, demand
5.   Consumers, supply

10-10   Multiple

Under _____ competition, no single buyer or seller has much effect on the going market price.

1.   Monopolistic
2.   Pure
3.   Oligopolistic
4.   Pure monopoly
5.   Competitive

10-11   Multiple

In a purely competitive market, all the following play little or no role except:

1.   Marketing research
2.   Product development
3.   Advertising
4.   Sales promotion
5.   All the above play no role

10-12   Multiple

In _____ competition, a company is never sure it will gain anything permanent through a price cut.

1.   Monopolistic
2.   Pure
3.   Oligopolistic
4.   Pure monopoly
5.   Competitive

10-13 Multiple

A company in a pure non-regulated monopoly is free to price whatever level it feels the market will bear. However, they do not always charge the full price for a number of reasons. One reason they do not consider is:

1. A desire not to attract competition
2. A desire to be perceived as socially responsible
3. A desire to penetrate the market faster
4. A fear of government regulation
5. All of the above are reasons

10-14 Multiple

The _____ curve shows the number of units the market will buy in a given period of time, at the different prices that might be charged.

1. Supply
2. Price
3. Market
4. Demand
5. Profit

10-15 Multiple

The price elasticity of demand equation divides _____ by _____

1. % change in quantity demanded, % change in price
2. % change in quality supplied, % change in price
3. % change in price, % change in quantity supplied
4. % change in price, % change in quantity demanded
5. % change in quantity demanded, % change in quantity supplied

10-16 Multiple

Nicolette is an up-and-coming executive for Nesbitt Burns. She is very happy with her promotion, as it has considerably increased her level of disposable income. She has become much less price-sensitive. Which of the following is not an additional reason for her being price sensitive?

1. The products she buys are unique
2. The products she buys are high in quality
3. The products she buys are usually gifts
4. The products she buys are prestigious
5. The products she buys are exclusive

10-17 Multiple

Canon wants to introduce a new colour printer. To help them decide whether or not they are operating at a cost advantage or disadvantage, Canon needs to _____ its costs against its competitor's costs.

1.   Compare
2.   Contrast
3.   Match
4.   Benchmark
5.   Analyze

10-18 Multiple

Companies set prices by selecting a general pricing approach that includes all of the following factors except:

1.   Cost-based approach
2.   Supplier-based approach
3.   Buyer-based approach
4.   Competition-based approach
5.   All of the above are factors

10-19 Multiple

The equation for unit costs is the following:

1.   Fixed costs + (variable costs/units sales)
2.   Unit sales + (fixed costs/variable costs)
3.   Variable costs + (fixed costs/unit sales)
4.   Fixed costs + (unit sales/variable costs)
5.   Variable costs + (unit sales/fixed costs)

10-20 Multiple

The _____ pricing strategy is used by utility companies, which are constrained to make a fair return on their investment.

1.   Break-even
2.   Target profit
3.   Cost-plus
4.   Value-based
5.   Value

10-20 Multiple

The equation for breakeven volume is the following:

1.   Fixed cost/(variable costs–price)
2.   Fixed cost/(price–variable cost)
3.   Variable cost/(price–fixed cost)
4.   Variable cost/(fixed cost–price)
5.   Price/(variable cost–fixed cost)

10-21 Multiple

In many business-to-business marketing situations, the pricing challenge is to find ways to adjust the value of the company's marketing offer in order to escape price competition and justify higher price margins. This is especially true for which of the following products?

1.   Consumer
2.   Industrial
3.   Convenient
4.   Commodity
5.   Manufactured

10-22 Multiple

In _____ industries that sell a commodity such as steel, paper or fertilizer, firms typically charge the same price.

1.   Pure competition
2.   Monopolistic
3.   Government
4.   Consumer
5.   Oligopolistic

10-23 Multiple

Companies are not free to do exactly what they want. In setting prices, a company's short-term sales, market share, and profit goals, as well as the ability of the vulnerable to afford them, may have to be tempered by _____. If consumers do not approve, they will not buy.

1.   Social concerns
2.   Government
3.   Resellers
4.   Economic conditions
5.   1 and 2

10-24 Multiple

Common mistakes companies make when it comes to pricing include:

1.   Pricing is too cost oriented
2.   Prices are not revised often enough to reflect market changes
3.   Pricing does not take the rest of the marketing mix into account
4.   Only 1 and 3
5.   All of the above

10-25 Multiple

Pricing to cover variable costs and some fixed costs, as in the case of automobile dealerships that sell below total costs, is typical of which of the following pricing objectives?

1.   Current profit maximization
2.   Product-quality leadership
3.   Survival
4.   Market-share leadership
5.   Price leadership

10-26 Multiple

Companies that price products to enhance current financial results rather than long-run performance are using which of the following pricing objectives?

1.   Survival
2.   Product-quality leadership
3.   Market-share leadership
4.   Current profit maximization
5.   Price leadership

10-27 Multiple

When a firm responds to a price change by the competition it must consider which of the following?

1.   It simplifies the pricing process
2.   It is based ultimately on demand for the product
3.   It reduces price competition when all firms in an industry use it
4.   Many people feel it is fairer to both buyers and sellers than other forms of pricing
5.   None of the above

10-21   Multiple

When a coffee shop in an airport and a fine restaurant in a luxury hotel charge different prices for the same meal to customers who find the atmosphere in the hotel worth the difference, which pricing method is being used?

1.   Cost-based pricing
2.   Going-rate pricing
3.   Value-based pricing
4.   Sealed-bid pricing
5.   Prestige pricing

10-28   Multiple

If a Nike tennis racket percentage demand change in the marketplace is greater than the percentage change in price, the demand is said to be:

1.   Elastic
2.   Weak
3.   Inelastic
4.   Unitary
5.   Indifferent

True/False Questions

10-1   True/False

If the company has selected its target market and positioning carefully, then its marketing-mix strategy, including price, will be fairly straightforward.

10-2   True/False

When determining a pricing strategy the key determination factor is market segmentation.

10-3   True/False

Prices have no bearing on keeping the loyalty and support of resellers or on avoiding government intervention.

10-4   True/False

Companies often make their pricing decisions first and then base other marketing-mix decisions on the prices they want to charge.

10-5   True/False

Target costing starts with an ideal selling price, and it then targets, or controls, costs to ensure this price is met.

10-6   True/False

The key to marketing is to charge the lowest price rather than product differentiation to meet the demands of the market.

10-7   True/False

The floor price that a company can charge for its product is based on company costs.

10-8   True/False

To price wisely, management needs to know how its costs vary with different levels of production.

10-9   True/False

An aggressive pricing strategy might give the product a superior image.

10-10   True/False

Both consumers and industrial buyers balance the price of a product or service against the benefits of using it.

10-11   True/False

Buyers may see differences in sellers' products, but are not willing to pay different prices for them.

10-12   True/False

A government monopoly has the flexibility and power to pursue a variety of pricing objectives.

10-13   True/False

Promotional pricing is based on a price at existing or higher prices. Pricing decisions, like other marketing-mix decisions, must be supplier-oriented.

10-14   True/False

Usually, the higher the price of a product, the lower the demand for that product is.

10-15 True/False

Companies may charge different prices for the same product in different countries because of economics, regulations, laws, and competition.

10-16 True/False

The simplest pricing method is cost-plus pricing.

10-17 True/False

Mark up pricing only works if that price actually brings in the expected level of profits.

10-18 True/False

Value-based pricing uses the seller's cost as well as the user's perception of value as the key to pricing.

10-19 True/False

Market penetration is based on establishing a low price to attract buyers quickly and obtaining a large market share.

10-20 True/False

More and more marketers have adopted the value pricing strategies, as it is based on the right combination of quality and goods and services at a fair price.

Applying Terms and Concepts

To determine how well you understand the materials in this chapter, read each of the following brief cases and then respond to the questions that follow. Answers are given at the end of this chapter.

Case #1   Polar Plate Incorporated

Polar Plate is an innovative retractable block heater extension cord located between a vehicle's bumper and licence plate. The re-innovation of a flawed past product allows Polar Plate to satisfy existing demand for this convenient product.

By offering a high-quality product with superior components, Polar Plate positions itself as a convenience item targeting "baby boomers" in the automotive aftermarket. Through the efforts of the founding members, Polar Plate will find a place in automotive parts stores where it can be made available to automobile enthusiasts and hobbyists. The convenient features will be communicated to consumers as a hassle-free time-saving device. Finally, Polar Plate will have a place at service stations as part of the options of different winterization packages.

Currently, traditional extension cords are the only alternative in the marketplace. These products require the user to manually attach the cord to the block heater and then into an active outlet. Polar Plate's features and benefits will help to avoid the traditional scenarios including stolen cords, damage to vehicles resulting from extension cords hanging from mirrors or antennas, and cords lost by individuals driving away, forgetting their vehicles were plugged in. Polar Plate's sturdy construction and retractable mechanism provide solutions for the hardships associated with traditional extension cords and block heater use.

1. What characteristics would Polar Plate's target market have?

_____

_____

_____

_____

2. What benefits of Polar Plate could be promoted to help price the product at a premium?

_____

_____

_____

_____

3. Polar Plate's fixed costs are $100,000, its variable costs are $12.50, and they expect to sell 9,000 in the first year. What is the unit cost?

_____

_____

_____

_____

4. If Polar Plate sells its product for $30.00, what is the break-even volume?

_____

_____

_____

_____

5. Do you believe value-based pricing could work in this situation? Why or why not?

_____

_____

_____

_____

Case #2   Scott Refining Company

The Scott Refining Company had been producing gasoline from the same refinery in Leduc, Alberta for over fifteen years, but the outlook over the near term was grim, and something had to be done soon. The members of the executive committee of Scott were involved in a heated discussion about price policy.

During the past four months, the gasoline industry had been engaged in a price war in the provinces of Alberta, Saskatchewan, and Manitoba. Prices had declined to the point where refiners were breaking even—at best. Industry prices had gone down by over 9 per cent, but gasoline sales volume had gone up by only 4 per cent.

The Sunpower Oil Company, one of Scott's competitors, had experienced sales gains of over 10 per cent, but this extra litreage was the result of luring away competitors' dealers by offering even lower prices than those offered to established Sunpower dealers. Scott experienced a 4.8 per cent gain in gasoline sales, while prices had declined 8 per cent as a result of the price war. Part of Scott's price decline had been offset by lower average production costs as the plant moved from 87 per cent to 96 per cent of rated capacity. The competitions' costs, however, had either remained stable or increased because all were operating at near rated capacity prior to the price war.

Clifford Cole, one member of Scott's executive committee, suggested getting together with some of the competitors to see if they could reach some kind of agreement to stop this cut-throat competition and set prices at a reasonable level. Linda Klein, another member, said she thought the company ought to set a resale (retail) price for its own dealers and refuse to sell to them if they cut prices below this level. Several other solutions were offered, but after several hours the meeting was adjourned without any decision.

_____ 1. The price elasticity of gasoline demand for the industry during the past four
months was:
   A.   very elastic.
   B.   slightly elastic.
   C.   inelastic.
   D.   declining substantially.
   E.   remaining constant.

_____ 2. The price elasticity of demand for Scott Gasoline during the past four months
was:
   A.   very elastic but not as much as that of the industry.
   B.   slightly elastic.
   C.   inelastic.
   D.   positive.
   E.   both (A) and (D)

_____ 3. The decline in Scott's production costs was probably a result of:
   A.   lower variable costs.
   B.   the experience curve.
   C.   lower total costs.
   D.   spreading fixed costs in order to offer greater volume.
   E.   higher variable costs.

_____ 4. Regarding the pricing practices of Sunpower Oil Company:
   A.   Scott should consider doing the same thing.
   B.   Scott should not meet Sunpower prices if Sunpower offers a lower price to
         a Scott dealer because matching competitors' prices is illegal.
   C.   it is probably illegal unless Sunpower can show lower costs in serving the
         dealers who get lower prices.
   D.   it is probably legal because sellers can lower their prices to whomever
         they wish.
   E.   both (A) and (D)

_____ 5. The suggestion that several competitors get together to set a "reasonable" price is:
   A.   probably illegal per se.
   B.   probably an acceptable practice as long as no small competitors are
         injured.
   C.   legal because firms can raise prices whenever they want to, with
         whomever they wish to.
   D.   illegal unless all parties to the agreement are selling below cost.
   E.   both (A) and (C)

Case #3   Sony Canada

Ron Jason is general manager of Sony Canada. Competition is severe and Sony is thinking of pulling out of Canada if expected profits are not realized, and that is Jason's biggest fear. Without expansion the company will fold. He has the opportunity to subcontract the work of a plastics company and retool their equipment for the production of videocassette boxes and stereo cassette boxes. This field is well represented in Canada but he sees these markets more on an international scale where replacement products of this type are difficult to get a hold of. He feels by being able to produce these products cheaply he will be able to find a new market for Sony and be able to move in with a super low price and still keep within the standard industry mark-up.

Their price will be based on an industry standard mark-up. Since this market is being served by a number of small plastic production houses, the opportunity, in his eyes, is one for moving in quickly, establishing themselves as a brand name manufacturer of this product, and capturing markets abroad in the future. This is an area to enter cautiously due to the nature of the product and the fact that customers, when purchasing replacement products of this type, are price sensitive. With its established name Sony hopes the weight this will carry will lead to success. At $2.00 an average replacement cost they feel they can easily compete. Price sensitivity will be the key deciding feature, not the long-term viability of the company.

1.   Sony is entering what kind of market situation?

   _____

2.   The pricing objective is:

   _____

3.   An industry standard markup gives indication that the company is using

   _____ pricing.

4.   What type of demand curve is Jason facing? Give reasons for your decision.

   _____

   _____

   _____

   _____

Multiple Choice Answers

1. Correct Answer: 5   Reference: pg. 418

2. Correct Answer: 1   Reference: pg. 418

3. Correct Answer: 3   Reference: pg. 420

4. Correct Answer: 4   Reference: pg. 418

5. Correct Answer: 1   Reference: pg. 421

6. Correct Answer: 5   Reference: pg. 423

7. Correct Answer: 3   Reference: pg. 423

8. Correct Answer: 4   Reference: pg. 429

9. Correct Answer: 1   Reference: pg. 425

10. Correct Answer: 2   Reference: pg. 428

11. Correct Answer: 5   Reference: pg. 428

12. Correct Answer: 3   Reference: pg. 424

13. Correct Answer: 2   Reference: pg. 424

14. Correct Answer: 4   Reference: pg. 426

15. Correct Answer: 1   Reference: pg. 427

16. Correct Answer: 3   Reference: pg. 428

17. Correct Answer: 4   Reference: pg. 428

18. Correct Answer: 2   Reference: pg. 429

19. Correct Answer: 3   Reference: pg. 430

20. Correct Answer: 1   Reference: pg. 430

21. Correct Answer: 2   Reference: pg. 431

22. Correct Answer: 4   Reference: pg. 432

23.	Correct Answer:	5	Reference:	pg. 433
24.	Correct Answer:	1	Reference:	pg. 444
25.	Correct Answer:	5	Reference:	pg. 418
26.	Correct Answer:	3	Reference:	pg. 421
27.	Correct Answer:	4	Reference:	pg. 418
28.	Correct Answer:	2	Reference:	pg. 443
29.	Correct Answer:	3	Reference:	pg. 433
30.	Correct Answer:	1	Reference:	pg. 426

True/False Answers

1.	TRUE	Reference:	pg. 418	Topic: Internal Factors Affecting Pricing Decisions
2.	FALSE	Reference:	pg. 418	Topic: Internal Factors Affecting Pricing Decisions
3.	FALSE	Reference:	pg. 419	Topic: Internal Factors Affecting Pricing Decisions
4.	TRUE	Reference:	pg. 420	Topic: Marketing-Mix Strategy
5.	TRUE	Reference:	pg. 420	Topic: Marketing-Mix Strategy
6.	FALSE	Reference:	pg. 420	Topic: Marketing-Mix Strategy
7.	TRUE	Reference:	pg. 421	Topic: Costs
8.	TRUE	Reference:	pg. 421	Topic: Costs
9.	FALSE	Reference:	pg. 422	Topic: Costs as a Function of Production Experience
10.	FALSE	Reference:	pg. 423	Topic: The Market and Demand
11.	FALSE	Reference:	pg. 423	Topic: The Market and Demand

12.	TRUE	Reference:	pg. 423	Topic: The Market and Demand
13.	FALSE	Reference:	pg. 425	Topic: Consumer Perceptions of Price and Value
14.	TRUE	Reference:	pg. 426	Topic: Analyzing the Price-Demand Relationship
15.	TRUE	Reference:	pg. 426	Topic: Analyzing the Price-Demand Relationship
16.	TRUE	Reference:	pg. 429	Topic: Cost-Plus Pricing
17.	FALSE	Reference:	pg. 429	Topic: Cost-Plus Pricing
18.	FALSE	Reference:	pg. 432	Topic: Value-Based Pricing
19.	TRUE	Reference:	pg. 432	Topic: Value-Based Pricing
20.	TRUE	Reference:	pg. 432	Topic: Value-Based Pricing

Applying Terms and Concepts Answers

Case #1   Polar Plate Incorporated

Question #1
- People who like to tinker with their cars
- People who are looking for convenience
- Baby boomers aged 30 to 52
- Incomes between $25,000 and $50,000

Question #2
- Security
- Prevents extension cord damage
- Convenience and ease of use
- Uniqueness
- Quality materials and construction to withstand harsh winter conditions
- Ease of installation

Question #3
- Unit Cost = $23.61

Question #4
- Breakeven volume = 5715

Question #5
- Value-based pricing is possible
- Consumers will find value in this product therefore manufacturers can price the product at a higher price to ensure that they cover their costs and do not hurt sales, because consumers are willing to pay more

Case #2   Scott Refining Company

1.   C
2.   C
3.   D
4.   C
5.   A

Case #3 Sony Canada

1.   Pure competition

2.   Survival

3.   Cost-plus

4.   Elastic demand curve

-       Industry characterized by many buyers and sellers, with no seller having much influence on the going market price.

-       Customers see the products as being homogeneous.

-       Company operating at roughly break-even. Customers do not exhibit brand loyalty.

-       Customers are price-sensitive.

Chapter 11

Distribution Channels and Logistics Management

Chapter Overview

Marketing channel decisions are among the most important decisions management faces. A company's channel decision directly affects every other marketing decision. Each channel system creates a different segment of target consumers and serves a different function. The role of the marketer is to be able to decide on the most effective channel and make an analytical decision on which to use. In this way profits can be raised without even increasing sales. Logistical decisions on movement of product is a key element to a firm's bottom line.

Therefore how company "A" and company "B" decide to distribute a similar product can spell the failure or success of that company. This is an area that is often overlooked by marketers as they become occupied with the selling of their product and forget the most economical way to logistically distribute their product. Management must make channel decisions carefully, incorporating today's needs with tomorrow's likely selling environment. While some companies pay too little attention to their distribution channels, others have used imaginative distribution systems to gain a competitive advantage.

Chapter Objectives

1. Explain why companies use distribution channels and explain the functions these channels perform.
2. Discuss how channel members interact and how they organize to perform the work of the channel.
3. Identify the major channel alternatives open to a company.
4. Discuss the nature and importance of physical distribution and integrated logistics management.
5. Analyze integrated logistics, including how it may be achieved and its benefits to the company

Chapter Topics

The Nature of Distribution Channels
- Why are Marketing Intermediaries Used?
- Distribution Channel Functions
- Number of Channel Levels

Channel Behaviour and Organization
- Channel Behaviour
- Vertical Marketing System
  - Corporate VMS
  - Contractual VMS
  - Administered VMS
- Horizontal Marketing System
- Hybrid Marketing System
- Changing Channel Organization

Channel Design Decisions
- Analyzing Consumer Service Needs
- Setting the Channel Objectives and Constraints
- Identifying Major Alternatives
  - Types of Intermediaries
  - Number of Marketing Intermediaries
  - Responsibilities of Channel Members
- Evaluating the Major Alternatives
- Designing International Distribution Channels

Channel Management Decisions
- Selecting Channel Members
- Motivating Channel Members
- Evaluating Channel Members

Physical Distribution and Logistics Management
- Nature and Importance of Physical Distribution and Marketing Logistics
- Goals of the Logistics System
- Major Logistics Functions
  - Order Processing
  - Warehousing
  - Inventory
  - Transportation
    - Rail
    - Truck
    - Water

- Pipeline
- Air
- Integrated Logistics Management
  - Cross-Functional Teamwork Inside the Company
  - Building Channel Partnerships
  - Third-Party Logistics

Chapter Summary

1. Why companies use distribution channels and the functions they perform.

Producers use intermediaries, because they may lack the financial resources to carry out direct marketing, for greater efficiency, contacts, and specialization. Expertise in one area does not mean expertise in all areas and marketers therefore seek out companies that will best serve their needs. Intermediaries perform the functions of providing information, promotion, contact, matching, negotiation, physical distribution, financing, and risk taking. Marketing decisions such as these can increase corporate profits.

2. The interaction of channels, how they relate to one another in a positive way to take advantage of what each has to offer, and the logistics of how they are put together in an organized manner to function as a channel.

Channel members interact in mutually interdependent ways. Channels consist of dissimilar firms that band together for the common good. Channel members may experience horizontal or vertical conflict. Types of vertical marketing systems include corporate, contractual, and administered. Corporate are wholly-owned while contractual may be wholesaler-sponsored voluntary chains, retailer co-operatives, or franchises. A franchise can be either manufacturer-sponsored or a service firm.

3. The major distribution channel alternatives open to a company.

Major alternatives include types of intermediaries (company sales force, manufacturer's agency, or industrial distributors), number of intermediaries (intensive, selective, exclusive distribution), and determining the responsibilities of each channel member.

4. How companies select, motivate, and evaluate channel members.

Selection involves determining the characteristics that distinguish better intermediaries: years in business, other lines carried, profit record, growth, profitability, cooperativeness, and reputation.

5. The issues firms face when setting up physical distribution systems.

Firms must consider the nature of physical distribution, the physical distribution objective, order processing, warehousing, inventory, transportation mode to be used, and organizational responsibility for physical distribution.

Key Terms

Multiple Choice Questions

11-1   Multiple

Caterpillar is a marketing intermediary used by a number of firms. What is the one factor Caterpillar cannot generally perform better than the firm itself?
1.   Contracts
2.   Experiences
3.   Financing
4.   Scale of operation
5.   All of the above

11-2   Multiple

Producers make _____ assortments of products in _____ quantities, but customers want _____ assortments of products in _____ quantities.

1.   Broad, large, narrow, small
2.   Narrow, large, broad, small
3.   Broad, small, narrow, large
4.   Narrow, small, broad, large
5.   None of the above

11-3   Multiple

A distribution channel overcomes all the following major gaps that separate goods and services from those who would use them except _____.

1.   Distance
2.   Time
3.   Place
4.   Possession
5.   All of the above

11-4   Multiple

Which of the following functions do members of the marketing channel not perform?

1.   Contact
2.   Physical distribution
3.   Negotiation
4.   Risk taking
5.   They perform all of the above

11-5   Multiple

Distribution channels provide the following function/s:

1.   Provide information for gathering and distributing research
2.   Provide promotion by developing persuasive communications.
3.   Contact and match by shaping and fitting buyers' needs.
4.   Provide physical distribution and transport and store goods.
5.   Provide finance and carry out channel work
6.   All of the above

11-6   Multiple

Several types of flows connect all of the institutions in the channel. Which of the following is not one of them?

1.   Physical flow
2.   Creative flow
3.   Flow of ownership
4.   Payment flow
5.   Promotion flow

11-7   Multiple

In the customer marketing channels, channel # _____ involves the manufacturer, wholesaler, retailer, and consumer.

1.   1
2.   2
3.   3
4.   4
5.   5

11-8   Multiple

In both the consumer and business marketing channels, there are complex systems of behaviour where people and companies interact to accomplish all of the following goals except:

1.   Profit
2.   Individual
3.   Company
4.   Channel
5.   All of the above

11-9   Multiple

When Coca-Cola came into conflict with some of its bottlers who agreed to bottle competitor Dr. Pepper, they were experiencing _____ conflict.

1.   Controversial
2.   Horizontal
3.   Vertical
4.   Bi-lateral
5.   Unilateral

11-10 Multiple

The vertical marketing system, which is a unified system, can be dominated by the:

1.   Producer
2.   Wholesaler
3.   Retailer
4.   Only 1 and 2
5.   All of the above

11-11 Multiple

Vertical marketing can prove to be profitable by all of the below with the exception of:

1.   Size
2.   Strong relationships
3.   Bargaining power
4.   Elimination of duplicate services
5.   All of the above

11-12 Multiple

Companies that are involved in each aspect of their selling are said to be practicing which type of vertical marketing?

1.   Contractual
2.   Administered
3.   Corporate
4.   Integrated
5.   Cooperative

11-13 Multiple

Some licensed bottlers in various markets buy Coca-Cola syrup concentrate and then carbonate, bottle and sell the finished product to retailers in the local market. They are practicing which type of vertical marketing system?

1.   Contractual
2.   Administered
3.   Corporate
4.   Integrated
5.   Cooperative

11-14 Multiple

In horizontal marketing systems, two or more companies at one level join together to follow a new marketing opportunity. Companies can combine all the following except _____ to accomplish more together than they could alone.

1.   Capital
2.   Production capabilities
3.   Marketing resources
4.   New product ideas
5.   All of the above

11-15 Multiple

Computers have emerged over the last few years as a necessity in today's business and home environment. Three things make up a winning computer product. Which of the following is not one of them?

1.	A product
2.	Customers
3.	Corporate relationships
4.	Distributors
5.	All of the above

11-16 Multiple

Which of the following questions would not be used in analyzing consumer service needs?

1.	Do customers want bargains or good quality?
2.	Do customers want to buy from nearby locations?
3.	Do customers want add-on services?
4.	Would they rather buy over the phone or through the mail?
5.	Do customers value breadth of product or do they want specialization?

11-17 Multiple

Which of the following channel objective characteristics greatly affects channel design?

1.	Product characteristics
2.	Characteristic of intermediaries
3.	Environmental factors
4.	Only 1 and 3
5.	All of the above

11-18 Multiple

After deciding on a channel objective the marketer is now ready to identify the major alternative. This is done by use of all of the following with the exception of:

1.	Types of intermediaries
2.	Number of intermediaries
3.	Stability of intermediaries
4.	Responsibility of each channel member
5.	All of the above

11-19 Multiple

Independent firms whose sales forces handle related products for many companies are known as:

1. Company sales forces
2. Manufacturer's agencies
3. Industrial distributors
4. Sales agencies
5. Wholesalers

11-20 Multiple

Producers of common raw materials and convenience products typically seek:

1. Selective distribution
2. Exclusive distribution
3. Expedient distribution
4. Intensive distribution
5. Reliable distribution

11-21 Multiple

The responsibilities of channel members are very important to articulate. This is the only item channel members do not need to agree on before entering into a contract:

1. Price policies
2. Conditions of sale
3. Marketing strategies
4. Territorial rights
5. Specific services

11-22 Multiple

A company that wants to keep the channel as flexible as possible would place greater importance on the _____ criteria in evaluating major alternatives.

1. Economic
2. Control
3. Financial
4. Adaptive
5. Replacement

11-23 Multiple

Channel management does not require _____:

1.   Selecting channel members
2.   Promoting channel members
3.   Motivating channel members
4.   Evaluating channel member performance
5.   All of the above

11-24 Multiple

When selecting intermediaries, a company will want to evaluate its channel members on everything except:

1.   Years in business
2.   Other lines carried
3.   Growth and profit recorded
4.   Cooperativeness
5.   All of the above

11-25 Multiple

Companies today are placing greater emphasis on logistics for several reasons. Which of the following is not one of them?

1.   To attain total quality management.
2.   Customer service and satisfaction have become the cornerstones of marketing
3.   Logistics is a major cost element for most companies
4.   The explosion in product variety has created a need for improved logistics
5.   Improvements in technology have created opportunities for major gains in distribution efficiency

11-26 Multiple

Shipping and transportation account for _____ % of an average product's price.

1.   20
2.   10
3.   5
4.   15
5.   25

11-27 Multiple

When firms decide on containerization for shipping of goods because of ease of transfer between two modes of transportation, it is said to be using which of the following?

1.   Fishyback
2.   Piggyback
3.   Trainship
4.   Airtruck
5.   None of the above

11-28 Multiple

Which of the following factors is not important in ranking the transportation modes?

1.   Speed
2.   Dependability
3.   Capability
4.   Availability
5.   All of the above

11-29 Multiple

Building channel partnerships is becoming increasingly popular. Which of the following is not considered a form of channel partnership?

1.   Cross-company teams
2.   Shared projects
3.   Bi-lateral teams
4.   Information sharing
5.   Continuous inventory replenishment

11-30 Multiple

Companies may use third-party logistics providers for several reasons. What is one reason they would cite for not using a third party?

1.   Getting product to market is their main focus
2.   Outsourcing logistics frees a company to focus more intensely on its core business
3.   Integrated logistics companies understand the increasingly complex logistics environment
4.   It is always cheaper
5.   All of the above

True/False Questions

11-1   True/False

Giving some of the selling jobs to intermediaries means a company gives up some control over how and to whom products are sold.

11-2   True/False

The role of marketing intermediaries is to transform the assortment of products made by producers into the assortment wanted by consumers.

11-3   True/False

Horizontal conflict does not occur between firms at the same level of a channel.

11-4   True/False

Producers, not final consumers, are part of every channel.

11-5   True/False

Channel systems do not stand still; new types of intermediaries surface, and whole new channel systems evolve.

11-6   True/False

Each channel member depends on the others.

11-7   True/False

A conventional channel consists of producers, wholesalers and retailers.

11-8   True/False

Individual channels are interested in the broad view, and therefore are more concerned with the success of the channel than with its own short-run goals.

11-9   True/False

Lack of conflict in a channel helps ensure healthy competition.

11-10 True/False

A vertical marketing system acts as a unified system.

257

11-11   True/False

The fact that most consumers can tell the difference between contractual and corporate vertical marketing systems shows how unsuccessfully the contractual organizations compete with corporate chains.

11-12   True/False

Forming successfully-horizontal marketing systems is absolutely essential in an era of global business and global travel.

11-13   True/False

Hybrid channels offer few advantages to companies facing large and complex markets.

11-14   True/False

Marketing channels can be thought of as customer value supply systems in which each channel member adds value for the customers.

11-15   True/False

Hybrid marketing channels organize two or more channels to reach one or more market segments.

11-16   True/False

A company need only identify one type of channel member who can carry out its channel work.

11-17   True/False

Three strategies are available with respect to the number of marketing intermediaries used. They are intensive, exclusive, and sequential distribution.

11-18   True/False

Mutual services and duties need to be spelled out carefully, especially in franchise and exclusive distribution channels.

11-19   True/False

In phase one of creating channels a company states its channel objective.

11-20 True/False

Logistics addresses the problem of outbound distribution, but fails to address the issue of inbound distribution.

Applying Terms and Concepts

To determine how well you understand the materials in this chapter, read each of the following brief cases and then respond to the questions that follow. Answers are given at the end of this chapter.

Case #1   Pro Image[1]

The marketing of professional and university team sportswear and novelty items is a $3 billion-a-year industry. Since 1985, approximately 300 sports fan shops have opened. Most are independent operations, but franchisers are an increasingly important part of the retailing scene. Pro Image wasn't the first franchiser of the one-stop sports fan shop, but they are battling to lead the pack. In the franchise field, Pro Image competes with such firms as SpectAthlete, Sports Fantasy, Fan Fair, and Sports Arena Ltd.

Fan shops seem to sell just about anything from T-shirts, sweatshirts, sweaters, and caps to coffee mugs, key chains, pennants, bedspreads, and football helmet telephones. While many items are licensed from teams and emblazoned with team logos, most shops also sell authentic merchandise like team jackets and jerseys.

Pro Image was founded in 1985 by Chad and Kevin Olson. Three years later they controlled over 130 stores, with an additional 100 franchised outlets. Each franchise store costs roughly $100,000, approximately $16,000 of which covers the franchise fee with the rest going towards inventory and store improvements.

Since Pro Image recognizes the importance of a good location, it requires franchisees to locate themselves in high-traffic regional malls. Pro Image assists franchisees in site selection, lease negotiation, and advertising. Storeowners must create an upscale image with glass storefronts and wood-slat wall displays. Pro Image requires new owners to attend a four-day training session. They also sponsor an annual convention. Other assistance includes a business hotline and a computerized inventory and sales system. As an added service, they stock hard-to-get items in a 4,500 square-foot warehouse, making them more readily available to franchisees.

Pro Image recognizes that consumers want to wear what their sports heroes wear during games. Therefore, they stock authentic merchandise that comes directly from the same manufacturers that supply leagues and teams. But authentic merchandise carries a relatively high price. Replica merchandise is available for the more price-conscious.

---

[1] *Principles in Marketing*, 3rd Edition, Kotler, Armstrong, Warren (Prentice Hall) – pg. 253.

259

Though it's very similar to the authentic merchandise, it's not exactly the same product worn by the pro players.

The main customer base for Pro Image is men between 18 and 40, although women are becoming increasingly important customers. Customers purchase the product for themselves, their spouses, or their children.

Competition for the sports fan market is intense. Pro Image must battle other franchise operations but also independents, department stores, general retailers, and athletic stores that sell similar merchandise. The latter three constitute the major competition for Pro Image since they control approximately 90 per cent of the total licensed merchandise market.

Retailers and their customers aren't the only ones benefiting from the boom in sports wear and novelty item merchandising. Consider NFL Properties, the licensing arm of the National Football League. Since 1980, NFL Properties has seen its souvenir revenues increase by nearly 400 per cent to approximately $1.5 billion US. The licensing division of NFL Properties oversees the authorization and sale of more than 700 items.

Team owners love NFL Properties. In the past decade, with two player strikes, relatively stagnant television income, and escalating player salaries, team owners have come to appreciate the approximately $1.5 million US they receive each year from Properties' activities.

Also benefiting is a variety of charities. Each year NFL Properties raises and distributes nearly $700,000 US to deserving organizations.

1.   In your opinion, is the sports merchandise "boom" a fad or a trend that will continue to be profitable?

_____

_____

_____

_____

2.   Would a conventional distribution channel work in this industry? Why or why not?

_____

_____

_____

_____

3.   Explain why an organization such as NFL Properties might choose to have independent retailers, franchise operations, department stores, mass merchandisers, and athletic stores sell NFL-authorized merchandise to consumers rather than sell the merchandise directly to consumers through their own chain of retail outlets.

_____

_____

_____

_____

4.   Discuss the nature of the vertical marketing system employed by Pro Image.

_____

_____

_____

_____

5.   Suppose you are interested in opening a sports fan shop. What do you see as the advantages and disadvantages of becoming part of a franchise operation?

_____

_____

_____

_____

Case #2   Ramer Gourmet Popcorn Shop

Cynthia Ramer opened her first Gourmet Popcorn Shop in November 1979, at the Riverside Mall in Victoria, BC. In addition to her fresh-popped popcorn, she sold a full range of popcorn merchandise, including unpopped corn, flavoured oils and salts, and various styles of corn poppers. She has since abandoned most of the popcorn merchandise and now concentrates on selling her flavoured popcorn and a small selection of flavoured salts.

Ramer's organization had grown since 1983 to include eight outlets in the Victoria and Richmond areas. Four shops were located in shopping malls, two in large hotel complexes, and two in office complexes, each location averaging $200,000 in sales per year.

In a bold venture, Ramer allowed her system of preparing and flavouring popcorn to become a franchise operation. She sold distribution rights to an independent group. The franchise contract set very strict requirements on nearly all facets of the operation, including pricing. Ramer also forced C.R. Purchasing to act as the wholesaler servicing the franchise locations.

After two years, Ramer Gourmet Popcorn Shops were a huge success, with over 30 franchise locations in operation in BC, in addition to their own eight shops. It seemed as if they were everywhere people were likely to congregate—hotels, subways, airports, and hospitals, in addition to shopping malls and office complexes. Ramer was beginning to experience some difficulty with her suppliers of popcorn and thought that if the operation continued to grow, she would consider moving into the farm business to assure a steady supply of corn. Ramer had no concern about the long-term viability of her organization. A report released in January by the Morden Manitoba-based Popcorn Institute indicated that popcorn consumption was expected to exceed 15 billion litres annually, up from the 10 billion litres consumed in 1988. Besides, Ramer's gourmet popcorn was so chic, it was sometimes purchased as a gift or used as hors d'oeuvres at parties.

Last month, Ramer began hearing complaints that several of the franchise locations were lowering their prices and/or selling new flavours of popcorn, even though this was clearly in violation of the franchise agreement.

_____1. The marketing strategy of Ramer Gourmet Popcorn Shops is to have _____ distribution.
  A.   intensive
  B.   selective
  C.   exclusive
  D.   market
  E.   blanket

_____2. The type of channel system currently used in marketing Ramer Gourmet Popcorn is:
  A.   conventional marketing system.
  B.   corporate vertical marketing system.
  C.   contractual vertical marketing system.
  D.   both (B) and (C)
  E.   none of the above.

_____3. What is occurring when several of the individual popcorn shop owners begin lowering their prices in violation of the franchise agreement?
  A.   channel cooperation
  B.   channel miscommunication
  C.   horizontal channel conflict
  D.   vertical channel conflict
  E.   channel interdependence

_____4. Ramer Gourmet Popcorn is currently sold through a _____-level channel system.
   A.   zero
   B.   one
   C.   two
   D.   direct
   E.   sub

Case #3   Jo Ann's Secrets

Jo Ann Andale has a successful clone of Victoria's Secret products and has been distributing them through clothing stores across Canada for 8 years. The idea was logical, as she would be able to benefit from Victoria's Secret's ideas, style and distribution through other stores and her own in the future. Her name is well known in the lingerie business as she has been a designer for ten years and has had her fair share of publicity. Though her name is not yet a household word, she feels with proper advertising the idea of a Canadian Victoria's Secret store will be turning heads and getting her more than her share of publicity. Products are still being made in Canada but due to increased production costs it appears that an intermediary will provide production within Asia within the year.

Orders are still filed to a central clearing house and sent out using various delivery services depending on availability, rather than investing in her own distribution network. By using a piggyback system she has been able to keep costs down while meeting shipping deadlines. Although she has been shipping goods by local carriers, she now sees the benefits of going to a specialist to deal with distribution and is in the process of changing her distribution channel. Her main concern now is to keep her products available in a very limited number of stores and not allow them to be available in such chain stores as Le Château. Interest in the stores is growing rapidly and the future looks bright. Some stores seem to be battling with the price of her products and it appears that pricing is now uniform. Rather than a small price range of 10%, stores vary as much as 35% and she seems to have little control over that decision.

_____1. What form of distribution is Jo Ann using?
   A.   intensive
   B.   exclusive
   C.   selective
   D.   market
   E.   blanket

_____2. It can be said that this firm is using which channel?
   A.   conventional marketing system.
   B.   corporate vertical marketing system.
   C.   contractual vertical marketing system.
   D.   two-level system.
   E.   zero-level system.

_____3. By continuing to open her own stores and limiting availability of her product in other stores, Jo Ann is said to be using which kind of marketing system:
   A.   horizontal
   B.   conventional
   C.   corporate
   D.   contractual
   E.   interdependent

_____4. A _____-level channel system is presently being used.
   A.   zero
   B.   one
   C.   two
   D.   three
   E.   sub

_____5. If her company were to decide to sell to clothing manufacturers, she would be said to be involved in:
   A.   operating a multichannel marketing system.
   B.   operating a hybrid marketing system
   C.   engaged in direct marketing.
   D.   all of the above
   E.   none of the above

6.   Which mode of transportation do you believe would be the most economical in this situation and why?

   _____

   _____

   _____

   _____

Multiple Choice Answers

1. Correct Answer: 3   Reference: pg. 460

2. Correct Answer: 2   Reference: pg. 460

3. Correct Answer: 1   Reference: pg. 461

4. Correct Answer: 5   Reference: pg. 461

5. Correct Answer: 6   Reference: pg. 459

6. Correct Answer: 2   Reference: pg. 464

7. Correct Answer: 3   Reference: pg. 462

8. Correct Answer: 1   Reference: pg. 463

9. Correct Answer: 3   Reference: pg. 465

10. Correct Answer: 5   Reference: pg. 465

11. Correct Answer: 2   Reference: pg. 465

12. Correct Answer: 3   Reference: pg. 465

13. Correct Answer: 1   Reference: pg. 466

14. Correct Answer: 4   Reference: pg. 467

15. Correct Answer: 2   Reference: pg. 467

16. Correct Answer: 1   Reference: pg. 470

17. Correct Answer: 5   Reference: pg. 470

18. Correct Answer: 3   Reference: pg. 473

19. Correct Answer: 2   Reference: pg. 473

20. Correct Answer: 4   Reference: pg. 475

21. Correct Answer: 3   Reference: pg. 475

22. Correct Answer: 4   Reference: pg. 476

23.	Correct Answer:	2	Reference:	pg. 478
24.	Correct Answer:	5	Reference:	pg. 478
25.	Correct Answer:	1	Reference:	pg. 482
26.	Correct Answer:	4	Reference:	pg. 484
27.	Correct Answer:	2	Reference:	pg. 485
28.	Correct Answer:	5	Reference:	pg. 485
29.	Correct Answer:	3	Reference:	pg. 486
30.	Correct Answer:	4	Reference:	pg. 487

True/False Answers

1.	TRUE	Reference:	pg. 460	Topic: Why are Marketing Intermediaries Used?
2.	TRUE	Reference:	pg. 460	Topic: Why are Marketing Intermediaries Used?
3.	FALSE	Reference:	pg. 464	Topic: Horizontal Conflict
4.	FALSE	Reference:	pg. 462	Topic: Number of Channel Levels
5.	TRUE	Reference:	pg. 463	Topic: Channel Behaviour and Organization
6.	TRUE	Reference:	pg. 463	Topic: Channel Behaviour
7.	TRUE	Reference:	pg. 465	Topic: Conventional Distribution
8.	FALSE	Reference:	pg. 464	Topic: Channel Behaviour
9.	FALSE	Reference:	pg. 464	Topic: Channel Behaviour
10.	TRUE	Reference:	pg. 465	Topic: Vertical Marketing Systems
11.	FALSE	Reference:	pg. 466	Topic: Contractual VMS
12.	TRUE	Reference:	pg. 467	Topic: Horizontal Marketing Systems

13.	FALSE	Reference:	pg. 468	Topic: Hybrid Marketing Systems
14.	FALSE	Reference:	pg. 473	Topic: Analyzing Consumer Service Needs
15.	TRUE	Reference:	pg. 468	Topic: Hybrid Marketing Systems
16.	FALSE	Reference:	pg. 473	Topic: Identifying Major Alternatives
17.	FALSE	Reference:	pg. 475	Topic: Number of Marketing Intermediaries
18.	TRUE	Reference:	pg. 476	Topic: Responsibilities of Channel Members
19.	TRUE	Reference:	pg. 478	Topic: Motivating Channel Members
20.	FALSE	Reference:	pg. 481	Topic: Nature and Importance of Physical Distribution and Marketing Logistics

Applying Terms and Concept Answers

Case#1   Pro Image

Question #1
- As long as professional and college sports teams continue to produce exciting games and quality entertainment, the sportswear industry will continue to flourish.
- In addition, the high profile of athletes and products also contribute to the sales.

Question #2
- A conventional distribution channel is a channel that consists of one or more independent producers, wholesalers, and retailers.
- Each is a separate business that seeks to maximize its own profits even at the expense of profits for the system as a whole.
- Since sports merchandise is more of a luxury product and carries high prices, a vertically integrated system would be most beneficial for this industry.
- Independent parties in a conventional system would result in higher-end prices for the consumer.
- Furthermore, the nature of the product requires that professional teams give permission for the use of their name and logo, thus the use of a vertical distribution system would be more cost-efficient, and less complex.

Question #3

- NFL Properties might choose to use a variety of retailers to reach target markets for several reasons, but two are especially important.
- First, NFL Properties may lack the financial resources to carry out direct marketing activities.
- Second, direct marketing activities would require NFL Properties to become an intermediary, which would not only mean that they would have to develop expertise in retailing and wholesaling activities, but might also mean they would have to carry products from other organizations to sell along with their own merchandise lest their own assortment be viewed as too narrow by target customers.
- The usefulness of intermediaries largely boils down to their greater efficiency in making goods and services available to target markets.
- Through their contacts, experience, specialization, and scale of operation, intermediaries usually offer the firm more than it can achieve on its own.

Question #4

- A conventional distribution channel consists of one or more independent producers, wholesalers, and retailers.
- Each is a separate business seeking to maximize its own profits, even at the expense of profits for the system as a whole.
- No channel member has much control over the other members, and there are no formal means of assigning roles and resolving channel conflict.
- By contrast, a vertical marketing system (VMS) consists of producers, wholesalers, and retailers acting as a unified system.
- One channel member either owns the others, has contracts with them, or wields so much power that all must cooperate.
- The vertical marketing system may be dominated by the producer, the wholesaler, or the retailer.
- VMSs came into being to control channel behaviour and manage channel conflict.
- They achieve economies through size, bargaining power, and elimination of duplicated services.
- Pro Image is a contractual vertical marketing system.
- Specifically, it's a service firm-sponsored retailer franchise organization wherein Pro Image licenses a system of retailers to bring selected products to customers.

Question #5

- The advantages of associating with a franchise organization such as Pro Image include company assistance with site selection, leave negotiation, advertising, financing, purchasing, inventory control systems, training, networking through newsletters, meetings and conventions, and a proven store design, layout and pricing strategy.
- There is also a greater likelihood of increased sales and profitability from associating with a franchise operation because of the name recognition.

<u>Case #2   Ramer Gourmet Popcorn Shop</u>

1.   A

2.   D

3.   C

4.   C

<u>Case #3   Jo Ann's Secrets</u>

1.   B

2.   A

3.   C

4.   B

5.   D

6.   The most effective way would be by truck, because of the geographic positioning of clients across Canada. The advantage of using a third party is that she incurs costs only as she needs them. As business improves she can reduce costs by going to an expert in an area and contracting their services over a long period of time.

Chapter 12

Retailing and Wholesaling

Chapter Overview

Although most retailing is conducted in retail stores, in recent years, non-store retailing has increased enormously. Therefore retailing is no longer restricted to the corner store or department store; there are door-to-door, telemarketing and the internet as examples of different ways consumers purchase goods. In addition, although many retail stores are independently owned, an increasing number are now banding together under some form of corporate or contractual organization. This allows companies to share data and to enter fields that they were not privy to before.

In this way new markets for their products are opened to them and it also allows them into different areas of business, be they wholesale or retail. Wholesalers have also experienced recent environmental changes, most notably mounting competitive pressures. Through new technological improvement and the advancement of retailing and wholesaling techniques they start, in some cases, to blend together. They have faced new sources of competition, more educated customers, new technologies, and more direct-buying programs on the part of large industrial, institutional, and retail buyers that merge their buying power and demand prices that match their buying power.

Chapter Objectives

1. Explain the roles of retailer and wholesaler in the distribution channel.
2. Describe the major types of retailers and give examples of each.
3. Identify the major types of wholesalers and give examples of each.
4. Explain the marketing decisions facing retailers and wholesalers.

Chapter Topics

Retailing
- Amount of Service
- Product Line
- Relative Prices
- Control of Outlets

Non-Store Retailing
- Direct Marketing
- Direct Selling
- Automatic Vending

Retailer Marketing Decisions
- Target Market and Positioning Decision
- Product Assortment and Services Decision
- Price Decision
- Promotion Decision
- Place Decision

The Future of Retailing
- New Retail Forms and Shortening Retail Life Cycles
- Growth of Non-Store Retailing
- Increasing Intertype Competition
- The Rise of Mega-Retailers
- Growing Importance of Retail Technology
- Retail Stores as "Communities" or "Hangouts"

Wholesaling

Types of Wholesalers

Wholesaler Marketing Decisions
- Target Market and Positioning Decision
- Marketing-Mix Decisions

Trends in Wholesaling

Chapter Summary

1.   The major types of retailers.

Store retailers can be classified by 5 major types: Amount of service, Product line sold, Relative price emphasis, Control of outlets, Type of store cluster. Non-store retailers include direct marketing, direct selling and automatic vending.

2.   The different types of retailers as distinguished by product line sold.

Speciality stores carry a narrow product line with a deep assortment. Department stores carry a wide variety of product lines, each managed as a separate department with specialist buyers and merchandisers. Supermarkets are large, low-cost, low-margin, high-volume, and self-service. Convenience stores carry a limited line of high-turnover convenience goods. Superstores are giant retailers carrying large assortments of many product lines.

3.   The types of retailers as distinguished by control of outlets.

Corporate chains consist of one or more outlets commonly owned using central buying and merchandising. Voluntary chains are wholesaler-sponsored while retailer co-operatives jointly own their wholesaler. Consumer co-operatives are owned by customers. Franchises are contractual agreements between the organizations and independent businesspeople. Merchandising conglomerates combine several different retailing forms and share distribution and management.

4.   The major types of wholesalers.

Merchant wholesalers are independently owned businesses that take title. Two broad types are full service (wholesale merchants and industrial distributors) and limited service (cash-and-carry, truck jobbers, drop shippers, rack jobbers, producer co-ops, mail order). Brokers bring two parties together and negotiate for them. Agents work for one party permanently. Sales branches carry inventory while offices do not.

5.   The marketing decisions faced by retailers and wholesalers.

Retailers and wholesalers both must first make target market decisions, and also decisions about product assortment and services (width, depth, store atmosphere, differentiation), price decisions (markup vs. volume), promotion (including special events, sponsorships, press conferences, and public relations), and place (location, location, location).

Key Terms

Agent	(pg. 523)	Retailer co-operative	(pg. 508)
Automatic vending	(pg. 523)	Retailers	(pg. 502)
Broker	(pg. 523))	Retailing	(pg. 502)
Central business districts	(pg. 517)	Service retailers	(pg. 506)
Chain Stores	(pg. 508)	Shopping centre	(pg. 517)
Convenience store	(pg. 505)	Specialty store	(pg. 504)
Department store	(pg. 507)	Supermarkets	(pg. 505)
Discount store	(pg. 504)	Superstore	(pg. 506)
Factory outlets	(pg. 507)	Voluntary chain	(pg. 508)
Franchise	(pg. 508)	Warehouse club (or wholesale club)	(pg. 507)
Independent off-price	pg. 507)		
Manufacturers' sales branches and offices	(pg. 523)	Wheel of retailing concept	(pg. 519)
		Wholesaler	(pg. 522)
Merchant wholesalers	(pg. 523)	Wholesaling	(pg. 522)
Off-price retailers	(pg. 507)		

Multiple Choice Questions

12-1   Multiple

Retail stores can vary from monster stores to your corner independent milk store. Of the following which is not common in classifying retail stores?

1.   Amount of service
2.   Product line
3.   Costs
4.   Relative prices
5.   Control of outlets

12-2   Multiple

Stores such as Wal-Mart and Saan provide sales assistance because they carry more shopping goods about which customers need information. These two stores would be classified as:

1.   Self-service retailers
2.   Limited-service retailers
3.   Full-service retailers
4.   Specialty-service stores
5.   Complementary-service stores

12-3   Multiple

Specialty stores are increasing in popularity for many reasons. Which of the following is not considered one of them?

1.   Increase use of market segmentation
2.   Market targeting
3.   Product specialization
4.   Time-poor society
5.   All of the above

12-4   Multiple

Stores that are relatively large and deal in low-cost/margin, high volume and self service operations are usually classified as:

1.   Supermarkets
2.   Department stores
3.   Specialty stores
4.   Superstores
5.   Discount stores

12-5   Multiple

When a store deals in high volume at low prices and sells common items it is said to be which kind of store?

1.   Supermarket
2.   Department store
3.   Specialty store
4.   Superstore
5.   Discount store

12-6   Multiple

If a store manufactures and sells its own goods, both regular and surplus goods, it is said to be a:

1.   Warehouse club
2.   Factory outlet
3.   Independent off-price retailer
4.   Convenience store
5.   Catalogue Showroom

12-7   Multiple

These stores once sold overpriced emergency goods, but are now offering automated teller and stamp machines, as well as faxes and photocopiers.

1.   Specialty stores
2.   Mail offices
3.   Convenience stores
4.   Supermarkets
5.   Superstores

12-8   Multiple

Hypermarkets are huge superstores that are very popular in Europe. The largest size of a hypermarket would be equivalent to _____ football fields.

1.   4
2.   7
3.   2
4.   6
5.   1

12-9   Multiple

Winners has become very popular in the last few years. They provide designer clothing at affordable prices. They get new stock every week and are able to clear most of it out because of its high quality and low price. Winners is a (n):

1.   Factory outlet
2.   Warehouse club
3.   Independent off-price retailer
4.   Discount store
5.   Specialty store

12-10 Multiple

Corporate chain stores have all but removed the independent stores. This is most evident in which of the following:

1.   Department stores
2.   Variety stores
3.   Drug stores
4.   Women's clothing
5.   All of the above

12-11 Multiple

Independent Grocers Alliance (IGA) is smaller in comparison to Safeway, but provides comparable services at similar prices. IGA engages in group buying to offer better deals to their consumers. IGA is part of a:

1.   Voluntary chain
2.   Corporate chain
3.   Retailer cooperative
4.   Joint-venture
5.   Collaborative retailing effort

12-12 Multiple

Franchises are very popular, with chains like McDonald's, Shoppers Drug Mart, and Bata Shoes International popping up everywhere. The differences between a franchise and a contractual system are that a franchise system is based on everything except:

1.   A unique product or service
2.   A trade name
3.   Goodwill
4.   Popular products
5.   All of the above

12-13 Multiple

_____ is growing in use with consumer markets in response to the increasing fragmentation of the world's mass markets into sub segments with distinct needs and wants.

1.   Direct selling
2.   Direct marketing
3.   Automatic vending
4.   Integrated marketing communications
5.   Advertising

12-14 Multiple

Automatic vending is increasing in frequency and popularity around the world. The only problem with vending machines is the high cost they incur. Prices of vended goods are often _____ % higher than those in retail stores.

1.   10 to 20
2.   25 to 40
3.   20 to 25
4.   15 to 20
5.   30 to 40

12-15 Multiple

Kiet is opening up a new retail outlet to sell men's grooming products. Which of the following product variables does he not have to consider before opening the store?

1.   Price points
2.   Product assortment
3.   Services mix
4.   Store atmosphere
5.   All of the above

12-16 Multiple

Product assortment must match the target shopper's expectations. Restaurants all have different product assortments, meaning they have different width and depth of products. Which of the following restaurants would have a narrow and deep assortment?

1.   Small lunch counter
2.   Delicatessen
3.   Cafeteria
4.   Larger restaurant
5.   Fast food

12-17 Multiple

A _____ is the largest and most dramatic type of shopping facility with from 40 to 200 stores under its roof.

1.   Central business district
2.   Community shopping centre
3.   Regional shopping centre
4.   Neighbourhood shopping centre
5.   Megamalls

12-18 Multiple

Shopping malls may be very profitable; however, the traffic flow in most malls has decreased over the last few years. All the following are reasons for this phenomenon except:

1.   People have less time to shop
2.   Large malls offer great selection but are less comfortable and convenient
3.   There are more alternatives available to shoppers, such as on-line shopping
4.   People have less disposable income to shop with
5.   None of the above

12-19 Multiple

What is one reason why there has been a huge rise in superpower mega-retailers?

1.   Vertical marketing systems
2.   Buying alliances
3.   Retail mergers
4.   Acquisitions
5.   All of the above

12-20 Multiple

Wholesaling is composed of all activities involved in selling goods and services to those buying for resale or business use. Which of the following functions would a wholesaler not perform?

1.   Selling and promoting
2.   Bulk-breaking
3.   Contract negotiations
4.   Financing
5.   Transportation

12-21 Multiple

Merchant wholesalers—independently owned businesses that take title to the merchandise they handl—are the largest single group of wholesalers, accounting for roughly _____ % of all wholesaling.

1.   50
2.   40
3.   75
4.   60
5.   90

12-22 Multiple

_____, upon receiving an order, select a manufacturer, who ships the merchandise directly to the customer.

1.   Wholesale merchants
2.   Drop shippers
3.   Cash-and-carry wholesalers
4.   Producer's co-operatives
5.   Rack jobbers

12-23 Multiple

_____ have a long-term relationship with buyers and make purchases for them, often receiving, inspecting, warehousing and shipping the merchandise to the buyers.

1.   Selling agents
2.   Purchasing offices
3.   Purchasing agents
4.   Commission merchants
5.   Sales branches and offices

12-24 Multiple

Wholesalers must also define their target markets and position themselves effectively—they cannot serve everyone. This is one method not used by wholesalers in selecting target markets.

1.   Size of customer
2.   Type of customer
3.   Need for service
4.   Price range of the customer
5.   All of the above

12-25 Multiple

Costco is an example of a grocery store wholesaler. They have very large stores, with few frills and large purchase quantities. They depend on large volumes to generate enough profit to survive as their average profit margin is often less than ___ %.

1.   5
2.   10
3.   7
4.   3
5.   2

12-26 Multiple

A retail firm owned by its customer would be called a (n):

1.   Volunteer chain
2.   Corporate chain
3.   Merchandising conglomerate
4.   Consumer co-operative
5.   Independent chain

12-27 Multiple

Creating and maintaining a store's atmosphere is part of which marketing decision?

1.   Target market
2.   Product assortment and services
3.   Price
4.   Promotion
5.   Store layout and décor

12-28 Multiple

This statement about retailing is not true.

1.   Retailing involves selling to final consumers
2.   Retailing is a major industry
3.   Manufacturers and wholesalers cannot make retailing decisions
4.   Retail sales may be done by person, mail, telephone, or vending machine
5.   None of the above

12-29 Multiple

A retailing operation that depends on location and long hours to attract customers for its limited line of frequently purchased products is called a:

1.   Convenience store
2.   Supermarket
3.   Specialty store
4.   Department store
5.   Superstore

12-30 Multiple

Which of the following types of retailing combines supermarket, discount and warehouse retailing principles?

1.   Discount operations
2.   Hypermarkets
3.   Self-service stores
4.   Superstores
5.   Both 1 and 3

True/False Questions

12-1   True/False

Today, self-service is the basis of all discount operations and typically is used by sellers of convenience goods.

12-2   True/False

Most supermarkets are facing steady sales growth despite slower population growth and an increase in competition from convenience stores and superstores.

12-3   True/False

Future Shop is considered a specialty store known as a "category killer."

12-4   True/False

For some businesses, the "product line" is actually a service.

12-5   True/False

Most retailers charge lower prices and offer normal-quality goods and customer service.

12-6   True/False

Off-price retailers buy at less than regular wholesale prices and charge consumers regular retail prices.

12-7   True/False

Specialty stores carry a narrow product line with a deep assortment.

12-8   True/False

Non-store retailing – direct marketing, direct selling and automatic vending – has been growing at the same rate as traditional store retailing.

12-9   True/False

Hypermarkets are another example of superstores.

12-10 True/False

The advantages of door-to-door selling are consumer convenience and personal attention.

12-11 True/False

Today's automatic vending machines use space age and computer technology to sell a variety of convenience and impulse goods such as $100 Armani ties and beer.

12-12 True/False

Large stores such as The Bay and Canadian Tire do not need to define their target markets because they are such large retailers they can cater to everybody.

12-13 True/False

In non-price competition the only factor that sets stores apart is the service mix.

12-14 True/False

Retail stores are not just assortment of goods; they are also environments to be experienced by people who shop in them.

12-15 True/False

Independent off-price retailers are owned and run by entrepreneurs or are divisions of larger retail corporations.

12-16   True/False

Retailers often cite three critical factors in retailing success: loyalty, location, and layout.

12-17   True/False

According to the International Council of Shopping Centres, 70% of Canadian retail sales occur in shopping centres.

12-18   True/False

A retailer's price policy is decided upon in relationship to market, product and competition.

12-19   True/False

Today's retailers are focusing on a share of particular product-market, rather than a share of wallet.

12-20   True/False

North American retailers are still significantly ahead of Europe and Asia when it comes to global expansion.

Applying Terms and Concepts

To determine how well you understand the materials in this chapter, read each of the following brief cases and then respond to the questions that follow. Answers are given at the end of this chapter.

Case #1   Chan's[1]

Cindy Chan is presently assembling the resources necessary to launch "Chan's," a retail chain designed to meet the clothing needs of the professional woman. Her intended customer is twenty-five to forty years old and willing to pay more to acquire the proper look.

Chan is planning to open three outlets in Vancouver. Each outlet will have approximately 5,000 square feet of selling space and feature suits, as well as coordinated separates for the working woman. Casual wear and sportswear will be limited. However, higher quality professional attire will be offered in a wide range of styles, fabrics, and sizes, in patterns and solids. Clothing accessories will include hats, scarves, belts, and stockings, with a small selection of handbags.

---

[1] *Principles of Marketing*, 3rd Edition, Kotler, Armstrong, Warren (Prentice Hall) – pg. 274.

Chan, a former vice president of purchasing for S. Altman Department Stores in Calgary, will function as the buyer while Joan Wilder will be responsible for sales and operations. Each store will have a manager with two assistants and two to four sales associates (depending upon sales and volume.) Each sales associate is expected to offer honest and objective opinions regarding the clothing and accessories that are "right" for the customer. Each sales associate must have prior personal sales experience and have demonstrated the ability to provide personalized attention to a client. The sales associates are to be from the same approximate age bracket as the intended target market.

As an extra service, Chan has hired a fashion consultant to service the three stores. She will be available by appointment to meet the fashion needs of individual customers.

1.   What type of retailer is Chan's? Explain.

_____

_____

_____

_____

2.   Describe Chan's merchandise assortment in terms of depth and selection.

_____

_____

_____

_____

3.   Where should Chan locate her three stores and why?

_____

_____

_____

_____

4.   Which type of services do you believe Chan's should offer its customers?

_____

_____

_____

_____

5.   How would you classify Chan's as a service retailer?

_____

_____

_____

_____

Case #2   Freed Slacks Company

Samuel Freed began the Freed Slacks Company in Winnipeg, in December 1981. Over the years his company has served the needs of approximately nine million mail order customers, over half as repeat customers.

Freed's current offering consists of men's double-knit dress slacks available in blue tweed, navy, brown, gray, tan, and green, in waist sizes 30" to 44" and inseam sizes from 28" to 35". The slacks are sold at $11.55 per pair with a minimum order of two pairs. They feature Quatral polyester, Tanalon nonsnag zippers, Bana-roll anti-roll waistline, and reinforced belt loops accommodating belts up to one and a half inches. Freed slacks are sold with a money back guarantee; however, returns average less than two percent. The customer pays postage of $4.85 per shipment.

Freed has indicated that the current production run will last approximately two years before it is changed. In the past Freed has featured casual slacks, sportswear, dress shirts, and work clothes. It is his practice to feature a type of menswear for a period of time, allowing him to concentrate his buying, manufacturing, and selling efforts on a limited product line, thereby reducing costs of operation.

Freed's literature boasts that his product's quality is comparable to that of slacks costing two or three times as much. A recent article in *Canadian Consumer* magazine agreed with this claim. Freed will quote the magazine in promoting his next dress slack offering.

Prospective customers receive a flyer, which describes the products and includes a small sample of material. Also included for their convenience is a postcard order blank, postage paid by the company. Freed acquires mailing lists of possible customers from the Addresser Company, a mailing list brokerage house in Moncton, New Brunswick.

_____1. The Freed Slacks Company should be classified as a(n) _____ service retailer.
    A.   self
    B.   limited
    C.   full
    D.   augmented
    E.   customer

284

_____2. The textbook would classify the Freed Slacks Company on the basis of:
   A.   type of store cluster.
   B.   control of outlets.
   C.   relative price.
   D.   nonstore retailing.
   E.   store retailing.

_____3. Freed's merchandise assortment is best described as _____ and _____.
   A.   wide, deep
   B.   wide, shallow
   C.   narrow, deep
   D.   narrow, shallow
   E.   wide, extensive

_____4. Which type of nonstore retailing is Freed involved in:
   A.   telemarketing.
   B.   direct mail marketing.
   C.   electronic shopping.
   D.   catalog marketing.
   E.   integrated marketing.

_____5. Comment on the pricing policy of the Freed Slack Company.

_____

_____

_____

_____

Case #3   Cell-Jam

Cell phones have turned into an annoyance for people in movie theatres, restaurants and places of worship. No matter how much advertising is done to ask these people to turn off their cell phones or put them on vibrate, you still hear them at the most inappropriate time. Cell-Jam is a new idea by a new company called Cell Control Company Limited.

Studies done by newspapers and by law enforcement agencies have found that people have had enough of these things. These people seem to think they have the right to talk to anyone anywhere. For some, privacy is still an issue and that is why Cell-Jam is so popular. Tony Miller, the president, finds his concept as one whose time has come. There is a demand for this product and he feels word of mouth will see sales soar. At this point independent businesses like restaurants, bookstores, even individual residences, are his main customers. But as word spreads he feels his major business will be from chains, be they theatres, restaurants, hotels or even hospitals, schools and other institutions. At $600 for a Cell-Jam that will eliminate incoming and outgoing calls over a 300 sq.m. space, the price seems right. Setup charges are non-existent as the product is simply bolted to the wall, is less than 20 cm by 8 cm and runs on direct current or battery and comes with a 10 year guarantee. To keep costs down he has decided to advertise in major Canadian papers across Canada and sell his product solely over an eight hundred number and over his web site. The free advertising through publicity and the positive public relations he has received have kept his manufacturers working regularly to keep up with a demand that has seen sales go from 50 a week to over 200 a week.

1.   What are the advantages of selling this over the internet?

_____

_____

_____

_____

2.   Where do you see the increase of sales of this product in the near future?

_____

_____

_____

_____

Multiple Choice Answers

1.   Correct Answer: 3   Reference: pg. 502

2.   Correct Answer: 2   Reference: pg. 502

3.   Correct Answer: 4   Reference: pg. 502

4.   Correct Answer: 1   Reference: pg. 503 (Table 12-1)

5.   Correct Answer: 5   Reference: pg. 503 (Table 12-1)

6.   Correct Answer: 2   Reference: pg. 503 (Table 12-1)

7.   Correct Answer: 3   Reference: pg. 505

8.   Correct Answer: 5   Reference: pg. 506

9.   Correct Answer: 3   Reference: pg. 507

10.   Correct Answer: 5   Reference: pg. 507

11.   Correct Answer: 1   Reference: pg. 508

12.   Correct Answer: 4   Reference: pg. 508

13.   Correct Answer: 2   Reference: pg. 509

14.   Correct Answer: 4   Reference: pg. 509

15.   Correct Answer: 1   Reference: pg. 511

16.   Correct Answer: 2   Reference: pg. 511

17.   Correct Answer: 3   Reference: pg. 516

18.   Correct Answer: 4   Reference: pg. 516

19.   Correct Answer: 5   Reference: pg. 520

20.   Correct Answer: 3   Reference: pg. 522

21.   Correct Answer: 1   Reference: pg. 522

22.   Correct Answer: 2   Reference: pg. 524 (Table 12-4)

23.	Correct Answer:	3	Reference:	pg. 524
24.	Correct Answer:	4	Reference:	pg. 525
25.	Correct Answer:	5	Reference:	pg. 526
26.	Correct Answer:	4	Reference:	pg. 509
27.	Correct Answer:	2	Reference:	pg. 512
28.	Correct Answer:	3	Reference:	pg. 502
29.	Correct Answer:	1	Reference:	pg. 503 (Table 12-1)
30.	Correct Answer:	2	Reference:	pg. 506

True/False Answers

1.	TRUE	Reference:	pg. 503	Topic:	Amount of Service
2.	FALSE	Reference:	pg. 505	Topic:	Product Line
3.	TRUE	Reference:	pg. 505	Topic:	Product Line
4.	TRUE	Reference:	pg. 505	Topic:	Product Line
5.	FALSE	Reference:	pg. 507	Topic:	Relative Prices
6.	FALSE	Reference:	pg. 507	Topic:	Relative Prices
7.	TRUE	Reference:	pg. 504	Topic:	Product Line
8.	FALSE	Reference:	pg. 509	Topic:	Non-Store Retailing
9.	TRUE	Reference:	pg. 506	Topic:	Direct Marketing
10.	TRUE	Reference:	pg. 506	Topic:	Direct Selling
11.	TRUE	Reference:	pg. 520	Topic:	Automatic Vending
12.	FALSE	Reference:	pg. 511	Topic:	Target Market and Positioning Decision

13.	FALSE	Reference:	pg. 512	Topic: Product Assortment and Services Decisions
14.	TRUE	Reference:	pg. 512	Topic: Product Assortment and Services Decisions
15.	TRUE	Reference:	pg. 507	Topic: Relative Prices
16.	FALSE	Reference:	pg. 517	Topic: Place Decisions
17.	FALSE	Reference:	pg. 517	Topic: Place Decision
18.	TRUE	Reference:	pg. 516	Topic: Price Decisions
19.	FALSE	Reference:	pg. 519	Topic: Increasing Intertype Competition
20.	FALSE	Reference:	pg. 520	Topic: Global Expansion of Major Retailers

Applying Terms and Concept Answers

Case #1   Chan's

Question#1
- Chan's should be classified as a limited line retailer.

Question#2
- Chan's is a specialty store, thus their product assortment is narrow and deep.

Question#3
- Cindy Chan should probably locate in regional and community shopping centres to facilitate comparison-shopping with the other specialty and department stores.

Question#4
Possible services include:
- Free alterations
- Evening and weekend hours
- Gift certificates
- Lay-away and credit programs
- Store-sponsored fashion show
- Garment bags with selected purchases
- Merchandise return policy
- Coupons for free dry-cleaning with selected purchases

Question#5
- Chan's is a full service retailer because the focus of the store is geared toward a particular segment of the market.
- Chan's is geared towards working women who want professional attire of superior quality.
- The employees will be trained to pay personal attention to all customers.
- The sales associates will ideally, offer one-on-one service.

Case #2   Freed Slacks Company

1.   A
2.   D
3.   C
4.   B
5.   The Freed Slacks Company can charge a relatively low price for its products because of long production runs, volume purchase of materials, specialization of labor, low overhead, and few services offered. The low price encourages customers to buy and try the product and for the low price customers probably do not expect expertly tailored clothing.

Case #3   Cell-Jam

1.   With the Internet growing by the second, more people are going on line for everything from banking to shopping to personal advice to medical advice it is no wonder that shopping for goods continues to grow. Advantages are that from the consumers' point of view it is fast and efficient and they can shop for a number of products from home. Advantages for Cell-Jam are that it is easy to have their product available to the consumer 24 hours a day, easy to make product updates available to consumers instantly and acts as direct marketing to a market that is growing daily. It also allows them access to a market without having to go to the undue expense of distributing their product to wholesalers and retailers and therefore they can keep their profits higher and sell at a more acceptable price for the consumer.

2.   Future sales will be in such areas as sales to chain restaurants, movie theatres and government institutions (schools, hospitals, etc.). As the growth to chains increasees, sales to their international locations will also increase. The possibility also exists for additional sales to individuals purchasing this product for their own use in their own home. As legislation appears to be going in the direction of banning cell phones in use in moving vehicles, car manufacturers are also a possible market.

Chapter 13

Integrated Marketing Communication Strategy

Chapter Overview

Modern marketing calls for more than just developing a good product, pricing it attractively, and making it available to target customers. Companies must also communicate with current and prospective customers, and what they communicate should not be left to chance. The steps in developing communications act to provide not just general communications to a general audience, but specific information geared to a target market. Areas of the promotion mix are not to be left to be on there own. They are meant to be integrated into the marketing mix, with each working in conjunction with the other. The communication process is therefore a tool that blends a company's product with a consistent clear message, derived through delivering this message through the proper communication channel. For most companies, the question is not whether to communicate, but how much to spend and in what ways to communicate more effectively.

Chapter Objectives

1. Name and define the five tools of the promotion mix.
2. Discuss the process and advantages of integrated marketing communications.
3. Outline the steps in developing effective marketing communications.
4. Explain the methods for setting the promotion budget and factors that affect the design of the promotion mix.

Chapter Topics

The Marketing Communications Mix
- A View of the Communication Process

Steps in Developing Effective Communication
- Identifying the Target Audience
- Determining the Response Sought
- Designing the Message
  - Message Content
  - Message Structure
  - Message Format

- Choosing Media
  - Personal Communication Channels
  - Non-Personal Communication Channels
- Selecting the Message Source
- Collecting Feedback

Setting the Total Promotion Budget and Mix
- Setting the Total Promotion Budget
  - Affordable Method
  - Percentage-of-Sales Method
  - Competitive-Parity Method
  - Objective-and-Task Method
- Setting the Overall Promotional Mix
  - The Nature of Each Promotional Tool
    - Advertising
    - Personal Selling
    - Sales Promotion
    - Public Relations
    - Direct Marketing
  - Promotion Mix Strategies
    - Type of Product/Market
    - Buyer Readiness Stage
    - Product Life-Cycle Stage

Integrating the Promotional Mix: The Changing Face of Marketing Communications
- Analyze Trends, Internal and External
- Audit Pockets of Communications Spending
- Identify Contact Points
- Team up in Communications Planning
- Create Compatible Themes
- Create Performance Measures
- Appoint a Director Responsible for Communications

Socially Responsible Marketing Communications
- Advertising
- Personal Selling

Chapter Summary

1.   The five tools of the promotion mix.

Advertising is any paid form of non-personal promotion of ideas, goods, or services by an identified sponsor. Personal selling is the oral presentation for the purpose of making a sale. Sales promotion consists of short-term incentives to encourage purchase or sales of a product or service. Public relations involve building good relations with the company's various publics by obtaining favourable publicity, building up a good "corporate image." Direct marketing carefully aims communications to individual consumers to obtain an immediate response.

2.   The elements of the communication process.

The nine elements are:

Sender—party sending the message to another

Encoding—putting thought into symbolic form

Message—set of symbols transmitted;

Media—communication channels used

Decoding—receiver assigning meaning to encoded symbols transmitted

Receiver—the target for the message

Response—the receiver's reaction to the message

Feedback—the part of the response returned to the sender

Noise—static or distortion

3.   Developing effective communications.

By identifying the target market, which includes existing users, potential users and those who make the buying decisions the marketer can design a message to obtain the desired response through message content and emotional appeal.

4.   The methods used for setting the promotion budget.

The affordable method sets the budget based upon available funds. The percentage-of-sales method bases the budget on a set fraction of current or forecasted sales. The competitive-parity method matches the competition's spending. The objective-and-task method defines goals; determines the tasks necessary to reach them; estimates the cost of the tasks and sets their budget. Only the objective-and-task method is proactive.

5.   The factors that affect the design of the promotion mix.

Factors used in setting the promotion mix are the type of product and market, the use of a push versus a pull strategy, the buyer readiness state, and the product's stage in the product life cycle.

6.   The buyer readiness states.

Awareness is the state at which the target audience is first aware of the product's existence. Knowledge is their degree of understanding of the product. Liking is the degree of positive or negative affect. Preference is the level at which the product is liked better than the competition. Conviction leads to demanding the product and not accepting substitutes. Purchase is buying. Promotion should be tailored to the appropriate state.

7.   Socially responsible.

People at all levels being aware of the responsibility they have surrounding communications from both a moral and legal foundation. Canadians expect companies to take a moral responsibility for their products and the advertising of these products.

Key Terms

Advertising   (pg. 542)

Affordable method   (pg. 559)

Buyer-readiness stages   (pg. 549)

Competitive-parity method   (pg. 559)

Direct marketing   (pg. 542))

Emotional appeals   (pg. 552)

Integrated marketing
      communications   (pg. 544)

Marketing communications
      mix. promotional mix   (pg. 542)

Moral appeals   (pg. 553)

Non-personal communication

      channels   (pg. 555)

Objective-and-task method   (pg. 560)

Percentage-of-sales method   (pg. 551)

Personal communication
      channels   (pg. 555)

Personal selling   (pg. 542)

Public relations   (pg. 542)

Pull strategy   (pg. 563)

Push strategy   (pg. 563)

Rational appeals   (pg. 551)

Sales promotion   (pg. 542)

Word-of-mouth influence   (pg. 555)

Multiple Choice Questions

13-1   Multiple

Discount books that provide incentive to shoppers is a form of marketing communications that is considered as:
1.   Advertising
2.   Personal selling
3.   Sales promotion
4.   Public relations
5.   Direct marketing

13-2   Multiple

The use of mail, telephone, fax, e-mail and other non-personal tools to communicate with specific customers is called:

1.   Advertising
2.   Personal selling
3.   Sales promotion
4.   Public relations
5.   Direct marketing

13-3   Multiple

Sales promotion is a very common sight in many stores. Which of the following is not considered a sales promotion?

1.   Point-of-purchase displays
2.   Premiums
3.   Coupons
4.   Billboards
5.   All of the above

13-4   Multiple

The communication process plays an important part in the consumer buying process. Different strategies are more beneficial at certain stages and less effective at others. Of the following which is not considered part of the customer buying process?

1.   Pre-selling
2.   Post-selling
3.   Post-consumption
4.   Consuming
5.   Selling

13-5   Multiple

There are nine elements of communication. The process of putting thought into symbolic form is part of which element?

1.   Feedback
2.   Message
3.   Decoding
4.   Encoding
5.   Response

13-6   Multiple

The communication element where the consumer is more aware of the attributes of a product, and may actually make a purchase is:

1.   Response
2.   Feedback
3.   Decoding
4.   Noise
5.   Message

13-7   Multiple

Communication starts with a sender's ability to get their message to a receiver. Without this the process could therefore not start. An efficient sender must have which of the following characteristics:

1.   Senders need to know what audiences they wish to reach and what responses they want
2.   They must be good at encoding messages
3.   They must send messages through media that reach target audiences
4.   They must develop feedback channels so that they can assess the audience's response to the message
5.   All of the above are required

13-8   Multiple

In developing an effective communication strategy for the promotion of a new or existing product there are a number of steps the marketer is responsible for. Of the following which one is a marketing communicator not responsible for:

1.   Identify the target audience
2.   Develop the product idea
3.   Choose a message
4.   Select the message source
5.   Collect feedback

13-9   Multiple

There are a number of stages the buyer goes through prior to purchasing. In the buyer readiness stage which of the following is not required:

1.   Awareness
2.   Linking
3.   Feeling
4.   Preference
5.   Conviction

13-10 Multiple

Enchantress Travel is trying out a new travel package for its loyal customers. This is a new concept and therefore in the marketing process, once the consumers feel favourable about the package, and learn to associate Enchantress with this great new travel package, Enchantress has reached the _____ stage in the buyer-readiness model.

1.   Linking
2.   Knowledge
3.   Preference
4.   Conviction
5.   None of the above

13-11 Multiple

Designing a message is a complex process. Many marketers use the AIDA model as a framework to help them with this step. Which of the following is not part of this model?

1.   Attention
2.   Desire
3.   Interest
4.   Idea
5.   Action

13-12 Multiple

Buckley's Mixture's advertising campaign has been very effective for the company. They have used the slogan "It tastes awful. And it works." This type of marketing approach would be considered a (n) _____ appeal.

1.   Emotional
2.   Moral
3.   Rational
4.   Reverse
5.   Controversial

13-13 Multiple

The message structure of a marketing communications mix is hard to establish. There are many different angles a company can take with the message they are trying to send. A one-sided argument is most effective in every case except when:

1.   The audience is highly educated
2.   The audience is young and easily influenced
3.   The audience is negatively disposed
4.   The audience is likely to hear opposing claims
5.   All of the above

13-14 Multiple

A marketer who decides to use print ads as their medium of communication does not need to consider?

1.   Eye-catching pictures
2.   Message size and position
3.   Message content
4.   Distinctive formats
5.   All of the above

13-15 Multiple

There are two different channels of communication: personal and non-personal. In which of the following scenarios does personal communication not carry much weight?

1.   Weekly groceries
2.   A Rolls Royce
3.   The stock markets
4.   A prom dress
5.   None of the above

13-16 Multiple

When a company starts with total revenues, deducts operating expenses and capital outlays, and then devotes some portion of the remaining funds to advertising, they are using the _____ method of calculating the promotion budget.

1.   Objective and task
2.   Competitive-parity
3.   Percentage-of-sales
4.   Affordable
5.   Simplistic

13-17 Multiple

The _____ method of calculating the promotion budget views sales as the cause of promotions rather than as the result.

1.   Objective and task
2.   Competitive-parity
3.   Percentage-of-sales
4.   Affordable
5.   Simplistic

13-18 Multiple

The objective-and-task method of calculating the promotion budget involves everything except:

1.   Determining the tasks needed to achieve these objectives
2.   Estimating the sales expected
3.   Defining specific promotion objectives
4.   Estimating the costs of performing these tasks
5.   All of the above

13-19 Multiple

_____ can reach masses of geographically dispersed buyers at a low cost per exposure.

1. Advertising
2. Personal selling
3. Sales promotions
4. Public relations
5. Direct marketing

13-20 Multiple

North American firms spend up to _____ times as much on personal selling as they do on advertising.

1. Two
2. Four
3. Six
4. Five
5. Three

13-21 Multiple

Direct marketing can be described by all the following except:

1. Non-public
2. Immediate
3. Simplistic
4. Customized
5. Interactive

13-22 Multiple

Using a _____ strategy, the producer directs its marketing activities toward the final consumers to induce them to buy the product.

1. Sales promotion
2. Pull
3. Direct marketing
4. Push
5. Intense advertising

13-23 Multiple

At which stage of the product life cycle does promotion play an important role in direct relationship to the advertising of the product?

1.   Early adoption
2.   Growth
3.   Maturity
4.   Decline

13-24 Multiple

In an integrated marketing communication system, a company must keep track of its promotional expenditures by:

1.   Product
2.   Promotional tool
3.   Product life cycle
4.   Observed effect
5.   All of the above

13-25 Multiple

Sellers must avoid the _____ advertising that attracts buyers under false pretenses, because governments in North America are cracking down on these practices.

1.   Pull-and-tug
2.   Bait-and-switch
3.   Foot-in-the-door
4.   Come-and-see
5.   None of the above

13-26 Multiple

In selling to businesses, this tactic is not used as part of the communication process.

1.   Offer bribes to purchasing agents
2.   Use technical or trade secrets of competition through bribery or industrial espionage
3.   Use false advertising with respect to competitors
4.   Copy competitors products and marketing ideas
5.   None of the above

13-27 Multiple

The "learn-feel-do" sequence of the buyer readiness states corresponds to:

1.   Cognitive, affective, behavioural
2.   Affective, behavioural, cognitive
3.   Behavioural, cognitive, affective
4.   Affective, cognitive, behavioural
5.   None of the above

13-28 Multiple

Using sales promotion to encourage early product trail emphasizes this factor in the promotion mix.

1.   Type of product/market
2.   Push versus pull strategy
3.   Buyer readiness state
4.   Product life cycle
5.   Both 1 and 4

13-29 Multiple

When advertising is primarily used to remind buyers already familiar with the brand, its features and availability, the marketer is emphasizing which factor in setting the promotion mix?

1.   Buyer readiness state
2.   Product life cycle stage
3.   Push versus pull strategy
4.   Type of product/market
5.   Both 1 and 3

13-30 Multiple

The concept by which a company carefully coordinates its communication channels to deliver a clear, consistent, and compelling message about the organization and its product is called:

1.   Integrated direct marketing
2.   The marketing mix
3.   Integrated marketing communications
4.   Direct marketing communications
5.   Coordinated marketing communications

True/False Questions

13-1   True/False

New technologies have encouraged more companies to move from mass communication to more targeted communication and one-on-one dialogue.

13-2   True/False

Too often, marketing communications has a short-term outlook.

13-3   True/False

The communication process should start with an audit of all the interactions target consumers have with the product and company.

13-4   True/False

A marketing communicator starts with a broad target audience in mind.

13-5   True/False

Noise is the receiving message sent by another party.

13-6   True/False

The marketing communicator must solve three problems: what to say, how to say it logically, and how to say it symbolically.

13-7   True/False

It has become accepted for a company not to draw conclusions in an advertisement but rather to leave it up to the consumer.

13-8   True/False

There are two broad types of communication channels—personal and industrial.

13-9   True/False

The target audience may be at any time in any of the six buyer readiness stages.

13-10   True/False

Non-personal communication affects buyers directly.

13-11 True/False

Mass communications should aim their messages directly at the public, and allow them to hear and see the messages for themselves.

13-12 True/False

Feedback on marketing communications can suggest changes in the promotion program or in the product offer itself.

13-13 True/False

There is sufficient evidence budgets based on competitive parity prevent promotion wars.

13-14 True/False

Companies within the same industry have similar designs in the promotion mix.

13-15 True/False

Advertising can be used to build a long-term image for a product or trigger quick sales.

13-16 True/False

Emotional appeals are used to obtain positive or negative responses to motivate sales.

13-17 True/False

Industrial companies tend to use a "pull" strategy more frequently and therefore put most of their funds into personal selling, followed by sales promotion.

13-18 True/False

Television, magazines and other mass media's dominance are declining and have been for the past few years.

13-19 True/False

Customers do not distinguish between message sources the way marketers do.

13-20 True/False

Percentage-of-sales method sets the budget in relationship to competition's promotions.

Applying Terms and Concepts

To determine how well you understand the materials in this chapter, read each of the following brief cases and then respond to the questions that follow. Answers are given at the end of this chapter.

Case#1   Bagelicious[1]

According to the AIDA concept, effective advertisements must get the Attention, hold the Interest, arouse consumer Desire and result in Action. The specific action is the purchase of the advertised product or service. This is difficult to accomplish when consumers are bombarded with over 1,500 advertisements per day. To accomplish this action marketers must use promotional methods that make them stand out.

Aaron Kaura is an articling student and part owner of Cafe Asante in Winnipeg. One day Aaron noticed that unlike the neighbouring cities of Regina and Minneapolis, Winnipeg did not have a restaurant specializing in bagels. Aaron saw this as a tremendous opportunity because of the increasing consumption of bagels by North Americans. Health conscious consumers were turning to bagels as a quick, healthy and nutritious substitute for doughnuts and bread product. Aaron, therefore, decided to create Bagelicious, Winnipeg's first restaurant specializing in bagels. The menu at Bagelicious consisted of 12 different types of bagels ranging from plain to one made from a combination of flax and bran. Bagels could be purchased to takeout or eat-in. Aaron planned to offer a wide selection of cream cheese spreads for use with the bagels and a selection of deli sandwiches made with the bagels.

To reach the largest possible market, Aaron planned a phased roll-out out of his concept. His first step was to build a restaurant in the southern section of Winnipeg close to the site of the new Jewish Congress Centre. This restaurant would have an oversized kitchen commissary area that would be fully utilized in the next phase. Phase Two called for Aaron to introduce kiosks and food carts in the downtown area, the Universities of Winnipeg and Manitoba and at Winnipeg's most popular tourist destination, The Forks. Aaron wanted six satellite locations in operation by the end of his second month of operation. A competitive analysis revealed there were currently no direct competitors, but that the Great Canadian Bagel was close to leasing space in Winnipeg. This analysis also revealed the existence of several small indirect competitors. None of these is a threat to Bagelicious due to their small size and out of the way locations.

Aaron needed to find a way to stand out from the competition. He decided the best way to do this was through a promotional campaign targeted to health conscious consumers. He built his plan around the name Bagelicious and the fact it contained information about the product and its taste. Aaron also decided to team up with the local "adult contemporary" radio station, for a series of promotions. This included becoming the

---

[1] *Principles of Marketing*, 3rd Edition, Kotler, Armstrong, Warren (Prentice Hall) – pg. 300.

305

lunch sponsor for the station's "Office of the Day" and sponsoring a series of remote broadcasts by the hosts of the drive-in program. Finally, Aaron decided to team up with a community group to display his social responsibility.

1.   Describe how Aaron's plan uses the AIDA model to get consumers to buy his products.

_____

_____

_____

2.   Aaron decides sales might improve if he had a spokesperson for his product. Describe the factors that make a spokesperson or source credible.

_____

_____

_____

3.   Aaron decides to hire former Winnipeger and current CNN anchor Lyndon Soles as his spokesperson. Does Mr. Soles meet the criteria described earlier?

_____

_____

_____

4.   Who do you think would be an appropriate spokesperson for Bagelicious?

_____

_____

_____

5.   Aaron plans on doing radio spots to promote Bagelicious. What is the medium? What is the message?

_____

_____

_____

_____

Case #2   Shock Cola

_____

_____

_____

_____

Larry Clark, a successful bottler of soft drinks, quietly introduced a cola last year, which is taking the industry by storm. Shock, short for "The Shock Treatment," defies the trend of reducing the sugar and caffeine in colas. Clark maintains that soft drinks were meant to be a treat--not a health food. And what a treat Shock is. It contains 6.0 milligrams of caffeine per ounce--twice what Coke and Pepsi offer and the maximum allowed by the Food and Drug Administration. And it is made with the highest quality beet and cane sugar, not the cheaper corn sweetener found in off-brand soft drinks. Clark has found that the combination of caffeine and sugar can give people a buzz unlike that of any other cola on the market.

Shock at $2.29 per six-pack and $1.19 for the two-litre bottle, is less expensive than name-brand colas. In fact, Clark views Shock as a premium cola at a popular price. And the public seems to agree. Last year Clark shipped only 60,000 cases of Shock; current sales projections are for 450,000. Interestingly, he spends very little on advertising as earnings are reinvested to improve bottling capacity and the distribution system. Any money left is then spent on newspaper advertising. Included in each ad is a coupon good for $.25 off the retail price of a six-pack or two-litre bottle.

Clark doesn't advertise very much because Shock's virtues are mostly spread by its aficionados. The messages, especially among younger drinkers include "It's cheap and it's legal," and "Get the treatment." Clark only smiles when he hears one of these lines.

_____ 1. Clark sets the promotional budget for Shock Cola using the _____ method.
   A.   affordable
   B.   percentage-of-sales
   C.   competitive-parity
   D.   objective and task
   E.   none of the above

_____2. The coupon included in the newspaper advertisement is an example of a(n)_____.
   A.   advertisement
   B.   personal selling
   C.   publicity
   D.   sales promotion
   E.   public relations

3.   Clark is using the coupon as a _____ (pushing, pulling) promotional strategy.

_____4. Clark's belief that Shock is an inexpensive treat suggests that a promotional campaign should stress a(n) _____ and _____ appeal.
   A.   emotional and rational
   B.   emotional and moral
   C.   rational and moral
   D.   sociological and psychological
   E.   emotional and moral

_____5. The word of mouth advertising used by the cola's fans, is an example of a(n) _____ communication channel.
   A.   personal
   B.   nonpersonal
   C.   suprapersonal
   D.   superpersonal
   E.   extrapersonal

Case #3   Mark's Graduation

College graduation is coming up and Mark is looking forward to the event, along with his girlfriend Marge and both their families. After 3 years of hard work Mark is graduating in engineering and wants the day to be perfect. He has recently seen ads for a local Chinese restaurant, Wong's that has gone into the catering business as well as offering a full sit down service at their banquet hall. His friends rave about the food and the facilities. Local papers have always voted the banquet hall as excellent value for the money. The price he has learned is competitive, and their ads look attractive and are geared to his age group and not his parents. Last year Mark's older brother wanted his graduation there but the price was just too high at $55.00. The price per person is now $35.00 and his parents think that is reasonable, for an expected turnout of 40 people. Wong's is offering a discount of 10%, over the graduation period to help encourage sales during this usually quiet period in their industry. All concerned seem to think it is a good idea and feel that the quality of the restaurant has to be good if it is constantly winning awards and picked as one of the best restaurants in town.

Henry said that she believed the best features included: automatic reverse, automatic

_____1. Local newspapers raving about Wong's is excellent publicity and can be see by
Wong's as an excellent reason for promoting the restaurant through which of the
following:
A.   rational
B.   moral
C.   emotional
D.   none of the above
E.   all of the above

_____2. Which channel best describes Mark's decision after hearing from his friends on
Wong's as a site for his graduation party?
A.   personal
B.   nonpersonal
C.   moral
D.   emotional
E.   social

_____3. Being constantly referred to as an excellent restaurant offering fine food and
excellent pricing and service is an excellent example of _____.
A.   sales promotion.
B.   publicity.
C.   advertising.
D.   personal selling.
E.   corporate communications.

_____4. By offering a discount of 10% over the graduation period, Wong's can be said to
be taking advantage of:
A.   sales promotion
B.   trustworthiness.
C.   point of sale promotion
D.   publicity
E.   both (A) and (B)

Multiple Choice Answers

1.	Correct Answer:	3	Reference:	pg. 540
2.	Correct Answer:	5	Reference:	pg. 542
3.	Correct Answer:	4	Reference:	pg. 542
4.	Correct Answer:	2	Reference:	pg. 542
5.	Correct Answer:	4	Reference:	pg. 545
6.	Correct Answer:	1	Reference:	pg. 546
7.	Correct Answer:	5	Reference:	pg. 546
8.	Correct Answer:	2	Reference:	pg. 547
9.	Correct Answer:	3	Reference:	pg. 548
10.	Correct Answer:	1	Reference:	pg. 549
11.	Correct Answer:	4	Reference:	pg. 549
12.	Correct Answer:	3	Reference:	pg. 549
13.	Correct Answer:	2	Reference:	pg. 550
14.	Correct Answer:	3	Reference:	pg. 550
15.	Correct Answer:	1	Reference:	pg. 553
16.	Correct Answer:	4	Reference:	pg. 557
17.	Correct Answer:	3	Reference:	pg. 557
18.	Correct Answer:	2	Reference:	pg. 558
19.	Correct Answer:	1	Reference:	pg. 560
20.	Correct Answer:	5	Reference:	pg. 558
21.	Correct Answer:	3	Reference:	pg. 560
22.	Correct Answer:	2	Reference:	pg. 561

23.	Correct Answer:	4	Reference:	pg. 560
24.	Correct Answer:	5	Reference:	pg. 561
25.	Correct Answer:	2	Reference:	pg. 562
26.	Correct Answer:	4	Reference:	pg. 562
27.	Correct Answer:	1	Reference:	pg. 547
28.	Correct Answer:	4	Reference:	pg. 560
29.	Correct Answer:	2	Reference:	pg. 560
30.	Correct Answer:	3	Reference:	pg. 561

True/False Answers

1.	TRUE	Reference:	pg. 542	Topic: The Marketing Communications Mix
2.	TRUE	Reference:	pg. 543	Topic: The View of the Communication Process
3.	FALSE	Reference:	pg. 543	Topic: A View of the Communication Process
4.	FALSE	Reference:	pg. 547	Topic: Identifying the Target Audience
5.	FALSE	Reference:	pg. 546	Topic: The Communicating Process
6.	TRUE	Reference:	pg. 549	Topic: Designing the Message
7.	TRUE	Reference:	pg. 551	Topic: Message Structure
8.	FALSE	Reference:	pg. 553	Topic: Choosing Media
9.	TRUE	Reference:	pg. 547	Topic: Developing Communications
10.	TRUE	Reference:	pg. 553	Topic: Non-Personal Communication Channels
11.	FALSE	Reference:	pg. 553	Topic: Non-Personal Communication Channels

12.	TRUE	Reference:	pg. 556	Topic:	Collecting Feedback
13.	FALSE	Reference:	pg. 556	Topic:	Competitive-Parity Method
14.	FALSE	Reference:	pg. 556	Topic:	Setting the Promotion Mix
15.	TRUE	Reference:	pg. 558	Topic:	Advertising
16.	TRUE	Reference:	pg. 550	Topic:	Message Design
17.	FALSE	Reference:	pg. 561	Topic:	Type of Product/Market
18.	TRUE	Reference:	pg. 562	Topic:	The Changing Communications Environment
19.	TRUE	Reference:	pg. 561	Topic:	Integrated Marketing Communications
20.	FALSE	Reference:	pg. 556	Topic:	Promotion Budget and Mix Communications

Applying Terms and Concept Answers

Case#1   Bagelicious

Question#1
- Attention: By teaming with the local "adult contemporary" station, Aaron will reach a large number of consumers in his target group. More importantly, by taking part in the station's promotions he will gain the attention of this group.

- Interest: Hearing the Bagelicious name and a description of its unique product offerings will attract the interest of consumers.

- Desire: Wanting to take part in a popular trend, eating bagels, and visiting a new restaurant will raise consumers' desire.

- Action: Once in the restaurant people will want to buy a bagel or bagel sandwich.

Question#2:
An effective spokesperson should have the following characteristics:

Expertise: The source is seen as having experience in the area.

Trustworthiness: This refers to how objective and honest consumers think the source is.

Likability: The audience wants a source they consider attractive in terms of being open, humorous and natural.

Question #3
Mr. Soles would have problems in the expertise area because the audience would see him as news anchor and not a bagel expert. His position and reputation as a fair and honest person makes him a trustworthy source. Mr. Soles is very likable because people in Winnipeg remember him as a good-natured, friendly person.

Question #4
Aaron needs someone who is an expert in the field of bagels. Sadly, bagel experts are hard to come by unless you hire some unknown, obscure dietitian. However, a local radio or TV personality should do the trick. They may not be a bagel expert, but they can profess to the good taste and fine quality of the Bagelicious products.

Question#5
• The medium is radio, and the message is "these bagels rock."

Case #2   Shock Cola

1.   A

2.   D

3.   pulling

4.   A

5.   A

Case #3   Mark's Graduation

1.   A

2.   A

3.   B

4.   E

Chapter 14

Advertising, Sales Promotion, and Public Relations

Chapter Overview

Companies must do more than make good products—they must inform consumers about product benefits and carefully position products in consumers' minds. To do this, they must skilfully use three mass-promotion tools in addition to personal selling, which targets specific buyers. The three mass-promotion tools are advertising, sales promotion, and public relations. The marketer must make the consumer aware of the product's existence its differentiation from other products and build an incentive to purchase the product. These tools, when used efficiently in a marketing plan, are blended together to inform the consumer of the product, distinguish it from others and encourage purchase of the product through adverting, sales promotion and public relations. In other words, let them know it exists, give them an incentive to buy and have them have faith in the company. These factors make up a consumer that is a repeat purchaser.

Chapter Objectives

1. Define the roles of advertising, sales promotion, and public relations in the promotion mix.
2. Describe the major decisions involved in developing an advertising program.
3. Explain how sales promotion campaigns are developed and implemented.
4. Explain how companies use public relations to communicate with their publics.

Chapter Topics

Advertising

Major Decisions in Advertising
- Setting Advertising Objectives
- Setting the Advertising Budget
- Developing Advertising Strategy
  - Creating the Advertising Message
    - Message Strategy
    - Message Execution
  - Selecting Advertising Media
    - Deciding on Reach, Frequently, and Impact
    - Choosing Among Major Media Types

- Evaluating Advertising
- Organizing for Advertising
- International Advertising Decisions

Sales Promotion
- Rapid Growth of Sales Promotion
- Sales Promotion Objectives
- Major Sales Promotion Tools
  - Consumer Promotion Tools
  - Trade Promotion Tools
  - Business Promotion Tools
- Developing the Sales-Promotion Program

Public Relations
- Major Public Relations Tools
- Major Public Relations Decisions

Chapter Summary

1.   The roles of advertising, sales promotion, and public relations in the promotion mix.Each is part of the tools for mass-production. Advertising helps build awareness, interest, and brand loyalty. Sales promotion provides incentive for buyers to purchase, now, within a specific time period. Public relations is used to create a favourable image of the company in a buyer's mind. Effective promotion strategy considers the strengths and limitations of each mass-promotion tool and assigns specific, coordinated objectives for each in support of an overall corporate objective.

2.   The major decisions involved in developing an advertising program.

Major decisions include setting objectives (communication, sales); setting the budget, which can be based on: affordable, percent of sales, comparative parity, objective-and-task; message decisions, based on, market, evaluation/selection and execution; media decisions which include such variables as; reach, frequency, impact, type, vehicles, timing; and campaign evaluation.

3.   How sales promotion campaigns are developed and implemented.

Sales promotion campaigns must determine the objective of the promotion, the size of the incentive, the ideal time to run the promotion, the conditions for participation, how to promote and distribute the promotion, the length of time it is to run, the budget for the promotion, and whether or not to protest the program. Following implementation, the company must evaluate the results by objective criteria as linked to sales and profit.

4.   How companies use public relations to communicate with their publics.

Public relations seeks to manage the presentation of the corporate image through press relations, product publicity, corporate communications, and lobbying efforts. Major tools for reaching various publics include news, speeches, special events, press releases, audio-visual materials, corporate identity materials, and public service activities.

5.   The different types of advertising used to meet advertising objectives.

Advertising objectives can be classified by purpose. Informative advertising is used heavily when introducing a new product category. Persuasive advertising becomes important as competition increases and the company seeks to build selective demand. Reminder advertising keeps consumers thinking about the product and is important for mature products as they proceed through the product life cycle.

Key Terms

Advertising agency	(pg. 593)	Patronage rewards	(pg. 599)
Advertising objectives	(pg. 580)	Persuasive advertising	(pg. 580)
Advertising specialities	(pg. 599)	Point-of-purchase promotions (POP)	(pg. 599)
Allowance	(pg. 600)		
Business promotion	(pg. 596)	Premiums	(pg. 599)
Cash refund offers (rebates)	(pg. 599)	Price packs (cents-off deals)	(pg. 599)
Comparison advertising	(pg. 580)	Public relations	(pg. 602)
Consumer promotion	(pg. 596)	Reach	(pg. 589)
Contests, sweepstakes, games	(pg. 599)	Reminder advertising	(pg. 581)
Coupons	(pg. 598)	Sales promotion	(pg. 596)
Discount	(pg. 600)	Sales-force promotion	(pg. 596)
Frequency	(pg. 589)	Samples	(pg. 597)
Informative advertising	(pg. 580)	Trade promotion	(pg. 596)
Media impact	(pg. 589)		
Media vehicles	(pg. 590)		

Multiple Choice Questions

14-1   Multiple

Advertising is a significant industry in Canada, employing more than 196,000 people. It is almost as important to the Canadian economy as the _____ industry.

1.   Agricultural
2.   Car manufacturing
3.   Tourism
4.   Government
5.   Natural resources

14-2   Multiple

Advertising is such a large industry, that in Canada we spend more than $8 billion annually on it while the US spends more than $250 billion and the worldwide advertising spending is approximately:

1. $600 billion
2. $900 billion
3. $500 billion
4. $ 1 trillion
5. $750 billion

14-3   Multiple

Each industry does not spend the same amount of money on advertising. Which of the following in not one of the top 5 advertising industries?

1.   Retailing
2.   Automotive
3.   Business equipment and services
4.   Entertainment
5.   Tourism

14-4   Multiple

Which of the following is not an important decision management has to make with regards to advertising?

1.   Setting objectives
2.   Setting and advertising budget
3.   Choosing an advertising agency
4.   Setting an advertising strategy
5.   Performing an advertising evaluation

14-5   Multiple

Home "parties" selling everything from, plastic food containers, to lingerie, has been in style for over fifty years and continues to grow; the newest trend is 'aroma' products to freshen each room with a different scent. But as it grows competition is springing up daily. A company in this business is said to be using which kind of advertising?

1.   Informative
2.   Persuasive
3.   Comparison
4.   Comparative
5.   Unique

14-6   Multiple

In designing an advertising budget for a new or existing product there are a number of factors to consider. Which of the following would not be considered a factor for a budget?
1.   Stage in the product life cycle
2.   Competition and clutter
3   Product differentiation
4.   Cost of different advertising mediums
5.   None of the above

14-7   Multiple

Advertising strategy consists of which of the following:

1.   Advertising messages
2.   Advertising market
3.   Advertising media
4.   Only 1 and 3
5.   All of the above

14-8   Multiple

In today's fast paced, over cluttered media society, consumers are not interested in sitting through commercials. They feel it is a waste of their time; therefore when commercials are on, they either fast-forward through them, or they channel surf. To combat these problems, today's advertising messages must be:

1.   Better quality
2.   Better planned
3.   More rewarding
4.   More imaginative
5.   All of the above

14-9   Multiple

When most TV viewers are armed with remote controls, a commercial has to cut through the clutter and seize the viewer's attention in:

1.   4-5 seconds
2.   1-2 seconds
3.   1-3 seconds
4.   3-6 seconds
5.   None of the above

14-10   Multiple

An effective message strategy is the basis for good advertising. This message portion of the message in this strategy can say to be identifying consumer_____, which is used in advertising appeal.

1.   Preferences
2.   Needs
3.   Wants
4.   Benefits
5.   All of the above

14-11   Multiple

Sherry is the advertising manger for Sabre Industries. From the following list, what is the one item Sherry does NOT need to consider in setting an advertising appeal?

1.   Compatible
2.   Meaningful
3.   Believable
4.   Distinctive
5.   All of the above are required

14-12   Multiple

Any message can be presented in different execution styles. A series of ads showing young Canadians with their faces painted, ready to attend Molson's Hockey Night in Canada, is an example of which advertising execution styles?

1.   Technical expertise
2.   Fantasy
3.   Slice of life
4.   Lifestyle
5.   Mood or image

14-13 Multiple

In some Cannon camera commercials, Cannon shows staff using high tech equipment as they put together quality components to produce their 35mm cameras. The adverting execution style they are using is:

1.   Testimonial evidence
2.   Technical expertise
3.   Scientific evidence
4.   Personality symbol
5.   Mood or image

14-14 Multiple

Which of the following is not a major step in the media selection process?

1.   Deciding on the reach, frequency and impact
2.   Choosing among the major media types
3.   Selecting specific media vehicles
4.   Deciding on media timing
5.   None of the above

14-15 Multiple

Media planners consider many factors when making their media choices. These factors include all the following except:

1.   Media habits of target consumers
2.   Spending habits of target consumers
3.   The nature of the product
4.   Cost
5.   All the following are factors

14-16 Multiple

There are advantages and disadvantages to using different media. Which of the following best reflects these characteristics: quality, long life, prestige, high geographic distribution and re-use is:

1.   Newspapers
2.   Direct mail
3.   Magazines
4.   Television
5.   Radio

14-17 Multiple

In selecting media vehicles, the media planner must balance media cost measures against the media impact factors. Which of the following is not an impact factor?

1.   Audience creativity
2.   Audience quality
3.   Audience attention
4.   Editorial quality
5.   None of the above

14-18 Multiple

Most large advertising agencies have the staff and resources to handle all phases of an advertising campaign for their clients. Agencies usually have four departments. Which of the following is not one of them?

1.   Media departments
2.   Creative departments
3.   Research departments
4.   Business departments
5.   None of the above

14-19 Multiple

_____ produces many benefits – lower advertising costs, greater coordination of global advertising efforts, and a more consistent worldwide company or product image.

1.   Globalization
2.   Standardization
3.   Media cooperation
4.   Integrated marketing communication
5.   None of the above

14-20 Multiple

Not all countries have an open media market like North America. In fact, many countries heavily regulate the media and advertising. From the following list, select the item least likely to be regulated.

1.   How much a company can spend on advertising
2.   The media used
3.   The people used in the advertising campaigns
4.   The nature of the advertising claims
5.   All of the above are regulated

14-21 Multiple

In many consumer packaged-goods companies, sales promotion accounts for ____ % or more of all marketing expenditures.

1.   50
2.   30
3.   90
4.   75
5.   65

14-22 Multiple

Sales promotion has grown immensely in the last few years. Which of the following is not one of the reasons?

1.   Product managers inside the company face greater pressures to increase their current sales
2.   Externally companies face more competition
3.   Advertising efficiency has declined due to rising costs and media clutter
4.   Retailers are demanding more deals from manufacturers
5.   Rise in the time-poor consumer

14-23 Multiple

Kraft Canada started a magazine called *What's Cooking*. This magazine contains letters from consumers, cooking tips, information on maintaining a healthy diet and recipes based on Kraft products. This magazine is used to meet which criteria of a good sales promotion strategy?

1.   Consumer promotions
2.   Customer relationship building
3.   Trade promotions
4.   Loyalty programs
5.   None of the above

14-24 Multiple

Goods offered either for free or at low cost as an incentive to buy – for example a bottle of hair spray with a bonus 50ml for the price of a regular bottle – would be considered:

1.   A price pack
2.   An advertising speciality
3.   A premium
4.   A patronage reward
5.   A point-of-purchase promotion

14-25 Multiple

A _____ calls for consumers to submit their names for a drawing.

1.   Sweepstake
2.   Game
3.   Contest
4.   Silent auction
5.   All of the above

14-26 Multiple

In developing a sales promotion program, a marketer must consider all the following except:

1.   Size of the incentive
2.   Conditions for participation
3.   Length of promotion
4.   Sales-promotion budget
5.   All the above must be considered

14-27 Multiple

Public relations departments in many companies are growing in importance and need. The following function performed by the pubic relations department, helps build relations with donors or members of non-profit organizations to gain financial or volunteer support.

1.   Press relations of press agentry
2.   Lobbying
3.   Investor relations
4.   Development
5.   Product publicity

14-28 Multiple

Evaluating public relations results can be very difficult, as public relations is usually accompanied by other means of marketing. However, a good measure of the effectiveness of a public relations campaign would be a change in all the following except:

1.   Product awareness
2.   Product consumption
3.   Product knowledge
4.   Product attitude
5.   Changes in all the above would be good

14-29   Multiple

The advantages of flexibility, timeliness, good local market coverage, broad acceptance, and high believability apply to which media type?

1.   Television
2.   Direct mail
3.   Radio
4.   Newspaper
5.   Magazines

True/False Questions

14-1   True/False

Advertising can be traced back to about the 1300s.

14-2   True/False

The sixth largest advertising spender is a non-profit organization – the Canadian government.

14-3   True/False

The Competition Act stipulates an advertisement using competitive claims must be based on adequate and proper tests that support it.

14-4   True/False

Advertising can and cannot achieve certain objectives. One thing it can do is affect the demand of a product by consumers.

14-5   True/False

The major steps in media selection do not include: reach frequency or impact.

14-6   True/False
Large advertising budget ensures a successful advertising campaign

14-7   True/False

The first step in creating effective advertising messages is to decide what general message will be communicated to consumers.

14-8   True/False

The impact of the message depends only on what is said, not on how it is said.

14-9   True/False

There are, quite often, small changes done to ads after they have been initially produced. These changes do not really change the effect the ad will have on the consumer.

14-10   True/False

The media planner ultimately decides which vehicles give the best reach frequency, and impact for the money.

14-11   True/False

Some companies do only seasonal advertising.

14-12   True/False

The sales effect of advertising is often easier to measure than the communication effect.

14-13   True/False

Frequency of an ad is will guarantee that commercials gain the attention of their audience and communicate the message.

14-14   True/False

Most international advertisers think globally but act locally.

14-15   True/False

Consumers are increasingly accepting sales promotions, therefore strengthening their ability to trigger immediate purchase.

14-16   True/False

If properly designed, every sales promotion tool has consumer-relationship-building potential.

14-17   True/False

Message strategy is based on deciding what general message will be relayed to the consumer.

14-18 True/False

Industrial advertising does not spend the same amount of money to advertise their products in comparison to consumer products.

14-19 True/False

In emerging countries like Russia, trade fairs are the only means of reaching potential buyers.

14-20 True/False

Public relations can have a strong impact on public awareness at a much lower cost than advertising.

Applying Terms and Concepts

To determine how well you understand the materials in this chapter, read each of the following brief cases and then respond to the questions that follow. Answers are given at the end of this chapter.

Case#1   Skin So Soft[1]

Is Skin So Soft a bath oil or an insect repellent? Avon, the makers of Skin So Soft (SSS), insists it is a bath oil. But while the company appreciates the revenue from sales to sports enthusiasts, pet owners, outdoorsmen, and even the military, Avon knows that those customers are purchasing Skin So Soft for a reason other than to smell nice. Some people believe that the product, when mixed with equal parts of water and applied to the skin, is an effective insect repellent.

Avon officials claim to be baffled why mosquitoes, fleas, and other bugs don't like their product. Scientists say there is no ingredient in SSS that should make it act like a repellent, but speculate the fragrance, a proven people pleaser is offensive to the keen sense of smell of some insects. SSS clearly doesn't ward off all bugs, and some research suggests it is effective on only one strain of mosquito. The research also suggests its effectiveness is short-lived. But that hasn't slowed the sales of SSS. Even pet owners are getting in on the act. According to one study, the flea count on dogs can be cut by one-third in just two days after a sponge bath with a mixture of SSS and water, and fleas seem to stay off longer than when regular flea dips are used alone. An added benefit is that the mixture leaves the dog's coat shinier and more pleasant-smelling. Unfortunately, the treatment doesn't work for cats; it seems their skin is too sensitive for the chemicals in the mixture. Horses, however, benefit from the treatment.

---

[1] *Principles of Marketing*, 3rd Edition, Kotler, Armstrong, Warren (Prentice Hall) – pg. 322.

Law prohibits Avon from touting SSS as an insect repellent. But advertisements such as "Millions of People Know the Secret of Skin So Soft, Do You?" are beginning to bug Avon's competitors, the makers of traditional insect repellents. They believe Avon should register the product with the EPA and subject it to the safety and effectiveness testing required by law. Avon professes innocence and maintains any benefits from secondary usage are spread by word-of-mouth among its devotees.

Recent findings some traditional insect repellents contain chemicals suspected of being hazardous to health have enhanced the sales of Skin So Soft, currently in the tens of millions of dollars—prompting one to wonder if SSS should really be translated as Sweet Smell of Success.

1.   Explain how Avon could use each of the following consumer promotion tools to increase the short-term sales of Skin So Soft and to help build long-tem market share. Sample

    _____
    _____
    _____
    _____

2.   Coupons

    _____
    _____
    _____
    _____

3.   Cash refund offers

    _____
    _____
    _____
    _____

4.   Price packs

    _____
    _____
    _____
    _____

5. Law prohibits Avon from advertising SSS as an insect repellent, so word of its effectiveness as a repellent is primarily spread by devotees. What are the relative advantages and disadvantages of this word-of-mouth advertising?

_____

_____

_____

_____

Case #2   Safeway Coupon Book

AMC Theatres is making a push to be the major movie going destination for Canadians. Most of the public, feel that movie prices are getting out of site as they hover around the $14.00 mark in the large stadium theatres. Realising this AMC is offering special promotion booklet on everything from admission to popcorn to help boost sales and get the public interested in seeing films on the super large screens and convinced the public that the prices are worth it for the quality they get. These are not your old small theatres but 10 storey high screens with comfortable seating and a sound system to impress any customer. The main purpose of the coupon book is to get the customer into the theatre, offer them value and that for a few dollars more they get a great deal more entertainment. Going to a movie is an evening experience and not just walk in see a movie and then leave. The Safeway coupon book was a monthly coupon book filled with reduced prices on a number of items, ranging from milk and dairy products to hair and beauty care products. The book was very popular and many people actually traded the coupons they did not want with their friends for ones they did want. The savings in each book totalled over $500 per month. The coupon book was used in an attempt to draw people into the stores and purchase items that they would not normally buy, but now were on sale. The book was also used to convince people that shopping at Safeway with the coupon book was almost as cheap as SuperValu, but the quality was better. The Safeway coupon book was delivered by Canada Post to all residents of an area and was a very successful venture for Safeway.

1. What are AMC's major objectives?

_____

_____

_____

_____

2. Evaluation is a major factor in advertising. How can they measure their success?

_____

_____

_____

_____

3. What are the advantages of getting other stores in the theatre involved in the promotion?

_____

_____

_____

_____

4. Will they succeed and why?

_____

_____

_____

_____

Case #3 Barone Wine

Marlo Barone opened his new winery in the Tuscany district of Italy with pageantry rivalling that of the opening ceremonies of the modern Olympic Games. Tuscan standard bearers hurled their flags into the air as the music of Nanini, Vivaldi, and Goldoni, Italy's renowned composers, was performed by the symphony orchestra of Milan. White doves were released to announce the arrival of the Cardinal of Siena, who bestowed his blessing on the winery and vineyards. Italian dignitaries looked on as a parade marched through town. Fireworks lit the evening sky, with Barone's winery, housed in a medieval castle, looming in the background.

The event last November, which was covered by media representatives from 12 countries writing for 32 different publications, signalled a major undertaking for Barone. The $100 million winery was built in the heart of Arezzo, Tuscany's most respected wine district. The winery, surrounded by 7,000 hectares of prime grape-growing land, is capable of producing 5.0 million litres of wine annually.

Barone had made his fortune by importing table wines such as Lambrusco and Sangria and bottling them under a variety of now popular brand names. Barone Wines, based in Toronto, had sales last year of $260 million.

The opening of the Arezzo Winery was a bold move not only because it would mark the first time Barone produced its own wines, but also because the winery would be Barone's entry into the high-quality premium wine market.

Barone hoped to break into the fast-growing market for fine wines now dominated by Californian and French vintners. A recent article in *Vintner*, the prestigious newsletter from the union of international oenologists, indicated that the worldwide market for premium wines had been growing by 15 percent annually, compared to only a 2.6 percent growth in the table wine market.

Barone's promotional campaign will be designed to build selective demand for the wine. One of the company's promotions is a magazine advertisement that shows an apparently wealthy couple leaning against a Rolls-Royce Silver Shadow on which has been placed a bottle of Barone's wine. (Starch Readership scores indicated the advertisement to be extremely effective.) This particular advertisement will be run in three consecutive issues of *Macleans*, *Canadian Business*, *Saturday Night* and *Psychology Today* magazines.

_____1. The winery's magazine promotion campaign would fall under which class of advertising objectives?
   A.   persuasive
   B.   comparison
   C.   information
   D.   reinforcement
   E.   remind

_____2. Which style of message execution is used by the magazine ad?
   A.   slice-of-life
   B.   life style
   C   personality symbol
   D.   testimonial
   E.   fantasy

_____3. The communication-effect research on the magazine advertisement (Starch Readership scores) is an example of:
   A.   a consumer panel.
   B.   direct ratings.
   C.   testimonial evidence.
   D.   a recognition test.
   E.   technical expertise.

_____4. Scheduling the magazine advertisement in three consecutive issues is an example of _____ (continuity/pulsing).

_____5. Which major promotional tool was Barone using to announce the opening of his winery?
   A.   advertisement
   B.   personal selling
   C.   public relations
   D.   sales promotion
   E.   trade promotion

Case #4   Toronto Honda—Tyco Car Wax Joint Promotion

Toronto Honda and Tyco Car Wax Company are planning to sponsor a sales promotion activity from October 1 to December 31 of this year. Tyco is allowing any resident of Canada who is 18 years of age with a valid driver's license to enter the activity. Each individual must complete an entry form and send it to Eltron Advertising—headquarters in Goose Bay, Labrador. No purchase is necessary, and each person may enter as many times as he or she wishes.

As part of their promotion they will be providing retailers with signs and cardboard displays to call attention to the promotion. Each display will contain a packet of entry forms which individuals may tear off, complete, and mail. By having these two companies be involved together in this promotion they are lowering production and distribution costs. This will help divide costs between both companies and help them reach a broader market then either one could reach on their own.

The prizes for this activity include:

	# of Prizes	Prize
First Prize	1	a Toronto Honda "CIVIC SUPREME"
Second Prize	10	free gasoline for one year (a value limit of $2500.00)
Third Prize	1,000	Toronto Honda t-shirts, value per prize $10.00
Fourth Prize	2,000	can of Tyco Car Wax, value per prize $5.00

In addition to the prizes listed above, each entrant receives a certificate entitling the bearer to a certain savings on the purchase of any Tyco car care product.

Each winner is responsible for the GST and any provincial sales tax. The activity is void where prohibited and all entries must be postmarked by December 31 of this year. The independent certified public accounting firm of Hartley and Sanger, whose decisions are final, will select winners. Tyco car wax /Toronto Honda employees and their immediate families are restricted from participating in this activity.

_____1. This sales promotion activity is best described as a:
   A.   contest.
   B.   sweepstakes.
   C.   game.
   D.   sales contest.
   E.   trade promotion.

_____2. The main tool of the sales promotion activity is for _____
        (consumer/trade) promotion.

_____3. The in store signage that was prepared for this promotion is called:
   A.   trade promotion.
   B.   advertising allowances.
   C.   point-of-purchase displays.
   D.   premiums.
   E.   advertising specialties.

_____4. Each individual who participated in the sales promotion activity was given a
        certificate entitling the bearer to a stated saving on the next purchase of any Tyco
        car care product or Toronto Honda service. These two firms were distributing:
   A.   samples.
   B.   coupons.
   C.   price packs.
   D.   premiums.
   E.   advertising specialty.

_____5. Each company placed a limit on the prizes they were distributing; when they did
        this they were deciding on:
   A.   conditions of participation.
   B.   distribution vehicle for promotion.
   C.   size of the incentive.
   D.   timing of promotion.
   E.   reach, frequency and impact.

Multiple Choice Answers

1.	Correct Answer:	3	Reference:	pg. 557
2.	Correct Answer:	1	Reference:	pg. 557
3.	Correct Answer:	5	Reference:	pg. 557
4.	Correct Answer:	3	Reference:	pg. 580
5.	Correct Answer:	2	Reference:	pg. 580
6.	Correct Answer:	4	Reference:	pg. 581
7.	Correct Answer:	4	Reference:	pg. 583
8.	Correct Answer:	1	Reference:	pg. 584
9.	Correct Answer:	3	Reference:	pg. 585
10.	Correct Answer:	4	Reference:	pg. 586
11.	Correct Answer:	1	Reference:	pg. 586
12.	Correct Answer:	3	Reference:	pg. 587
13.	Correct Answer:	2	Reference:	pg. 588
14.	Correct Answer:	5	Reference:	pg. 588
15.	Correct Answer:	2	Reference:	pg. 589
16.	Correct Answer:	4	Reference:	pg. 590
17.	Correct Answer:	3	Reference:	pg. 590
18.	Correct Answer:	1	Reference:	pg. 593
19.	Correct Answer:	5	Reference:	pg. 593
20.	Correct Answer:	2	Reference:	pg. 594
21.	Correct Answer:	3	Reference:	pg. 594
22.	Correct Answer:	4	Reference:	pg. 596

23.	Correct Answer:	5	Reference:	pg. 596
24.	Correct Answer:	2	Reference:	pg. 597
25.	Correct Answer:	3	Reference:	pg. 597
26.	Correct Answer:	1	Reference:	pg. 599
27.	Correct Answer:	5	Reference:	pg. 599
28.	Correct Answer:	4	Reference:	pg. 602
29.	Correct Answer:	2	Reference:	pg. 607
30.	Correct Answer:	4	Reference:	pg. 590

True/False Answers

1.	FALSE	Reference:	pg. 577	Topic: Advertising
2.	TRUE	Reference:	pg. 577	Topic: Advertising
3.	TRUE	Reference:	pg. 588	Topic: Setting Objectives
4.	TRUE	Reference:	pg. 581	Topic: Setting the Advertising Budget
5.	FALSE	Reference:	pg. 588	Topic: The Advertising Media
6.	FALSE	Reference:	pg. 583	Topic: Creating the Advertising Message
7.	TRUE	Reference:	pg. 585	Topic: Message Strategy
8.	FALSE	Reference:	pg. 587	Topic: Message Execution
9.	FALSE	Reference:	pg. 587	Topic: Message Execution
10.	TRUE	Reference:	pg. 590	Topic: Selecting Specific Media Vehicles
11.	TRUE	Reference:	pg. 590	Topic: Selecting Specific Media Vehicles

12.	FALSE	Reference:	pg. 583	Topic: Advertising Message
13.	TRUE	Reference:	pg. 593	Topic: Organizing for Advertising
14.	TRUE	Reference:	pg. 593	Topic: Organizing for Advertising
15.	FALSE	Reference:	pg. 596	Topic: Rapid Growth of Sales Promotion
16.	TRUE	Reference:	pg. 585	Topic: Message Strategy
17.	TRUE	Reference:	pg. 597	Topic: Consumer-Promotion Tools
18.	FALSE	Reference:	pg. 601	Topic: Business-Promotion Tools
19.	TRUE	Reference:	pg. 601	Topic: Business-Promotion Tools
20.	TRUE	Reference:	pg. 602	Topic: Public Relations

Applying Terms and Concepts Answers

Case#1   Skin So Soft

Question #1
- Samples: Samplers are offers of a trial amount of a product.
- A small container of Skin So Soft could be included free of charge along with each Avon order delivered to a customer.

Question #2
- Coupons: Coupons are certificates that give buyers savings when they purchase specified products.
- A coupon for specified savings off the regular price of Skin So Soft could be included in each Avon catalogue or distributed by the Avon salesperson when servicing customers.

Question #3
- Cash refund offers: Rebates are price reductions given after the purchase rather than at the time of sale.
- Avon could allow the consumer to receive a portion of the retail price back, after the consumer sends a "proof-of-purchase" to them.

Question #4

- Price packs: Price packs offer consumers savings off the regular price of a product, Skin So Soft could be sold as a single item at a reduced price, or it could be bundled with another product and sold at a price below what both would cost if sold separately.

Question #5

- Personal communication channels involve two or more persons communicating directly with one another.
- They might communicate face-to-face, person-to-person, over the telephone, or through the mail.
- Personal communication channels are effective because they individualize presentation and feedback.
- There are three types of personal communication channels: advocate channels, consisting of company salespeople contacting buyers in the marketplace; expert channels, consisting of independent persons with expertise making claims to target buyers; and social channels, consisting of neighbours, friend, family members, and associates talking to target buyers.
- This last channel, known as word-of-mouth influence, is the most persuasive in many product areas.
- Word-of-mouth has the advantage of being more believable in that acquaintances have nothing to gain financially from the advice they are giving to potential buyers.
- Most of the time, they are simply trying to provide assistance.
- The disadvantages of word-of-mouth are that it may be inaccurate and biased.
- The product's supporters may be well intentioned but ill informed, and therefore impart poor information.
- Personal influence is especially important when the product is expensive, risky, purchased infrequently, or has significant social status.
- But even with a product as "simple" as Skin So Soft, personal influence can greatly impact sales.

Case #2   Safeway's Coupon Book

Question #1

- To get people to buy products they would not normally buy if they weren't on sale
- To get people to buy more products than normal since they are on sale
- To increase sales of slower moving products
- To get rid of ageing merchandise before it becomes outdated

Question #2

- They can compare sales of the products before, after and during the promotion to see if there was any effect—for example brand loyalty as a result of trying the product on sale
- They can compare the number of the same items purchased and see if the coupons influenced people to buy more than what they really needed

Question #3
- Yes, if the results of the coupon book were positive—people buy more of the products that are in the book—then Safeway could charge the company a fee to place their products in the book
- The book is not just a coupon book, it also allows companies to advertise their products so consumers will see and buy, therefore this is a form of promotion, therefore Safeway can charge a fee

Question #4
- For new products, sampling is more effective as people are not familiar with the product, therefore if they can form an educated opinion about it before they buy, they are more likely to buy it
Coupons are good for repeat purchases where people are really indifferent about the different brands and are price sensitive

Case #3   Barone Wines

1.   A

2.   B

3.   D

4.   continuity

5.   C

Case #4   Tyco Car Wash—Toronto Honda

1.   B

2.   consumer

3.   C

4.   B

5.   C

Chapter 15

Personal Selling and Sales Management

Chapter Overview

Selling and sales management make up the sales team after the product has been designed, modified and packaged: it is know time to put it to its final test, selling it to the buyer. At this point the sales team enters the picture with one main objective, to get the product into the consumer's hands. The sales force builds a strategy built on individuals that have been selected for their sales ability and building relationships with their other sales representatives and their buyers. And as a key to any marketing endeavour we must be able to measure the success of our sales teams and how we compensate them for their work. Like every aspect of marketing it builds on a strong base. How do we recruit, how do we select, and how much time and effort do we put into our sales team before the training is complete and salespeople finally hired? People that sell are known by a variety of names including salespeople, sales representatives, account executives, sales consultants, sales engineers, agents, district managers, and marketing representatives. Regardless of their titles, members of the sales force play a key role in modern marketing organizations.

The term salesperson covers a wide spectrum of positions. Salespeople may be order takers, such as the department-store salespeople who stand behind the counter. Or they may be order getters—salespeople engaged in the creative selling of products and services such as appliances, industrial equipment, advertising, or consulting services. To be successful in these more creative forms of selling, a company must first build and manage an effective sales force.

Chapter Objectives

1. Discuss the role of a company's salespeople in creating value for customers and building customer relationships.
2. Explain how companies design sales-force strategy and structure.
3. Explain how companies recruit, select, and train salespeople.
4. Describe how companies compensate and supervise salespeople, and how they evaluate sales-force effectiveness.
5. Discuss the personal selling process, distinguishing between transaction-oriented marketing and relationship marketing.

Chapter Topics

The Role of Personal Selling
- The Nature of Personal Selling
- The Role of the Sales Force

Managing the Sales Force
- Designing Sales Force Strategy and Structure
  - Sales-Force Structure
    - Territorial Sales-Force Structure
    - Product Sales-Force Structure
    - Customer Sales-Force Structure
    - Pyramid Structures
    - Complex Sales-Force Structures
  - Sales-Force Size
  - Other Sales-Force Strategy and Structure Issues
    - Outside and Inside Sales Forces
    - Team Selling
- Recruiting and Selecting Salespeople
  - What Makes a Good Salesperson?
  - Recruiting Procedures
  - Selecting Salespeople
- Training Salespeople
- Compensating Salespeople
- Supervising Salespeople
  - Directing Salespeople
  - Motivating Salespeople
- Evaluating Salespeople
  - Sources of Information
  - Formal Evaluation of Performance
    - Comparing Salespeople's Performance
    - Comparing Current Sales with Past Sales
    - Qualitative Evaluation of Salespeople

Principles of Personal Selling
- The Personal Selling Process
- Steps in the Selling Process
  - Prospecting and Qualifying
  - Preapproach
  - Approach
  - Presentation and Demonstration
  - Handling Objections
  - Closing
  - Follow-up
- Relationship Marketing

Chapter Summary

1.   The steps in the selling process.

There are seven major steps in the selling process. Prospecting involves identifying qualified potential customers. Preapproach involves learning about the target customer. Approach meets the buyer and gets things off to a good start. Presentation tells the story to the buyer. Handling objections solves logical and psychological problems. Closing asks for the order. Follow-up ensures consumer satisfaction and repeat business. In this way the seller takes the buyer logically through the selling process and ensures future sales.

2.   The six major sales-force management steps.

Major steps are: designing sales-force strategy and structure; recruiting and selecting salespeople; training salespeople; compensating salespeople; supervising salespeople; evaluating salespeople.

3.   How companies design sales-force strategy and structure.

Companies set different strategic goals for sales forces. Some use general guidelines such as "sell, maintain, develop, and serve" while others provide specific instructions on time/activity allocation. Designing sales-force strategy involves determining the type of selling (individual, team, conference, seminar), the structure (territory, product, customer, complex), and size.

4.   The companies recruit, select, and train salespeople.

Recruitment and selection are based upon the company's perception about what type of person will be successful representing the company. Personnel look at applications, prospects from employees, places ads, interview college students. Training is increasingly seen as an investment and may run several months, even more than a year, with planned continuing development during the salesperson's tenure with the company.

5.   How companies supervise salespeople and evaluate their effectiveness.

Supervision involves developing customer targets and call norms, using sales time efficiently and motivating salespeople through organizational climate, sales quotas, and positive incentives. Evaluating salespeople relies on sources of information such as sales reports (work plan, annual territory marketing plans, expense reports, call reports) and formal procedures such as current to past sales comparison and qualitative evaluations.

Key Terms

Approach	(pg. 640)	Prospecting	(pg. 625)
Closing	(pg. 642)	Pyramid sales-force structure	(pg. 642)
Complex sales force structure	(pg. 627)	Relationship marketing	(pg. 642)
Customer sales force structure	(pg. 624)	Sales-force management	(pg. 623)
Follow-up	(pg. 642)	Salesperson	(pg. 621)
Handling objections	(pg. 642)	Sales quotas	(pg. 636)
Inside sales force	(pg. 626)	Selling process	(pg. 639)
Outside sales force (field sales)	(pg. 626)	Team selling	(pg. 627)
Preapproach	(pg. 640)	Telemarketing	(pg. 626)
Presentation	(pg. 640)	Territorial sales-force structure	(pg. 623)
Product sales-force structure	(pg. 639)	Workload approach	(pg. 625)

Multiple Choice Questions

15-1   Multiple

Modern salespeople are a far cry from the stereotypes of the past. Today sales people are:

1.   Well-educated professionals
2.   Well-trained professionals
3.   Well-dressed professional
4.   Only 1 and 2
5.   All of the above

15-2   Multiple

Personal selling today is much more than closing a sale. Salespeople must ensure the following is (are) done.

1.   Satisfy customer needs
2.   Listen to their customers
3.   Solve their customers problems
4.   Only 1 and 2
5.   All of the above

15-3   Multiple

Salespeople whose positions demand the creative selling of products and services are considered:

1.   Order takers
2.   Order getters
3.   Missionary sellers
4.   Aggressive sellers
5.   None of the above

15-4   Multiple

Salespeople should be concerned with more than just _____. They must also know how to produce _____ and _____.

1.   Sales, customer satisfaction, company profit
2.   Company profit, sales, customer satisfaction
3.   Company profits, customer satisfaction, customer loyalty
4.   Sales, company profits, customer loyalty
5.   None of the above

15-5   Multiple

Sales-force management is made up of a number of components. All if the following can be included in sales force management except for which one of the following:

1.   Analyzing
2.   Financing
3.   Implementing
4.   Planning
5.   All the following

15-6   Multiple

A key component of sales force management is the successful designing of sales strategy. When dealing with the sales force which of the following is not part of their role?

1.   Training
2.   Evaluating
3.   Surveying
4.   Recruiting
5.   Compensating

15-7   Multiple

Which of the following descriptions of sales-force structure clearly defines the
salesperson's job and improves selling effectiveness.

1.   Pyramid
2.   Complex
3.   Customer
4.   Territorial
5.   Product

15-8   Multiple

There are a variety of sales-force structures. If a company decides to deal in sales of
product, for example, software, for their existing clients they could be said to be which
type of sales structure?

1.   Pyramid
2.   Complex
3.   Customer
4.   Territorial
5.   Product

15-9   Multiple

These sales forces are often composed of people with different skills, who are employed
to accomplish different tasks ranging from merchandisers who help retailers, to
telemarketers, to information managers.

1.   Pyramid
2.   Complex
3.   Customer
4.   Territorial
5.   Product

15-10 Multiple

A company has 1000 Type-A accounts and 2000 Type-B accounts. Type A accounts
require 36 calls a year and Type B accounts require 12 calls per year. In this case, the
sales-force's workload – the number of calls it must make per year – is:

1.   60,000
2.   84,000
3.   194
4.   138
5.   None of the above

15-11 Multiple

Inside sales force conduct business from their offices via a number of different methods. All of the following are included with the exception of:

1.   Technical support people
2.   Sales assistants
3.   Telemarketers
4.   Managers
5.   All of the above

15-12 Multiple

As companies continue to grow and diversify sales teams become more and more popular and effective as a style. In a sales team which of the following would not be included?

1   Engineering
2   Finance
3   Upper management
4   Technical support
5   All of the above would participate

15-13 Multiple

In a typical sales force, the top _____ % of the salespeople might bring in _____ % of the sales.

1.   25, 75
2.   30,60
3.   40,50
4.   20,80
5.   15,60

15-14 Multiple

The hiring of staff is a major decision of any company. In dealing with a sales hiring there are certain characteristics that are looked for by management. They include a sales rep that is:

1.   Outgoing
2.   Aggressive
3.   Energetic
4.   Soft-spoken
5.   All of the above are good traits

15-15   Multiple

Selecting salespeople is quite a challenge. Most companies administer a series of tests, either prior to all interviews, or after the first interview. These formal tests can measure all the following except:

1.   Sales aptitude
2.   Education level
3.   Analytical skills
4.   Personality traits
5.   All of the above can be measured

15-16   Multiple

There are many different compensation packages offered to salespeople. Packages can include base salary, commission, bonuses, and fringe benefits. The average plan consists of about _____ % salary and _____ % incentive pay.

1.   60,40
2.   50,50
3.   70,30
4.   55,45
5.   30,70

15-17   Multiple

The relationship between overall marketing strategy and sales-force compensation is very important and easily identifiable. Which strategic goal would a company be trying to achieve if its ideal salesperson was a competitive problem-solver, the sales focus was consultative selling and its compensation role was to reward new and existing accounts sales?

1.   To rapidly gain market share
2.   To maximize profitability
3.   To solidify market share
4.   To solidify market leadership
5.   To maximize shareholder wealth

15-18 Multiple

Not all a salesperson's time is spent selling. Some other activities may include service calls, administrative tasks, telephone selling and waiting/travelling. On average a salesperson only spends _____ % of their time engaged in face-to-face selling.

1.   40
2.   50
3.   30
4.   20
5.   15

15-19 Multiple

_____ is the motivation tool, which helps salespeople have a positive view about their opportunities, values, and regard for a good performance within the company.

1.   Sales quotas
2.   Positive incentives
3.   Performance based reward system
4.   Organizational climate
5.   None of the above

15-20 Multiple

There are many sources of information companies use to evaluate salespeople. _____ outlines salespeople's plans for building new accounts and increasing sales from existing accounts.

1.   Work plan
2.   Expense reports
3.   Annual territory marketing plans
4.   Call reports
5.   Projected sales reports

15-21 Multiple

Formal evaluation produces many benefits. Which of the following is not one of them?

1.   Management must develop and communicate clear standards for judging performance
2.   Management must gather well-rounded information about salespeople
3.   Salespeople receive constructive feedback that helps them to improve future performance
4.   Salespeople are motivated to perform well because they know they will have to sit down with the sales manager and explain their performance
5.   All the above are benefits

15-22 Multiple

Salespeople cannot make sales calls to every company in their territory. They must carefully select companies according to certain criteria. During the prospecting and qualifying stage, salespeople evaluate and qualify potential companies on all the following except:

1.   Competitive take-over possibilities
2.   Financial ability
3.   Volume of business
4.   Special needs
5.   All of the above are used for qualifying potential companies

15-23 Multiple

Companies who are interested in just making the sales are _____.

1.   Profit oriented
2.   Transaction oriented
3.   Relationship oriented
4.   Product oriented
5.   Customer oriented

15-24 Multiple

Companies that specialize in relationship marketing when looking for possible new prospects are looking for clients that have all of the following traits except:

1.   That they prefer suppliers who can sell and deliver a coordinated set of products and services to many locations
2.   That they want suppliers who can quickly solve problems
3.   That they want suppliers who can work closely with customer teams to improve products and processes
4.   That they want suppliers who emphasize service over technical support
5.   All the above are characteristics

15-25 Multiple

A company that is looking at new customers as possible clients and studying the wants and needs of these companies can be said to be:

1.   Prospecting
2.   Communications
3.   Selling
4.   Information gathering
5.   Presentation and demonstration

15-26 Multiple

Which of the following involves the most creative form of selling?

1.   Order taking
2.   Technical specialist
3.   Selling intangible products
4.   Selling tangible products
5.   Detailing

15-27 Multiple

When a sales representative brings resource people from the company to meet with one or more buyers to discuss problems and mutual opportunities, the firm is engaged in _____ _____ selling.

1.   Sales representative to buyer group
2.   Conference
3.   Seminal
4.   Sales team to buyer group
5.   Group

348

15-28 Multiple

Many companies determine the size of the sales force by using:

1.   Industry averages
2.   The build-up approach
3.   The customer-contact approach
4.   The relationship marketing approach
5.   The workload approach

15-29 Multiple

Which of the following elements in a compensation package provides the greatest incentive for sales representatives?

1.   Salary
2.   Fringe benefits
3.   Expense allowances
4.   Commissions
5.   Use of company vehicles

15-30 Multiple

Which of the following has not been identified as a desirable trait of a sales representative?

1.   Sympathy
2.   Enthusiasm
3.   Self-confidence
4.   Initiative
5.   All of the above are good traits

True/False Questions

15-1   True/False

Selling is the oldest profession in the world.

15-2   True/False

Personal selling can be more effective than advertising in more complex selling situations.

15-3   True/False

All companies have some salespeople.

15-4   True/False

Salespeople constitute one of the company's most productive – and most expensive – assets.

15-5   True/False

Increasing the number of salespeople in a company will increase both costs but not sales.

15-6   True/False

Inside sales staff conduct their business form within their office.

15-7   True/False

Team selling is not based on the team approach but on the salesperson in the field for management, delivery and production schedules.

15-8   True/False

According to one study, sales superstars sell an average of 2-4 times more than the average salesperson.

15-9   True/False

Companies still find it difficult to convince university students a career in selling is a lucrative and rewarding one.

15-10   True/False

Sales people are paid by a number of different methods and not just salary. To attract salespeople, a company must have an appealing compensation plan.

15-11   True/False

The sales-force plan can only be used to motivate salespeople, but cannot be used to direct their activities.

15-12   True/False

Companies are now designing compensation plans that reward salespeople for building customer relationships and growing the long-run value of each customer and not so much the short-term sales.

15-13 True/False

Sales-force automation not only lowers sales force costs and improves productivity, but it also improves the quantity of sales management decisions.

15-14 True/False

Training for sales people today can take up to a year for completion. Some salespeople will do their best without any special urging from management.

15-15 True/False

Generally sales quotas are set equal to sales forecasts to encourage sales managers and salespeople to give their best effort.

15-16 True/False

Sales reports are divided into summaries for future activities and plans of completed activities.

15-17 True/False

Because of the lack of good sales people, management no longer has to worry about organizational climate, and sales quotas or incentives

15-18 True/False

The problem-solver salesperson fits better with the marketing concept than does the hard-seller salesperson.

15-19 True/False

A salesperson when starting the selling process must first become involved in prospecting for clients.

15-20 True/False

Companies are realizing that when operating in maturing markets and facing stiffer competition, it costs more to keep a current customer than to secure new customers.

Applying Terms and Concepts

To determine how well you understand the materials in this chapter, read each of the following brief cases and then respond to the questions that follow. Answers are given at the end of this chapter.

Case#1   Goodwin Publishing Co.[1]

Nikki Lawson was sales manager for Goodwin Publishing Company, a small firm located in Charlottetown, PEI. Goodwin specializes in business texts used at both the undergraduate and graduate levels. Cathy Goodwin, founder of the company, focused on business texts because she had been a professor of marketing at Mount Allison College. Goodwin was dissatisfied with the quality of available books so she wrote her own, *Marketing in Canada*. The text sold well—so well in fact that she left teaching to devote herself to the publishing business. Goodwin's book is still in print, now co-authored by two of Goodwin's colleagues at Mount Allison. Goodwin controls 23 other titles, several of which are industry standards selling in excess of 20,000 copies per year. Sales for the company totalled $14 million last year and returned a respectable profit.

There had been considerable consolidation in the publishing business the last few years. The industry is now dominated by a few firms. Individual company names still appear as publishers but most are now subsidiaries of some conglomerate. Goodwin is still one of the few true independents and she wanted to stay that way.

Goodwin decided the company needed to increase profits. The profits would be used to increase the stockholder dividend and to begin buying back company stock. There was little indication of stockholder discontent and Goodwin wanted that to continue. And what better way than to increase the value of their holdings and their dividends. Sales projections were flat so the only way to increase profits was to reduce costs.

Goodwin had always treated her employees well. Her 20 sales representatives enjoyed privileges that were the envy of the industry. The sales staff was paid a straight salary and enjoyed generous fringe benefits including a company car and a liberal expense account. Goodwin thought that perhaps the company was too generous. Goodwin asked Carlson to review several aspects of the sales department operation. Company records indicated that approximately 10,200 sales calls to college faculty were made last year, with each sales representative averaging 17 visitations per week, over a 30-week academic year. Carlson was also asked to review the compensation program and general role of the sales force.

1.   Using workload analysis, calculate how many sales representatives could be terminated, if Goodwin instructed Carlson to increase the average number of sales calls per representative from 17 to 19 per week holding the total number of calls constant.

_____

_____

_____

_____

---

[1] *Principles of Marketing*, 3rd Edition, Kotler, Armstrong, Warren (Prentice Hall) – pg. 345.

2. Discuss the relative merits of each of the following compensation programs for a sales representative: Straight salary

_____

_____

_____

_____

3. Straight commission

_____

_____

_____

4. Salary plus bonus

_____

_____

_____

_____

5. Salary plus commission

_____

_____

_____

_____

Case #2   Nonverbal Communication

In recent years marketers have begun to pay close attention to the role of nonverbal factors in the communication process. Communication is a complex process composed of many elements with signals, both verbal and nonverbal, continually flowing back and forth between the communicators. Studies have indicated that such wordless signals as the vocal element (tone, pitch, volume, resonance), the facial element (expression, eye contact), the proximity element (physical distance between communicators), the kinetic element (body and limb movements), the physical element (grooming, dress), and general deportment all play a role in the communication process. Nonverbal clues may actually alter what the receiver has "heard." Receivers tend to search out such cues to determine the "real" message.

1.   Explain the significance of such findings for a salesperson.

_____

_____

_____

_____

____2. Nonverbal skills would be *most* useful to salespeople in which of the following
sales positions?
A.   inside order takers
B.   outside order takers
C.   sales engineers
D.   creative sales
E.   detailers

____3. The adept use of nonverbal communication would be evidence of which of the
following traits of a successful salesperson?
A.   empathy
B.   ego drive
C.   aggressiveness
D.   deceptiveness
E.   perseverance

____4. A salesperson that believes in the usefulness of nonverbal behavior would be most
likely to use which of the following types of sales presentations?
A.   canned approach
B.   formulated approach
C.   need-dissatisfaction approach
D.   AIDA approach
E.   none of the above

Case #3   Jackson Recruiting Company

Jackson Electronics has been in business for over twenty years. Their specialty has been
to hire experienced sales reps with ten years or more in business and with an outstanding
track record. Turnover in this field has always been small, which makes it hard to attract
experienced sales reps. But Jackson has always paid their reps well and strictly on
commission. Because of the nature of their business they have offices set up in all
provinces except the east coast. The Halifax office handles the entire Maritimes. Their
compensation is based on 2% of total sales and 1% on maintenance and service contracts,
which is considered quite high in the industry. They sell a large line of electronic
components to the television industry. Components are industry based and highly
specialized, with strong competition. Sales reps need to be experienced in sales as their
top priority and Jackson's will provide the training they need to be effective sales reps.

Companies that come to Jackson's are repeat customers that can depend on a resourceful staff that is well supported.

1.   What method does this company use for compensating its sales force and why?

_____

_____

_____

_____

2.   Is this company more apt to have a two-day or four week training period, explain?

_____

_____

_____

_____

3.   What sales force structure best suits Jackson Electronics and state why?

_____

_____

_____

_____

Jackson recruiting has been in business for 20 years in Canada and been quite successful. Its major strength has been the hiring of sales staff.

Multiple Choice Answers

1.	Correct Answer:	4	Reference:	pg. 620
2.	Correct Answer:	5	Reference:	pg. 621
3.	Correct Answer:	2	Reference:	pg. 622
4.	Correct Answer:	1	Reference:	pg. 622
5.	Correct Answer:	2	Reference:	pg. 623
6.	Correct Answer:	3	Reference:	pg. 623
7.	Correct Answer:	4	Reference:	pg. 623
8.	Correct Answer:	3	Reference:	pg. 624
9.	Correct Answer:	2	Reference:	pg. 625
10.	Correct Answer:	1	Reference:	pg. 625
11.	Correct Answer:	4	Reference:	pg. 626
12.	Correct Answer:	5	Reference:	pg. 627
13.	Correct Answer:	2	Reference:	pg. 627
14.	Correct Answer:	5	Reference:	pg. 628
15.	Correct Answer:	2	Reference:	pg. 629
16.	Correct Answer:	1	Reference:	pg. 631
17.	Correct Answer:	4	Reference:	pg. 632 (Table 15-1)
18.	Correct Answer:	3	Reference:	pg. 635 (Figure 15-2)
19.	Correct Answer:	4	Reference:	pg. 635
20.	Correct Answer:	3	Reference:	pg. 636
21.	Correct Answer:	5	Reference:	pg. 636
22.	Correct Answer:	1	Reference:	pg. 638

23.	Correct Answer:	2	Reference:	pg. 639
24.	Correct Answer:	4	Reference:	pg. 642
25.	Correct Answer:	1	Reference:	pg. 639
26.	Correct Answer:	3	Reference:	pg. 639
27.	Correct Answer:	2	Reference:	pg. 641
28.	Correct Answer:	5	Reference:	pg. 625
29.	Correct Answer:	4	Reference:	pg. 631
30.	Correct Answer:	1	Reference:	pg. 629

True/False Answers

1.	TRUE	Reference:	pg. 621	Topic:	The Nature of Personal Selling
2.	TRUE	Reference:	pg. 621	Topic:	The Role of the Sales Force
3.	FALSE	Reference:	pg. 621	Topic:	The Role of the Sales Force
4.	TRUE	Reference:	pg. 625	Topic:	Sales-Force Size
5.	FALSE	Reference:	pg. 625	Topic:	Sales-Force Size
6.	TRUE	Reference:	pg. 625	Topic:	Other Sales-Force Strategy and Structure Issues
7.	FALSE	Reference:	pg. 627	Topic:	Team Selling
8.	FASLE	Reference:	pg. 627	Topic:	Recruiting and Selective Salespeople
9.	FALSE	Reference:	pg. 629	Topic:	What Makes a Good Salesperson
10.	TRUE	Reference:	pg. 631	Topic:	Compensating Salespeople
11.	FALSE	Reference:	pg. 631	Topic:	Compensating Salespeople
12.	TRUE	Reference:	pg. 632	Topic:	Compensating Salespeople

13.	FALSE	Reference:	pg. 633	Topic: Directing Salespeople
14.	TRUE	Reference:	pg. 630	Topic: Training Salespeople
15.	FALSE	Reference:	pg. 550	Topic: Motivating Salespeople
16.	FALSE	Reference:	pg. 636	Topic: Evaluating Salespeople
17.	FALSE	Reference:	pg. 635	Topic: Comparing Salespeople's Performance
18.	TRUE	Reference:	pg. 639	Topic: The Personal Selling Process
19.	TRUE	Reference:	pg. 639	Topic: Steps in the Selling Process
20.	FALSE	Reference:	pg. 642	Topic: Relationship Marketing

Applying Terms and Concept Answers

Case#1   Goodwin Publishing Company

Question #1
- Carlson currently supervises 20 sales representatives who average 17 visitations per week.
- Given Goodwin's directive, the number of sales representatives could be reduced by 2.
- The calculations are as follows: 10, 200 calls divided by 30 weeks equals 340 calls per week.
- 340 divided by 19 calls per sales representative equals (approximately) 18 sales representatives.
- A relatively modest increase in the required number of sales calls per week per sales representative, reduced the sales force by 2.

Question #2
Straight salary provides maximum security for the sales representative. Their earnings are guaranteed regardless of sales. There may be minimal incentive for the sales representative to make additional calls to generate additional sales.

Question #3
Straight commission provides maximum incentive for the sales representative since their earnings are based on how much they sell. While there is relatively little security for the sales representative, the company only pays a commission when sales are generated.

Question #4
Salary plus bonus provides some security for the sales representative but also provides an incentive. The incentive is based on the bonus to be received after other goals and objectives have been met. The bonus may be paid based on such goals and objectives as an increase in sales, increase in profitability, reduction of costs, increase in new accounts, or sales of certain products.

Question #5
Salary plus commission provides some security for the sales representatives but also provides an incentive. The incentive is based on the commission earned from the generation of sales.

Case #2   Non verbal Communication

1.   The salesperson must communicate effectively to sell effectively. Insights into nonverbal communication can assist a sales representative in better preparing the sales presentation to be more effective in dealing with a client. These insights also allow the sales representative to better understand the customer's responses and attitudes and can help the salesperson frame, tailor, and adjust the sales presentation.

2.   D

3.   A

4.   D

Case #3   Jackson Electronics:

1.   Straight commission is the best method of compensation for this company. It is most effective because of: the sales people they are trying to recruit, they are experienced and will have to be encouraged to join this firm. Because of the small turn over in staff and difficulty in hiring new people the level of compensation must be at or above the norm. To pay just salary or commission plus salary would not attract the best of the best and result in staff that would leave to go to the next better paying job.

2.   Training because of the nature of the job would be a minimum of 4 weeks. This will give the sales reps the confidence they need to sell this product and instil in them faith in the company and a feeling of teamwork. In this way the chances of success are also higher, than if sending out an under qualified rep which would result in customers feeling wary of dealing with such an unqualified representative.

3.   Because of the distribution of offices the best way would be a territorial sales
        force structure. This breaks the salesperson's territory into preassigned
        geographical areas. This is beneficial because it clearly lays out the area that the
        rep is responsible for and it helps give them incentive to do a good job because
        the company know exactly who is in an area and the rep realizes that he/she will
        get the credit they deserve for growth within a specific geographic area.

Chapter 16

Direct and Online Marketing

Chapter Overview

Mass marketers typically try to reach millions of buyers with a single product and a standard message communicated via the mass media. Consequently, most mass marketing communications are one-way communications directed at consumers rather than two-way communications with consumers. Rapid growth of online marketing; at present there are over 170 countries connected to the internet with over 327 million people that have access. Industries that never existed are now some of the largest industries in Canada with e-commerce revenue expected to hit $151 billion by the year 2004. Today, many companies are turning to direct marketing in an effort to reach carefully targeted customers more efficiently and to build stronger, more personal, one-to-one relationships with them. From catalogue marketing to infomercials starring both the product (the ab-buster) that have developed there own following to a new kind of TV star, the star of the info commercials, like George Foreman and his famous Grilling Machine; direct and online marketing works its way into our homes daily.

Chapter Objectives

1. Discuss the benefits of direct marketing to customers and companies and the trends fuelling its rapid growth.
2. Define a customer database and list the four ways companies use databases in direct marketing.
3. Identify the major forms of direct marketing.
4. Compare the two types of online marketing channels and explain the effect of the Internet on electronic commerce.
5. Identify the benefits of online marketing to consumers and marketers and the four ways that marketers can conduct online marketing.
6. Discuss the public policy and ethical issues facing direct marketers.

Chapter Topics

What is Direct Marketing?

Growth and Benefits of Direct Marketing
- The Benefits of Direct Marketing
- The Growth of Direct Marketing

Customer Databases and Direct Marketing

Forms of Direct Marketing Communication
- Face-to-Face Selling
- Telemarketing
- Direct-Mail Marketing
- Catalogue Marketing
- Direct-Response Television Marketing
- Kiosk Marketing

Online Marketing and Electronic Commerce
- Rapid Growth of Online Marketing
- The Online Consumer
- Conducting Online Marketing
- Online Marketing Channels
  - Creating an Electronic Online Presence
  - Placing Advertisements Online
  - Participating in Forums, Newsgroups, and Web Communities
  - Using E-mail and Webcasting
- The Promise and Challenges of Online Marketing

Integrated Direct Marketing

Public Policy and Ethical Issues in Direct Marketing
- Irritation, Unfairness, Deception, and Fraud
- Invasion of Privacy

362

Key Terms

Catalogue marketing	(pg. 669)	Electronic commerce	(pg. 675)
Commercial online service	(pg. 673)	Integrated direct marketing	(pg. 685)
Corporate web site	(pg. 678)	Internet (or the Net)	(pg. 673)
Customer database	(pg. 663)	Marketing web site	(pg. 679)
Direct marketing	(pg. 657)	Online ads	(pg. 680)
Direct-mail marketing	(pg. 668)	Online marketing	(pg. 673)
Direct-response television marketing	(pg. 671)	Telemarketing	(pg. 667)
		Webcasting	(pg. 682)

Multiple Choice Questions

16-1   Multiple

When commenting on home shopping consumers report that home shopping is:

1.   Fun
2.   Convenient
3.   Offers a large selection of merchandise
4.   Offers everyday low prices
5.   All of the above

16-2   Multiple

Direct marketing has surpassed mass marketing in the 1990s. Which of the following is not an advantage of direct marketing?

1.   Marketers are able to measure the type and rate of response
2.   Marketers are able to compile databases
3.   Direct marketing provides security
4.   Only 2 and 3
5.   All of the above

16-3   Multiple

While retail sales are growing at a rate of 3% per year, catalogue and direct-mail sales are growing at around ___ % per year.

1.   5
2.   7
3.   9
4.   11
5.   15

16-4   Multiple

Many customers shop out of either necessity or the joy of shopping. For those that are tired of the crowds the stores and the attitude or lack of staff, which of the following is not a factor of going to the net:

1.   Less disposable income
2.   Higher costs of driving
3.   Shortage of sales retail help
4.   Lack of time
5.   Lines at checkout counters

16-5   Multiple

When dealing with millions of customers which of the following is the most difficult to customize to an individual's needs?

1.   Messages
2.   Structure
3.   Delivery modes
4.   Payment methods

16-6   Multiple

To succeed marketers rely on databases for a variety of information. Databases collect data collect data on all of the following with the exception of
1.   Demographic
2.   Physiological
3.   Behavioural
4.   Geographic
5.   All of the above

16-7   Multiple

A business-to-business database or a salesperson's customer profile will probably not contain data on this subject.

1.   Products and services a customer has bought
2.   Status of current contracts
3.   An assessment of competitive strengths and weaknesses
4.   Financial stability
5.   Competitive suppliers

16-8   Multiple

Which of the following groups most frequently uses databases?

1.   Non-profit organizations
2.   Commodity product producers
3.   Service retailers
4.   1 and 3
5.   All of the above

16-9   Multiple

The collecting and proper usage of data gives marketers a wealth of information for the marketing of their products. Of all the 4 ways they can use this information which of the following is not one:
1.   Identifying prospects
2.   Deciding which customers should receive a particular offer
3.   Deepening customer loyalty
4.   Reactivating customer purchases
5.   All of the above are used

16-10   Multiple

Like many other marketing tools, database marketing requires a special investment. Companies must invest in all the following except _____ to have an efficient and productive database.

1.   Skilled personnel
2.   Proper Internet links
3.   Hardware
4.   Analytical programs
5.   All of the above

16-11 Multiple

For the personal touch many companies rely on long term relationship with their clients. It can be said that this is best referred to as_____.
1.   Face-to-face selling
2.   Direct-mail marketing
3.   Catalogue marketing
4.   Telemarketing
5.   Direct-response television marketing

16-12 Multiple

Direct mail marketing has evolved immensely over the last few years. All the following except _____ are new forms of direct mail marketing.

1.   Fax mail
2.   E-mail
3.   Snail mail
4.   Voice mail
5.   3 and 4

16-13 Multiple

While catalogue sales represent _____ % of retail sales in the United Sates, they represent _____ % of sales in Canada.

1.   4,6
2.   5,8
3.   2,1
4.   8,3
5.   10,15

16-14 Multiple

George runs a catalogue publishing firm. He receives many orders to make catalogues for different businesses that wish to market directly to other businesses. He tells them all the following except _____ are different types of catalogues for business-to-business marketing.

1.   Brochures
2.   Three-ring binders
3.   Encoded video tapes
4.   Encoded computer disks
5.   All of the above are forms of catalogues

16-15 Multiple

Infomercials are also growing in popularity along with direct marketing. However, few companies use infomercials to:

1.   Sell their wares over the phone
2.   Collect information from callers to compile company databases
3.   Refer customers to retailers
4.   Send out coupons and product information
5.   All of the above

16-16 Multiple

Online marketing has taken off at an enormously fast pace. Every day hundreds of new companies put their services online in an attempt to increase their market share. Which of the following is not part of these new online services?

1.   Provide subscribers with new information
2.   Provide entertainment
3.   Provide dialogue opportunities
4.   Provide e-mail
5.   All of the above are services

16-17 Multiple

The Internet is a vast and flourishing global web of computer networks. The Internet was created by:

1.   The Russian Government
2.   IBM
3.   The US Government
4.   The US Defense Department
5.   Microsoft

16-18 Multiple

Dilbert has a computer at home and just purchased the necessary software to be hooked up to the Internet 5 weeks ago. He has made a routine of surfing the Net every Wednesday night for about 3 hours. He looks for information on different topics, and likes to download some of the different games offered. Dilbert would be considered a (n):

1.   Casual user
2.   Heavy user
3.   Frequent user
4.   Intermittent user
5.   Compulsory user

16-19 Multiple

Internet users come in all shapes and sizes; however, the typical Internet user is probably not _____:

1.   Young
2.   Wealthy
3.   Well educated
4.   French-speaking
5.   Professional

16-20 Multiple

Because of its one-to-one interactive nature, online marketing is a good tool for building:

1.   Customer relationships
2.   Brand loyalty
3.   Product knowledge
4.   Short-term sales
5.   Long-term sales

16-21 Multiple

The reason online marketing has become so popular over the last few years is not because _____.

1.   It reduces costs
2.   It is a fad
3.   It increases efficiency
4.   It is flexible
5.   None of the above

16-22 Multiple

There are a number of web sites available that have different functions; some are designed to handle communications by the consumer. Which of the following web sites act in this capacity?

1.   Advertising
2.   Product placement
3.   Corporate
4.   Independent
5.   Customer-oriented

16-23   Multiple

One of the major problems with online marketing is privacy and security issues. To solve
these problems, companies are now using _____ extensions of their internal computer
networks that allow them to link with their suppliers, members of their distribution
channels and corporate customers.

1.   Intranets
2.   Supportnets
3.   Transnets
4.   Extranets
5.   Conglomernets

16-24   Multiple

_____ provide a place where members can congregate online and exchange
views on issues of common interest.

1.   Web communities
2.   Newsgroups
3.   Bulletin board systems
4.   Forums
5.   All of the above

16-25   Multiple

Webcasting, also known as _____ programming, provides an attractive channel for
online marketers to deliver their Internet advertising or other information content.

1.   Pull
2.   Direct web
3.   Market
4.   Online
5.   Push

16-26   Multiple

One study found a site must capture web surfers' attention within _ seconds or lose them
to another site.

1.   3
2.   6
3.   8
4.   10
5.   2

16-27 Multiple

Irritation, unfairness, deception and fraud are becoming associated more and more with
online marketing and markets. All the following except _____ are reasons why
fraudulent direct marketers are hard to catch.

1.   Customers often respond quickly
2.   Customers usually do not understand all they see and read on their screen
3.   Customers do not interact personally with the sellers
4.   Customers usually expect to wait for delivery
5.   All of the above are reasons

16-28 Multiple

The direct marketing industry is addressing issues of ethics and public policy because
they know if these issues are left unattended everything except _____ is
likely to happen.

1.   Increasing negative consumer attitudes
2.   Lower response rates
3.   Increase in company liability
4.   Increase in more restrictive provincial and federal legislation
5.   All of the above are bound to happen

16-29 Multiple

The creation of the "information superhighway" promises to revolutionize commerce.
Today more than ____ % of the 11.6 million Canadian households has a personal
computer.

1.   15
2.   52
3.   24
4.   36
5.   48

16-30 Multiple

A database can help a company make attractive offers of product replacements, upgrades, or complementary products just when customers might be ready to act. This capability would qualify as which of the following uses of databases?

1.   Reactivating customer purchases
2.   Deepening customer loyalty
3.   Deciding which customers should receive a particular offer
4.   Identifying prospects
5.   None of the above

True/False Questions

16-1   True/False

Most marketing communications consist of two-way communication with consumers, not directed at them.

16-2   True/False

The telephone has become the most direct marketing tool.

16-3   True/False

Of all the things a database is capable of doing, it cannot identify prospects.

16-4   True/False

The growth of affordable computer power and customer databases has enabled direct marketers to single out the best prospects for a limited number of items that they wish to sell.

16-5   True/False

A recent survey found that almost two-thirds of all large consumer-products companies currently use or build databases for targeting their marketing efforts.

16-6   True/False

A well-managed database always leads to sales gains that will more than cover its costs.

16-7   True/False

E-mail for many has turned into junk mail that takes up room on their computer and time out of their busy day. Many are now looking for programs or 'agents' that will help edit out the 'junk'.

16-8   True/False

Sears Canada, which has 1,700 catalogue stores across the country, traditionally used their catalogues as a speciality products merchandising tactic.

16-9   True/False

Marketers use inbound telephone marketing to sell directly to consumers and businesses.

16-10   True/False

Many experts think that advances in two-way, interactive television and linkages with Internet technology will eventually make video shopping one of the major forms of direct marketing.

16-11   True/False

The Internet is being overtaken by the commercial online services as the primary online marketing channel.

16-12   True/False

Online marketing is conducted through interactive online computer systems. Electronic markets are "marketspaces" in which sellers offer their products and services electronically.

16-13   True/False

The fundamental principle that businesses must understand when considering marketing on the Internet is consumers have greater control over the marketing process than ever before.

16-14   True/False

Buyers will increasingly become consumers of product information, not creators of it.

16-15   True/False

A company can create a presence by buying space on a commercial service or by its own web site.

16-16 True/False

With a marketing web site, the consumer initiates communication and interaction.

16-17 True/False

Barriers to growth for online business commerce include the belief that firms are not offering the right products or services and that there are security and privacy issues.

16-18 True/False

Although web advertising is on the increase, many marketers still question its value as an effective advertising tool.

16-19 True/False

There is a very clear line between adding value and the consumer feeling that you are being intrusive.

16-20 True/False

In an integrated direct marketing campaign, the marketer seeks to improve response rates and profits by adding media and stages that contribute more to additional sales than to additional costs.

Applying Terms and Concepts

To determine how well you understand the materials in this chapter, read each of the following brief cases and then respond to the questions that follow. Answers are given at the end of this chapter.

Case #1   Quenching Small Businesses' Thirst[1]

Coca-Cola USA's research found there are approximately 1 million American workplaces, employing less than fifty people that do not have soft drinks available on - site. For this market, Coca-Cola developed a small fountain-drink dispenser that it called the BreakMate. To promote the new machine to small businesses, Coke mailed to office managers and presidents of small businesses a direct mail piece that focused on the convenience of having an in-house soda dispenser. Coca-Cola now has about 60,000 BreakMate machines pumping more than 1 million gallons of syrup in workplaces.

---

[1] *Marketing*, 5th Edition, Schoell, Guilitinan (Allyn and Bacon) – pg. 168.

1.   What was the measurable response Coca-Cola was seeking with this mailing?

       _____

       _____

       _____

       _____

2.   By using direct mail as its primary advertising medium to reach prospective
       customers, what advantage(s) of direct marketing is Coca-Cola using?

       _____

       _____

       _____

       _____

3.   Why is Coca-Cola gathering information from those who respond to its mailing
       for a database?

       _____

       _____

       _____

       _____

4.   Who would consider this mailing to be junk mail?

       _____

       _____

       _____

       _____

5.   Besides direct mail, identify other forms of direct marketing.

       _____

       _____

       _____

       _____

Case #2   Infomercials[2]

What would life be like without such necessities as a Vege-Matic or a complete set of Ginzu knives? Producers of infomercials don't intend to let us find out. Their extended commercials, often masquerading as talk shows or news programs, continue to bombard our airwaves. While many of the products on direct-response television in the early days made dubious claims about their ability to promote weight loss or make long-lost hair grow back, the industry is evolving as mainstream corporations begin to get into the act.

Still pitfalls remain. One pitfall is infomercials may dupe consumers into changing their attitudes towards advertised items by making them believe the information they are receiving is more credible and objective than is really the case. By presenting product information in a news or talk show format, receivers of these pervasive communications may not counter-argue as heavily as if they message were clearly identified as coming from a commercial sponsor. For example, in a controversial campaign for Maxwell House coffee, TV newscaster Linda Ellerbee and Willard Scott plugged the product in a setting resembling a news show. This format attempted to capitalize on the actors' backgrounds to produce the inference that their reports were news rather than commercials. So look carefully next time you are channel surfing and happen to land on an adoring crowd applauding a demonstration of the latest juicer, glassmaker or other "must have" product. The money you save may be your own.

1.   What are the benefits of direct-response television?

_____

_____

_____

_____

2.   What are disadvantages of direct-response television?

_____

_____

_____

---

[2] *Consumer Behaviour*, 3rd Edition, Michael Solomon (Prentice Hall) – pg. 218.

3. Do you believe direct-response marketing is replacing door-to-door selling? Why or why not?

_____

_____

_____

_____

4. Would infomercials be as (more) effective if they went online?

_____

_____

_____

_____

5. Do you watch infomercials? What do you think of them?

_____

_____

_____

_____

Case #3   You Can't Hide[3]

For years Lisa Tomaino kept her address secret. She and her husband, Jim, a police office, wanted to make it as hard as possible for the crooks he put away to find out where they lived. But last year Lisa had a baby. So much for her big secret. Within six weeks she was inundated with junk mail aimed at new mothers. The hospital had sold her name and address to a direct-marketing company, and soon she was on dozens of other lists. Efforts to get their names removed from these lists proved fruitless. "It was a complete violation of our right to privacy," she declares.

Private citizens, private watchdogs, and a handful of lawmakers have railed for years about Big Brotherism by business. But when politicians balance industry's interest in reaching markets against the customer's right to privacy, marketing usually wins. "Existing laws regulating privacy simply aren't effective," gripes Robert Bulmash, president of Private Citizen, Inc., a public advocacy group.

---

[3] *Introduction to Marketing Communications*, Burnett, Moriarty, pg. 390.

Marketers are keenly aware of the public's reaction to their unwanted attention. After all, it's their job to stay in touch with the preferences of consumers. Vendors of marketing data argue that any intrusion on privacy from selling lists is offset "by the significant potential gain to consumers from the special offers and products offered by direct marketers."

The industry has largely staved off regulation by convincing the federal government that it can police itself. The Information Monitoring Association (IMA), for example, runs a phone number for people who want their names removed from mailing lists. Or, you can register with the Mail Preference Service (MPS), at the following address: Mail Preference Service, Direct Marketing Association, P.O. Box 9008, Farmingdale, New York, 11735-9008.

But relatively few consumers use it, and those who do contend their names come off some, but no all, lists. Even long-standing laws, such as the 1970 Fair Credit Reporting Act, aren't effective. The statute is supposed to prevent credit agencies such as TRW, Equifax, and TransUnion from releasing financial information about a person except for "legitimate" business needs, such as a credit check. Unfortunately, it doesn't always do so.

As marketing techniques become more sophisticated, the privacy of the Lisa Tomainos of the world will grow increasingly difficult to protect.

1.   As a direct marketer, how would you justify this perceived invasion of privacy?

_____

_____

_____

_____

2.   Suppose the Tomainos started receiving threats from a criminal that Officer Tomaino had apprehended. Suppose also that the criminal had found their personal phone number and address through access to a direct-marketing database. Do you think the Tomainos should have any recourse against the hospital?

_____

_____

_____

_____

3.   Now assume that you are the director of a non-profit hospital. Direct marketers offer hundreds of thousands of dollars for the database you maintain of those who recently had a baby in the hospital. By accepting the money for selling your database, you can lower your delivery and newborn care costs and upgrade medical equipment. However, you're worried about privacy issues. Can you suggest a data collection process that does not violate a patient's right to privacy?

_____

_____

_____

_____

4.   What inconveniences can consumers be subjected to regarding direct marketing?

_____

_____

_____

_____

5.   Discuss the public policy and ethical issues facing direct marketers.

_____

_____

_____

_____

Case #4   The Ethical Issues of Direct Marketing

As consumers rely more and more on their computers the question of ethics comes up. Are marketers becoming too pushy as they phone our houses at dinner time, leave hundreds of fax messages at our workplace over night, and the dependability of their products becomes questionable. The question of privacy and invasion of our personal space become issues that concerned marketers must deal with. A negative article in a newspaper on how a company conducts their marketing can harm a firm's sales and profits as they are looked at as the big bad company prying into society's life a little too hard and a little too much.

1.   What are the main objections consumers have towards telemarketers?

_____

_____

_____

_____

2.   Where can customers turn for help?

_____

_____

_____

_____

3.   What areas are government looking at for legislation to protect the consumer?

_____

_____

_____

_____

Multiple Choice Answers

1.   Correct Answer: 4   Reference: pg. 659

2.   Correct Answer: 5   Reference: pg. 659

3.   Correct Answer: 2   Reference: pg. 661

4.   Correct Answer: 1   Reference: pg. 662

5.   Correct Answer: 3   Reference: pg. 662

6.   Correct Answer: 2   Reference: pg. 663

7.   Correct Answer: 4   Reference: pg. 664

8.   Correct Answer: 4   Reference: pg. 663

9.   Correct Answer: 5   Reference: pg. 664

10.	Correct Answer:	2	Reference:	pg. 666
11.	Correct Answer:	1	Reference:	pg. 666
12.	Correct Answer:	3	Reference:	pg. 668
13.	Correct Answer:	1	Reference:	pg. 669
14.	Correct Answer:	5	Reference:	pg. 669
15.	Correct Answer:	2	Reference:	pg. 671
16.	Correct Answer:	5	Reference:	pg. 673
17.	Correct Answer:	4	Reference:	pg. 673
18.	Correct Answer:	3	Reference:	pg. 675
19.	Correct Answer:	4	Reference:	pg. 676
20.	Correct Answer:	1	Reference:	pg. 676
21.	Correct Answer:	2	Reference:	pg. 677
22.	Correct Answer:	3	Reference:	pg. 584
23.	Correct Answer:	4	Reference:	pg. 678
24.	Correct Answer:	1	Reference:	pg. 680
25.	Correct Answer:	5	Reference:	pg. 682
26.	Correct Answer:	3	Reference:	pg. 684
27.	Correct Answer:	2	Reference:	pg. 686
28.	Correct Answer:	3	Reference:	pg. 689
29.	Correct Answer:	4	Reference:	pg. 662
30.	Correct Answer:	1	Reference:	pg. 666

True/False Answers

1.	FALSE	Reference:	pg. 657	Topic:	What is Direct Marketing
2.	TRUE	Reference:	pg. 667	Topic:	Telemarketing
3.	TRUE	Reference:	pg. 659	Topic:	The Growth of Direct Marketing
4.	FALSE	Reference:	pg. 661	Topic:	The Growth of Direct Marketing
5.	TRUE	Reference:	pg. 662	Topic:	Customer Databases and Direct Marketing
6.	FALSE	Reference:	pg. 662	Topic:	Customer Databases and Direct Marketing
7.	TRUE	Reference:	pg. 668	Topic:	Direct-Mail Marketing
8.	FALSE	Reference:	pg. 669	Topic:	Catalogue Marketing
9.	FALSE	Reference:	pg. 667	Topic:	Telemarketing
10.	TRUE	Reference:	pg. 671	Topic:	Direct-Response Television Marketing
11.	FALSE	Reference:	pg. 673	Topic:	Window on the Future: Online Marketing and Electronic Commerce
12.	TRUE	Reference:	pg. 675	Topic:	Rapid Growth of Online Marketing
13.	TRUE	Reference:	pg. 676	Topic:	Understanding Empowered Consumers
14.	FALSE	Reference:	pg. 676	Topic:	Understanding Empowered Consumers
15.	TRUE	Reference:	pg. 677	Topic:	Online Presence
16.	FALSE	Reference:	pg. 678	Topic:	Creating Electronic Storefront

17.	TRUE	Reference:	pg. 678	Topic:	Creating Electronic Storefront
18.	TRUE	Reference:	pg. 680	Topic:	Placing Advertisements Online
19.	FALSE	Reference:	pg. 681	Topic:	Using E-mail and Webcasting
20.	TRUE	Reference:	pg. 685	Topic:	Integrated Direct Marketing

Applying Terms and Concept Answers

Case #1   Quenching Small Businesses' Thirst

Question #1
- The measurable response was calls to Coke's 800 number.

Question #2
- Coke is enjoying the following advantages: selectivity, precise targeting of prospects, measurement of results with possible adjustments to the strategy based on these results, demonstration of size of product and how easily it will fit into the prospect's office, less expensive than face-to-face personal sales calls.

Question #3
- Coke is creating a database in order to better target future promotions.

Question #4
- Executives and office managers would receive this mail as junk mail who were not interested in providing soft drinks for their employees or who already have soda vending machines.

Question #5
- Telemarketing (over the telephone)
- Television marketing
- Online shopping

Case #2   Infomercials:

Question #1
- They can go in-depth
- You can have various different visual demonstrations of the product
- You can get well-known people on your infomercials at most likely a reduced cost
- You can give the customer a lot of additional information if they are interested

Question #2

- Not face-to-face
- People can easily flip the channel and not listen
- It may be too long and people will not watch the whole thing
- It may be expensive and overdone

Question #3

- Yes, door-to-door selling is becoming harder and harder as many households have both partners working therefore there is no one at home
- Infomercials are on usually at night when they know people are home
- They are able to give the same amount of information in the infomercial as they would face-to-face

Question #4

- It may not be as effective if the Internet site is not well developed
- There are limitations with the Internet, not enough visual appeal etc.
- More people have TVs than PCs

Case #3   You Can't Hide

Question #1

- As a direct marketer, I would claim that I was informing potential customers and the general public of goods and services that I have to offer.
- They may learn of products through my mailing that they otherwise, would be unaware of.

Question #2

- The Tomainos could be old-fashioned Americans and sue the hospital for millions.

Question #3

- The hospital could ask the patients if they minded their names being given out.
- Or, the hospital could maybe have a sign-up or registration for patients who are interested in new products.

Question #4

- Consumers are irritated, let's talk about dinner-time phone calls
- Unfairness, smooth talking sales representatives can take advantage of people
- Deception, mail designed to mislead buyers
- Fraud, crooked direct marketers

Question #5

- Invasion of privacy
- Too much financial information
- Access to information that most people would not disclose

Case #4   The Ethical Issue in Telemarketing

Question #1

Consumers are most concerned about:

--invasion of privacy

--irritation, deception and fraud

--unfairness and irritation

Question #2

Canadian consumers can direct their concerns to the Privacy Commissioner of Canada at,

www.privcom.gc.ca/

Question #3

Legislation is helping the consumer by studying the changes of law in such areas as:
> ---Obtaining consumer consent
> ---Limitations on the type of information to be gathered
> ---Firms must insure the accuracy of the information they collect
> ---Individuals have the right to know what information firms have about them

Chapter 17

The Global Marketplace

Chapter Overview

In the past, North American companies paid little attention to international trade. If they could pick up some extra sales through exporting, that was fine. But the big market was at home, and it teemed with opportunities. Companies today can no longer afford to focus only on their domestic market, regardless of its size. With computers and the internet the smallest company can go global along with the largest. Global marketing is a reality and those that will succeed in industry are those that will have their product accessible to the world. Marketers now face competition that in the past was not conceivable, but now all that has changed as more and more competition battles for the consumer and business dollars of industry. Many industries are global industries, and firms that operate globally achieve lower costs and higher brand awareness. At the same time, global marketing is risky because of variable exchange rates, unstable governments, protectionist tariffs and trade barriers, factors that few companies had to deal with in the past but that are now of concern even to one person companies that operate from their home. Given the potential gains and risks of international marketing, companies need a systematic way to make their international marketing decisions.

Chapter Objectives

1. Discuss how the international trade system, economic, political-legal and cultural environment affects a company's international marketing decisions.
2. Describe three key approaches to entering international markets.
3. Explain how companies adapt their marketing mixes for international markets.
4. Identify the three major forms of international marketing organization.

Chapter Topics

Global Marketing in the Twenty-First Century

Looking at the Global Marketing Environment
- The International Trade System
  - The World Trade Organization and GATT
  - Regional Free Trade Zones
- Economic Environment
- Political-Legal and Ethical Environment
- Cultural Environment

Deciding Whether to Go International

Deciding How to Enter the Market
- Exporting
- Joint Venture
- Licensing
- Contract Manufacturing
  - Management Contracting
  - Joint Ownership
- Direct Investment

Deciding on the Global Marketing Program
- Product
- Promotion
- Price
- Distribution Channels

386

Chapter Summary

1.   The elements of the international trade system.

International trade is regulated and restricted by various governments. A tariff is a tax levied by a foreign government on certain products. A quota sets limits on the amount of goods that an importing company will accept. This is done to control the amount of product coming into the country and act as a method of protection for the importing company which also produces the same product. An embargo totally bans some imports. Exchange controls limit the amount of foreign exchange and the exchange rate against other currencies. Non-tariff barriers include bias against firms and unfair product standards, which in turn help protect the host country's companies.

2.   The major forces operating in the economic, political, legal, and cultural environments that affect international marketing decisions.

Foreign economies may be subsistence, raw material exporting, industrializing, or industrial. Income distribution may be mostly low incomes, very-low/very-high, low/medium/high, and mostly medium family incomes. Political-legal environments vary on attitudes toward international buying, political stability, monetary regulations, and government bureaucracy. Cultural factors include differences in values, proximities, and symbolism.

3.   The three key approaches to entering international markets.

International markets' entry strategies include exporting (indirect, direct), joint venture (licensing, contract manufacturing, management contracting, and joint ownership), and direct investment (assembly facilities, manufacturing facilities). Each form varies in the amount of commitment, risk, control, and profit potential.

4.   How companies might adapt their marketing mixes for international markets.

Mix variations include standardized marketing mix with virtually no adaptation and several adaptation strategies. Product adaptation includes straight product extension, product adaptation, and product invention. These must be able to meet local standards and can vary from country to country. Promotion adaptation involves language, symbolism, and value translations and message modifications to meet both legal and ethical requirements. Price adaptation must consider economic and cultural differences. Distribution must take a whole-channel approach.

5.   The three major forms of international marketing organizations.

Export departments simply ship out the goods. International divisions manage the different forms of international marketing for each foreign country the company is in. Global organizations no longer view themselves as belonging to one or another domestic market as a primary or host country and plan, promote, and market according to worldwide organizational needs.

Key Terms

Adapted marketing mix	(pg. 725)	Joint venturing	(pg. 722)
Communication adaptation	(pg. 729)	Licensing	(pg. 722)
Contract manufacturing	(pg. 723)	Management contracting	(pg. 723)
Counter-trade	(pg. 715)	Non-tariff trade barriers	(pg. 708)
Direct investment	(pg. 724)	Product adaptation	(pg. 727)
Economic community	(pg. 709)	Product invention	(pg. 728)
Embargo	(pg. 706)	Quota	(pg. 708)
Exchange controls	(pg. 708)	Standardized marketing mix	(pg. 725)
Exporting	(pg. 722)	Straight product extension	(pg. 725)
Global firm	(pg. 706)	Tariff	(pg. 708)
Global industry	(pg. 706)	Whole-channel view	(pg. 732)
Joint ownership	(pg. 724)		

Multiple Choice Questions

17-1   Multiple

The world is shrinking rapidly as a result of everything except:

1.   Faster communications
2.   Faster transportation
3.   Faster financial flows
4.   Faster cultural adaptations
5.   All of the above

17-2   Multiple

Companies that go global confront every problem except this one.

1.   High debt, inflation and unemployment in many countries
2.   Oversaturation
3.   Governments are placing more regulations on foreign firms
4.   Corruption
5.   None of the above

17-3   Multiple

A global firm is one that, by operating in more than one country, gains every advantage except:

1.   Marketing
2.   Production
3.   R&D
4.   Financial
5.   None of the above

17-4   Multiple

International trade restrictions that allow countries to be biased against bids or restrictive towards product standards, are considered:

1.   Non-tariff trade barriers
2.   Tariffs
3.   Quotas
4.   Embargoes
5.   Exchange controls

17-5   Multiple

The General Agreement on Tariffs and Trade (GATT) is a treaty designed to promote world trade by reducing tariffs and other international trade barriers. The date of its inception was:

1.   1930
2.   1948
3.   1964
4.   1952
5.   1976

17-6   Multiple

The GATT agreement went through several rounds of negotiations before coming to a consensus. The first seven rounds of negotiations reduced average worldwide tariffs on manufactured goods from _____ % to just _____ %.

1.   80, 25
2.   75, 10
3.   45, 5
4.   50, 7
5.   30, 2

17-7   Multiple

To become more competitive countries have formed trade zones and the countries included in these zones are referred to as:

1.   Trading communities
2.   Partnership countries
3.   Trade cooperatives
4.   Economic communities
5.   None of the above

17-8   Multiple

In January 1994, the North America Free Trade Agreement was signed between Canada, Mexico and the US. This agreement created a single market of _____ million people.

1.   120
2.   190
3.   260
4.   300
5.   360

17-9   Multiple

The Asian-Pacific Economic Cooperation is composed of 18 member countries and accounts for _____ % of world trade.

1.   80
2.   30
3.   45
4.   65
5.   15

17-10 Multiple

MERCOSUL is an example of countries of Latin and South America as free trade areas. Which of the countries below is not a member?

1.   Brazil
2.   Chile
3.   Columbia
4.   Mexico
5.   All of the above are linked

17-11   Multiple

Despite NAFTA's many successes, a number of challenges have been posed to maintain the smooth trade relations between Canada and the US. All the following except _____ explain why these relationships are hurting.

1.   Salmon fishing rights along the shores of Vancouver Island
2.   Canada's protection of its dairy and poultry industries
3.   Canada's insistence of protection for its cultural industries
4.   Canada's trading status with Cuba
5.   All of the above are causing problems

17-12   Multiple

Of the economies that are ideal markets for companies producing industrial equipment and tools which of the following are ideal economies?

1.   Industrial economies
2.   Industrializing economies
3.   Raw-material-exporting economies
4.   Subsistence economies
5.   None of the above

17-13   Multiple

In a (n) _____ economy, manufacturing accounts for 10 to 20% of the country's economy.

1.   Industrial
2.   Industrializing
3.   Raw-material-exporting
4.   Subsistence
5.   2 and 3

17-14   Multiple

Marketers use four political-legal factors prior to the decision of doing business with a foreign company. The factor that is not considered is_____.
1.   Attitudes towards international buying
2.   Government bureaucracy
3.   Political stability
4.   Ethical standards
5.   Monetary regulations

17-15 Multiple

The counter-trade form whereby the seller sells a plant, equipment or technology to another country and agrees to take payment in the resulting products is called:

1.   Compensation
2.   Counter purchase
3.   Barter
4.   Delayed payment
5.   Reciprocity

17-16 Multiple

The average _____ man uses almost twice as many cosmetic and beauty aids as his wife.

1.   German
2.   Japanese
3.   Canadian
4.   Russian
5.   French

17-17 Multiple

Companies must take into account a variety of factors when deciding upon going international. Which of the following would a company not consider?

1.   Global competitors might attack the company's domestic market
2.   Government regulations may force companies to globalize
3.   The company might want to counter-attack these competitors
4.   The company might want to reduce the risk of depending too much on one country
5.   All of the above are reasons

17-18 Multiple

Not all global markets are equally attractive. Westsun Communications is thinking about expanding its operation to some countries in the Pacific Rim. Which of the following were not important factors in their assessment?

1.   Market growth
2.   Competitive advantage
3.   Cost of doing business
4.   Financing opportunities
5.   Risk level

17-19 Multiple

_____ is the simplest way for a manufacturer to enter international markets.

1.   Licensing
2.   Exporting
3.   Contract manufacturing
4.   Joint ownership
5.   Management contracting

17-20 Multiple

_____ prevents a company from setting up its own operations for a period of time.

1.   Licensing
2.   Exporting
3.   Contract manufacturing
4.   Joint ownership
5.   Management contracting

17-21 Multiple

In an investment, from funds to involvement, the biggest direct involvement of a firm moving into a foreign market is:

1.   Joint ownership
2.   Joint ventures
3.   Direct investment
4.   Exporting
5.   Integrated marketing efforts

17-22 Multiple

The philosophy to "take the product as is and find customers for it" is:

1.   Product invention
2.   Product adaptation
3.   Communication adaptation
4.   Straight product extension
5.   None of the above

17-23 Multiple

If a company decides not to change the product but to adapt their promotion when entering new markets, they are performing:

1.   Product invention
2.   Product adaptation
3.   Communication adaptation
4.   Straight product extension
5.   Integrated marketing strategy

17-24 Multiple

The channel concept for international marketing includes everything except:

1.   Seller's headquarters
2.   Marketing intermediaries
3.   Channels between nations
4.   Channels within nations
5.   Final users or buyers

17-25 Multiple

The international divisions corporate staff includes all the following except:

1.   Marketing
2.   Research
3.   Personnel
4.   Finance
5.   None of the above

17-26 Multiple

The European Community Free Trade zone was founded in:

1.   1947
2.   1957
3.   1967
4.   1977
5.   1987

394

17-27 Multiple

Canada has proven to be quite successful in international markets. What factors were decisive in Canada entering international markets?

1.   The weakening of domestic marketing opportunities
2.   A very strong dollar compared to other currencies
3.   Growing opportunities for their products in other countries
4.   Both 1 and 3
5.   All of the above

17-28 Multiple

The Canadian government has been considering the adoption of safety and emission standards that must be met by all companies wishing to sell automobiles in Canada. Such an action is an example of a (n):

1.   Revenue tariff
2.   Non-tariff barrier
3.   Quota
4.   Embargo
5.   Constrictive tariff

17-29 Multiple

Economic communities usually strive to do which of the following?

1.   Raise tariffs within the community
2.   Expand employment and investment
3.   Reduce prices
4.   Only 1 and 2
5.   Only 2 and 3

17-30 Multiple

Which of the following is not a component of a country's industrial structure?

1.   Product and service requirements
2.   Employment levels
3.   Values and norms
4.   Income levels
5.   Both 1 and 2

True/False Questions

17-1   True/False

Companies who stay at home and play it safe not only lose their chance to enter other markets, but also risk losing their home market.

17-2   True/False

You must be an industry giant to venture into international markets.

17-3   True/False

The global company sees the world as many different markets.

17-4   True/False

A company looking abroad must first understand the international trade system

17-5   True/False

Industrial economies are major importers of manufactured goods and investment funds.

17-6   True/False

As a result of increased unification, European companies will grow bigger and more competitive.

17-7   True/False

Canadian exports to the US have grown faster than imports from the US.

17-8   True/False

Nations do not differ greatly in their politico-legal environments.

17-9   True/False

Industrialization usually creates a new rich class and a large and growing middle class, both demanding more goods.

17-10 True/False

International marketers never find it profitable to do business in an unstable country.

17-11 True/False

Exporting, joint venturing and direct investment are three strategies for entry into foreign markets. Most international trade involves cash transactions.

17-12 True/False

Many local firms must be increasingly aware of the globalization of competition even if they never plan to go overseas themselves.

17-13 True/False

Because of the risks and difficulties of entering international markets, most companies do not act until some situation or event thrusts them into the global arena.

17-14 True/False

Direct exporting involves less investment because the firm does not require an overseas sales force or set of contacts.

17-15 True/False

Coca-Cola markets internationally by contract manufacturing its bottlers around the world and supplying them with the syrup to produce the product.

17-16 True/False

Licensing provides a simple way to enter international markets.

17-17 True/False

Global standardization is an all-or-nothing proposition.

17-18 True/False

Product invention might mean reintroducing earlier product forms that happen to be well adapted to the needs of a given country.

17-19 True/False

The media used by a company also needs to be adapted internationally because its availability varies from country to country.

17-20 True/False

Companies keep the same form of promotion from country to country and do not have to change for the different markets.

Applying Terms and Concepts

To determine how well you understand the materials in this chapter, read each of the following brief cases and respond to the questions that follow. Answers are given at the end of this chapter.

Case #1   Modern-Day Pirates[1]

You're traveling in Southeast Asia and have an opportunity to visit the outdoor market in Chinatown in Kuala Lumpur, Malaysia. Covering many city blocks, the market is a shopper's fantasy with stalls selling everything from Calvin Klein T-shirts and jeans to Ralph Lauren's signature Polo shirts, Coach bags, and Rolex watches. The question is: Would you buy? The problem is that many of these products are counterfeit.

Marketers with big brands, worried more about their loss of image than monetary loss, are battling with international pirates who steal their logos, packages, and sometimes counterfeit their products. In negotiations with the Chinese, the U.S. trade representative held up two boxes of Microsoft Word—one legitimate, one a copy. There was no way to tell the difference, other than the price.

China has been indifferent to its citizens' unauthorized copyright and trademark use of international marketers' software, music, film, apparel, and sporting goods. However, it agreed to enforce its own laws against piracy and undertook a nationwide crackdown in 1995 in order to be awarded the 1996 Olympiad trademark licenses. The Chinese are not the only marketing pirates. The International Intellectual Property Alliance (IIPA) also cites Turkey, Bulgaria, and Indonesia on its list of priority-watch countries.

The IIPA also estimates that Japan and Germany were the leading sources of monetary loss to piracy. The Software Publishers Association (SPA), representing 1,200 business, education, and consumer software marketers, estimates that the Singapore market cost U.S. software marketers $33 million last year, small potatoes compared to markets like German with an estimated $1.1 billion loss and Japan where the SPA estimates U.S. industry losses at $1.3 billion a year, the world's highest rate. And that's only one industry. Germany, as concerned as the United States about the piracy problem, has passed a tough new law called the Brand Law that enables marketers to protect not only their brand logo but also the logo's colors and the product's packaging design.

As piracy has escalated, marketers and industry trade associations worldwide have increased their vigilance in lobbying lawmakers, instigating local police seizures, and even ad campaigns. International marketers, such as Reebok and Levi-Strauss, are fighting their battles with public relations campaigns. Reebok, fighting piracy in China and South Korea, reaches its trade audience with its message about supporting legitimate brands through articles in business and trade publications.

---

[1] *Advertising Principles & Practice*, 4th Edition, Wells, Burnett, Moriarty, pg.672.

The Motion Picture Association is running an ongoing cinema and videocassette trailer campaign in Belgium, Germany, Italy, and the United Kingdom. In Latin America the group has targeted Venezuela, a growing piracy market, for an antipiracy poster campaign. A spokesperson for the association said, "The video trailer in Europe is working very well, with a toll-free hot line [for consumers reporting piracy]."

Washington-based Software Publishers Association this month broke a Singapore antipiracy campaign in both Singapore and Malaysia. The education-and-enforcement campaign is the association's first outside the United States. Previously the association has distributed ads in Spanish for Mexico and Costa Rica, in Portuguese for Brazil, and in Hebrew for Israel.

The bottom line is that piracy hurts brands and consumers of brands. If Ralph Lauren's Polo brand gets copied so much that the original brand is unrecognizable, then why buy Polo? As the marketplace becomes more and more international, the problem only becomes greater. Regardless of where you live, the money you invest in buying a brand is wasted if the brand loses it cachet. How can that message be communicated through advertising and other forms of marketing communication? What message makes that point?

So go back to your imaginary trip through the marketplace in Kuala Lumpur (or walk down a street in New York City). Would you buy that incredibly cheap Rolex watch?

1.   Why would it be difficult for companies to prosecute pirates in a foreign country?

_____

_____

_____

_____

2.   How can companies persuade and motivate consumers to help eliminate piracy?

_____

_____

_____

_____

3. How can companies persuade foreign governments to implement laws against piracy?

_____

_____

_____

_____

4. Why would the Chinese government be indifferent to the piracy that occurs in their country?

_____

_____

_____

_____

5. Germany has passed the Brand Law, but will this be effective to prosecute pirates in other countries?

_____

_____

_____

_____

Case #2   PepsiCo: Swapping Pepsi for Chickens and Tomato Paste[2]

Pepsi-Cola was the first foreign consumer product to be sold in the USSR and it took the firm's chairman David Kendall many years to ensure PepsiCo's long-term presence there. With the fall of the Berlin Wall, many firms expected large financial returns on relatively little investment in market extension activities. These companies ignore the lesson PepsiCo had learned "the hard way." Democracy has a difficult job moving East Europeans toward Western-style capitalism and consumption.

Just as the sociocultural environment made it difficult to enter the new markets, so did its lack of technology. East European factories are antiquated; they are not competitive. But, they are the major source of employment. In addition the political environment did not welcome foreign marketers. It is now obvious that many of the predictions about Eastern European economic growth were overly optimistic for most companies. PepsiCo, however, having learned its lessons from its dealings with the Soviet Union has been able to make substantial inroads into the new markets.

---

1.   It took more than a decade for PepsiCo to execute its plan to enter the Soviet market. Discuss some possible ways in which PepsiCo managers may have (1) assured goal-directed actions, (2) assigned resources, and (3) built interpersonal relationships and informal networks.

_____

_____

_____

_____

2.   What unanticipated environmental changes are more likely to affect marketers doing business in the Soviet Union and Eastern Europe than Western marketers who confine themselves to domestic marketers? What are the implications for marketers?

_____

_____

_____

_____

3.   How successful do you think PepsiCo's counter-trade strategy has been?

_____

_____

_____

_____

4.   Many Western marketers initially assumed that Eastern European consumers would be essentially equivalent to Western European consumers once they were allowed to access a free market. How may Eastern Europeans differ from their Western cousins?

_____

_____

_____

5.   How could a company successfully enter the Eastern European market?

_____

_____

_____

_____

Case #4   Hard Decisions for Nike

Nike has had to face marketing decisions both domestically and abroad that have resulted in their huge success as a company with a broad product line and depth. If we look at this international company there are issues and discussions that you should understand and be able to argue intelligently as would-be marketers. If one has a base knowledge of the company, its size, and brand name/loyalty it is easy to consider the following questions.

1.   How would Nike choose to adapt or standardize a marketing mix?

_____

_____

_____

_____

2.   What are three adaptation strategies that were and still are available to Nike?

_____

_____

_____

_____

3.   What are the problems faced by Nike when establishing foreign pricing?

_____

_____

_____

_____

Multiple Choice Answers

1.   Correct Answer: 4   Reference: pg. 703

2.   Correct Answer: 2   Reference: pg. 705

3.   Correct Answer: 5   Reference: pg. 706

4.   Correct Answer: 1   Reference: pg. 708

5.   Correct Answer: 2   Reference: pg. 708

6.   Correct Answer: 3   Reference: pg. 709

7.   Correct Answer: 4   Reference: pg. 709

8.   Correct Answer: 5   Reference: pg. 710

9.   Correct Answer: 3   Reference: pg. 710

10. Correct Answer: 2   Reference: pg. 710

11. Correct Answer: 5   Reference: pg. 710

12. Correct Answer: 3   Reference: pg. 712

13. Correct Answer: 2   Reference: pg. 712

14. Correct Answer: 4   Reference: pg. 713

15. Correct Answer: 1   Reference: pg. 715

16. Correct Answer: 5   Reference: pg. 716

17. Correct Answer: 2   Reference: pg. 717

18. Correct Answer: 4   Reference: pg. 718

19. Correct Answer: 1   Reference: pg. 722

20. Correct Answer: 5   Reference: pg. 723

21. Correct Answer: 3   Reference: pg. 724

22. Correct Answer: 4   Reference: pg. 727

23.	Correct Answer:	3	Reference:	pg. 729
24.	Correct Answer:	2	Reference:	pg. 732
25.	Correct Answer:	5	Reference:	pg. 732
26.	Correct Answer:	2	Reference:	pg.733
27.	Correct Answer:	4	Reference:	pg. 703
28.	Correct Answer:	2	Reference:	pg.708
29.	Correct Answer:	5	Reference:	pg. 709
30.	Correct Answer:	3	Reference:	pg. 721

True/False Answers

1.	TRUE	Reference:	pg. 703	Topic: Global Marketing into the Twenty-First Century
2.	FALSE	Reference:	pg. 703	Topic: Global Marketing into the Twenty-First Century
3.	FALSE	Reference:	pg. 704	Topic: Global Marketing into the Twenty-First Century
4.	TRUE	Reference:	pg. 704	Topic: Looking at the Global Marketing Environment.
5.	FALSE	Reference:	pg. 706	Topic: The International Trade System
6.	TRUE	Reference:	pg. 709	Topic: Regional Free Trade Zones
7.	TRUE	Reference:	pg. 709	Topic: Regional Free Trade Zones
8.	FALSE	Reference:	pg. 713	Topic: Politico-Legal and Ethical
9.	FALSE	Reference:	pg. 712	Topic: Economic Environment
10.	FALSE	Reference:	pg. 713	Topic: Political-Legal and Ethical Environment

11.	TRUE	Reference:	pg. 713	Topic: Political-Legal and Ethical Environment
12.	TRUE	Reference:	pg. 717	Topic: Deciding Whether to Go International
13.	TRUE	Reference:	pg. 717	Topic: Deciding Whether to Go International
14.	FALSE	Reference:	pg. 722	Topic: Exporting
15.	FALSE	Reference:	pg. 722	Topic: Licensing
16.	TRUE	Reference:	pg. 724	Topic: Direct Investment
17.	FALSE	Reference:	pg. 724	Topic: Deciding on the Global Marketing Program
18.	TRUE	Reference:	pg. 727	Topic: Product
19.	TRUE	Reference:	pg. 728	Topic: Promotion
20.	FALSE	Reference:	pg. 724	Topic: Deciding on the Global Marketing Organization

Applying Terms and Concepts Answers

Case #1   Modern-Day Pirates

Question #1
- Companies may have a hard time prosecuting pirates due to foreign governments, who may not realize the severity of the problem. In addition, foreign governments may not have sufficient or adequate laws to properly reprimand the pirates.
- Furthermore, other countries may have different standards and perceptions regarding piracy.

Question #2
- 1-800 telephone numbers that are open 24 hours a day would facilitate the process for consumers.
- In addition, offering incentives such as large sums of money would motivate the ordinary, average Joe.
- Companies could also try to appeal to society's moral side, and try to educate the public with ads and publicity spots on television.
- The key is to educate foreign populations where the piracy occurs.

Question #3

- Companies have to appeal to the foreign governments' morals. Is piracy fair?
- How would they feel if their country were being cheated out of billions of dollars?
- US/German/and Japanese governments could also help foreign governments create anti-piracy laws.
- The key to upholding the law is to have strict enforcement and a severe penalty.

Question #4

- It could be that the Chinese government is pre-occupied with Asian gangs and they are too busy to deal with small annoyances like piracy.
- However, it is more realistic that the Chinese government realizes that their country is profiting in millions and billions from piracy and unauthorized rip-offs.
- If you were the Chinese government, what would be a priority—satisfying the demands of already prosperous companies, or grabbing a few bucks for your people?

Question #5

- The German law could have minimal impact on foreign pirates.
- Can the Germans even prosecute pirates in another country?
- What are the penalties for violating these laws?
- Can the German companies and the German government really make an impact with their local policies when pirates in Venezuela, Turkey, China, Indonesia, and so forth are copying merchandise like rabbits? I think not.

Case #2   PepsiCo: Swapping Pepsi for Chickens and Tomato Paste

Question #1

Managers should ensure goal-directed actions by:

(1) making sure that those involved understand that the ultimate goal is beating Coke into the Soviet and Soviet-satellite markets rather than short-term sales figures and

(2) making sure managers are rewarded for advancing relations with Soviets and not penalized for being in a group that does not bring in sales for many years.

They should assign resources to make sure that those involved:

(1) have the resources to pay for the time of translators, lawyers, and consultants on Soviet culture and politics, and

(2) have the equipment and money for taking it to the USSR for demonstrations.

They should make sure that those involved are willing to and are interested in developing relationships with their Soviet counterpart and with all the many people in the home office who will need to be involved.

Question #2

Some environmental changes that affect marketers include

(1) basic political instability and uncertainty,

(2) sudden changes in regime that have a more profound effect than political changes in

the West,

(3) sudden changes in the currency, and

(4) the possibilities of civil unrest. The implications for marketers are that they should:
  a. construct crisis control plans in anticipation of such event
  b. assess the balance of such risks against the possible gains in assets
  c. make sure that business in other parts of the world will offset the possible loss of business in the areas.

Question #3

PepsiCo's counter-trade strategy has been very successful. It has allowed PepsiCo to

(1) establish strong market positions in countries where it would have been impossible to do business otherwise,

(2) obtain a steady supply of products that it needs in its other businesses—tomato paste, chickens, etc.—at prices that are lower than in the West,

(3) work out long-term relationships that create goodwill with foreign governments because it helps them to gain credibility for their own products overseas, and

(4) establish relationships that are deeper than simple cash-purchase relationships—it would be hard, for instance, for Hungarians to find another such large purchaser for its tomato paste (which provide agricultural and industrial jobs) whereas it might be fairly easy to find another Western marketer who could offer the equivalent amount of cash.

Question #4

- Although many Eastern Europeans crave Western products, their attitudes toward products and marketing may be very different because they were cut off from the West before the great boom of the post-war marketing era.
- First, it may take many years if not decades before they are equally affluent.
- Second, it seems that many do not want to abandon socialist ideas entirely—they may turn out to be just as materialistic but many need different advertising and promoting campaigns.
- Also, many people in Eastern Europe are not "European" in the cultural sense, but rather come from Eurasian, Turkish, or other traditions.

Question #5

- Research and investigate whether there is a need or demand for a product
- Ensure that the marketing and packaging meet local tastes and standards
- Be familiar with local culture

Investigate the economic and political environment. Is it feasible to expand into this country?

Case # 4 Nike

Question #1

World brands sold the same way to different countries
Expected quality to be similar
Prices to be similar

Question #2

　　　　Straight product extension
　　　　Product adaptation
　　　　Product invention

Question #3

　　　　Keep pricing the same world wide
　　　　Foreign governments may insist on plants in their country
　　　　Value of the currency and its volatility
　　　　May be seen as *dumping* product to get an unfair advantage

Chapter 18

Marketing and Society: Social Responsibility And Marketing Ethics

Chapter Overview

Responsible marketers discover what consumers want and respond with the right products, priced to give good value to buyers and profit to the producer. A marketing system should sense, serve, and satisfy consumer needs and improve the quality of consumers' lives. Marketers must now more than ever deal with the pressures placed on them from consumers, legislation and how their products do or do not affect the environment. No longer can marketers work in isolation from society, but now more than ever they are part of everyday society and the way their product reacts within society. In working to meet consumer needs, marketers may take some actions that are not to everyone's liking or benefit. From the plants that produce the finished product to the components that make up the finished product marketers are responsible not only to the consumers who use their goods but society as well, and the criticisms, and their responsibilities.

Chapter Objectives

1. Identify the major social criticisms of marketing.
2. Define consumerism and environmentalism and explain how they affect marketing strategies.
3. Describe the principles of socially responsible marketing.
4. Explain the role of ethics in marketing.

Chapter Topics

Social Criticisms of Marketing
- Marketing's Impact on Individual Consumers
  - High Prices
    - High Costs of Distribution
    - High Advertising and Promotion Costs
    - Excessive Markups
  - Deceptive Practices
  - High Pressure Selling
  - Shoddy or Unsafe Products
  - Planned Obsolescence
  - Poor Service to Disadvantaged Consumers
- Marketing's Impact on Society as a Whole
  - False Wants and Too Much Materialism
  - Too Few Social Goods
  - Cultural Pollution
  - Too Much Political Power
- Marketing's Impact on Other Businesses

Citizen and Public Actions to Regulate Marketing
- Consumerism
- Environmentalism
- Public Actions to Regulate Marketing

Business Actions Toward Socially Responsible Marketing
- Enlightened Marketing
  - Consumer-Oriented Marketing
  - Innovative Marketing
  - Value Marketing
  - Sense-of-Mission Marketing
  - Societal Marketing
- Marketing Ethics

Chapter Summary

1.   The social criticisms of marketing's impact on individuals.

Criticisms of marketing include the impact on individual consumers of high prices, high advertising, promotion, and distribution costs, excessive mark-ups, deceptive practices, high pressure selling, unsafe products, planned obsolescence and poor service to disadvantaged consumers. Where is the consumer in all of this and what are the responsibilities of the marketer?

2.   The social criticisms of marketing's impact on society as a whole.

Marketing is accused of fostering several societal "evils" including false wants and too much materialism, too few social goods, cultural pollution and too much political power.

3.   Defining consumerism and environmentalism and explaining how they affect marketing strategies.

Consumerism is an organized movement of citizens and government agencies to improve the rights and powers of buyers in relation to sellers. Environmentalism is an organized movement of concerned citizens and government agencies to protect and improve people's living environment. Marketing strategies often seek to position the company as more consumer-oriented and/or environmentally responsible (green marketing).

4.   The principles of socially responsible marketing.

Socially responsible or enlightened marketing consists of five principles. Consumer-oriented marketing organizes marketing activities from the consumer's viewpoint. Innovative marketing seeks continuous real product and marketing improvements. Value marketing puts resources into value-building marketing investments. Sense-of-marketing defines the company mission in broad social terms. Societal marketing blends social, company and consumer needs.

5.   The role of ethics in marketing.

Enlightened companies realize that marketing ethics are an important component of a long-term consumer orientation. Responsibilities fall on the market be they ethical or legislation introduced by government for the protection of society and the environment. Ethics is an integral part of the corporate culture and should not be pushed aside to a junior employee but should have the full and active participation of upper management for a company to succeed.

Key Terms

Consumerism	(pg. 764)	Innovative marketing	(pg. 763)
Consumer-oriented marketing	(pg. 762)	Pleasing products	(pg. 767)
Deficient products	(pg. 766)	Salutary products	(pg. 767)
Desirable products	(pg. 767)	Sense-of-mission marketing	(pg. 764)
Enlightened marketing	(pg. 762)	Societal marketing	(pg. 766)
Environmentalism	(pg. 756)	Value marketing	(pg. 763)

Multiple Choice Questions

18-1   Multiple

Many critics charge the marketing system causes prices to be higher than they would be under more "sensible" systems. All the following factors are attributed to this fact except:

1.   High costs of distribution
2.   High advertising and promotion costs
3.   High levels of competition
4.   Excessive markups
5.   All of the above

18-2   Multiple

Companies are defending themselves against allegations they are raising their prices to make more of a profit. Which of the following would not be considered a good statement of defense?

1.   Intermediaries do the work that would otherwise be done by manufacturers or consumers
2.   Markups reflect services that consumers themselves want
3.   Costs of operating stores keep rising, forcing retailers to raise their prices
4.   Retail competition is so intense margins are actually quite low
5.   None of the above

18-3   Multiple

Companies must also defend themselves against critics who insist companies are spending too much on advertising and promotion, which is increasing the price of goods unnecessarily. From the following list, choose the one option that does not explain why companies have such large advertising budgets.

1.   Heavy advertising is needed to establish companies as Fortune 500 companies
2.   Heavy advertising is needed to make consumers feel wealthy, beautiful, or special, which is what they want
3.   Heavy advertising is necessary to create branding, which gives buyers confidence
4.   Heavy advertising is needed to inform millions of potential buyers of the merits of a brand
5.   Heavy advertising and promotion may be necessary for a firm to match a competitor's efforts

18-4   Multiple

Deceptive practices fall into all the following groups except:

1.   Deceptive pricing
2.   Deceptive placing
3.   Deceptive promotion
4.   Deceptive packaging
5.   All of the above are deceptive

18-5   Multiple

Consumers have many complaints regarding products and they are not shy about voicing these to company agencies. Which of the following is not a common complaint?
1.   Many products deliver little benefit
2.   Many products are not safe to use
3.   Many products are too expensive
4.   All of the above are common complaints

18-6   Multiple

Disadvantaged neighbourhoods face discrimination in many ways including large companies refusing to set up shop in certain areas. This form of economic discrimination is referred to as:_____ Streamlining
1.   Embargoing
2.   Redlining
3.   Price-lining
4.   Location-lining

18-7   Multiple

Marya is doing a paper on factors influencing people's wants and needs. She knows marketers do not have the ultimate influence. Which of the following does not have an influence on people's wants and needs?

1.   Peer groups
2.   Income
3.   Religion
4.   Ethnic background
5.   Education

18-8   Multiple

"Cultural pollution is becoming more of a problem," claim many critics of marketing systems. Cultural pollution continuously pollutes people's minds with messages about everything except:

1.   Materialism
2.   Sex
3.   Power
4.   Status
5.   All of the above messages lead to pollution

18-9   Multiple

Critics charge a company's marketing practices can harm other companies and reduce competition. What is one factor that does not contribute to this allegation?

1.   Acquisition of competitors
2.   Marketing practices that create barriers to entry
3.   Only large companies can afford to compete
4.   Unfair competitive marketing practices
5.   All of the above are problems

18-10 Multiple

Government continues to play an ever-increasing role in consumerism and marketing and their dependency on one another. Consumers are now entitled to a number of rights. All the following are rights with the exception of _____.
1.   The right to be informed
2.   The right to be heard
3.   The right to everyday low prices
4.   The right to consumer education

18-11 Multiple

Which of the following is not included in the fundamental right to be informed?

1.   The true intention of advertising
2.   The true interest on a loan
3.   The true cost per unit of a brand
4.   The ingredients in a product
5.   The true benefits of a product

18-12 Multiple

The marketing system's goal should not be to maximize consumption, consumer choice or consumer satisfaction, but rather to maximize:

1.   Consumer quality
2.   Service quality
3.   Societal quality
4.   Product quality
5.   Life quality

18-13 Multiple

_____ minimizes not only pollution from production, but also all environmental impacts throughout the full product life cycle.

1.   Environmental sustainability
2.   Product stewardship
3.   Environmental technologies
4.   Sustainability vision
5.   Sustainable development

18-14 Multiple

Many new regional agreements such as NAFTA and the EC have posed complex environmental problems for many countries. Environmental policies vary widely from country to country and uniform worldwide standards are not expected for another _____ years or more.

1.   5
2.   10
3.   15
4.   20
5.   25

18-15 Multiple

Legal issues facing marketing managers include everything except:

1.   Selling decisions
2.   Packaging decisions
3.   Competitive relations decisions
4.   Financing decisions
5.   Product decisions

18-16 Multiple

Customer-oriented marketing means the company should view and organize its marketing activities from the consumer's point of view. This is the one thing a company does not have to do for the needs of a defined group of customers.

1.   Solidify
2.   Sense
3.   Serve
4.   Satisfy
5.   The must do all of the above

18-17 Multiple

Value marketing is a basic in marketing and is based on value building. Which of the following is not considered to be a value-adding strategy?

1.   Lowering costs and prices
2.   Advertising effectively
3.   Improving product quality
4.   Making services more convenient
5.   None of the above

18-18 Multiple

A product, which possesses high immediate satisfaction but low long-run consumer benefits, is a _____ in the societal classification of products scale.

1.   Salutary product
2.   Desirable product
3.   Impulse product
4.   Deficient product
5.   Pleasing product

18-19 Multiple

Under the _____, companies and mangers must look beyond what is legal and allowed and develop standards based on personal integrity, corporate conscience, and long-run consumer welfare.

1.   Marketing ethics standard
2.   Integrated marketing concept
3.   Social marketing concept
4.   Environmentalism concept
5.   Consumerism concept

18-20 Multiple

The principles for public policy toward marketing reflect certain assumptions that underlie much of modern marketing theory and practice. Which of the following is not one of these principles?

1.   The principle of consumer and producer freedom
2.   The principle of curbing potential harm
3.   The principle of economic efficiency
4.   The principle of innovation
5.   All of the above are principles

18-21 Multiple

When marketers answer charges that they generate undesired "commercial noise" by pointing out that ads help reduce the cost of magazines and newspapers, it is responding to which of the following criticisms?

1.   Marketing emphasizes too much materialism
2.   Marketing spreads cultural pollution
3.   Marketing creates too few social goods
4.   Marketing exercises too much political power
5.   All of the above

18-22   Multiple

When large companies use patents and heavy promotion spending to prevent new competitors entering their markets, then marketing is sometimes criticized for its:

1.   Impact on other businesses
2.   Impact on the economy
3.   Impact on the individual
4.   Impact on society as a whole
5.   Impact on fair marketing practices

18-23   Multiple

All the following relate to proposals on consumer protection except:

1.   Strengthening consumer rights in cases of business fraud
2.   Reducing the level of advertising noise
3.   Requiring greater product safety
4.   Giving more power to government agencies
5.   None of the above

18-24   Multiple

From a societal marketing perspective, dental floss is a:

1.   Desirable product
2.   Pleasing product
3.   Deficient product
4.   Salutary product
5.   None of the above

18-25   Multiple

From a societal marketing perspective, a candy bar is a:

1.   Desirable product
2.   Pleasing product
3.   Deficient product
4.   Salutary product
5.   All of the above

18-26   Multiple

From a societal marketing perspective, bad-tasting mouthwash that doesn't work is a:

1.   Desirable product
2.   Pleasing product
3.   Deficient product
4.   Salutary product
5.   Rejected product

18-27   Multiple

In order to be truly effective, ethics and societal responsibility in business:

1.   Must be a component of the overall corporate culture
2.   Must be written into codes
3.   Should be left to the individual's sense of right and wrong
4.   Should be determined on a case-by-case basis
5.   Only 1 and 2

18-28   Multiple

Corporate marketing ethics policies are broad guidelines everyone in the organization must follow. These policies should cover everything except:

1.   Distributor relations
2.   Advertising standards
3.   Product development
4.   Supplier contracts
5.   All of the above are covered

18-29   Multiple

Environmental sustainability means developing strategies that both _____ the environment and produce _____ for the company.

1.   protect, customers
2.   protect, profits
3.   sustain, customers
4.   sustain, benefits
5.   sustain, profits

18-30 Multiple

Differentiated products like cosmetics, detergents, toiletries, include promotion and packaging costs that can amount to _____ % or more of the manufacturer's price to the retailer.

1. 30
2. 40
3. 50
4. 60
5. 70

True/False Questions

18-1 True/False

Surveys usually show consumers hold mixed or even slightly unfavourable attitudes toward marketing practices.

18-2 True/False

Consumers usually can buy functional versions of products at lower prices but often are willing to pay more for products providing desired psychological benefits.

18-3 True/False

Deceptive practices have led to legislation and other consumer protection actions, but not to industry self-regulation standards.

18-4 True/False

Critics say that marketing causes prices to be higher than so called "sensible systems" of marketing.

18-5 True/False

Deceptive practices do not fall into the categories of: pricing, promotion and packaging.

18-6 True/False

Marketing is seen as creating false wants that benefit industry more than they benefit consumers.

18-7   True/False

Marketers are most effective when they create new wants rather than appealing to existing ones.

18-8   True/False

Advertisers are accused of holding too much power over the mass media, limiting their freedom to report independently and objectively.

18-9   True/False

The two major movements in citizen and public action groups have been commercialism and environmentalism.

18-10   True/False

Urban residents often have to shop in poorer stores with inferior goods.

18-11   True/False

Pollution control means eliminating or minimizing waste before it is created.

18-12   True/False

Design for environment (DFE) practices not only help to sustain the environment, but they can also be highly profitable.

18-13   True/False

Most companies today invest heavily in pollution prevention.

18-14   True/False

Ethical questions are not a concern of marketers as their goal is to increase sales and not become restricted by legislation or consumer rights groups.

18-15   True/False

Alert companies view societal problems as threats.

18-16   True/False

The challenge posed by pleasing products is they sell very well, but may end up hurting the consumer.

18-17 True/False

Managers need a set of principles to help them determine the moral importance of each situation and decide how far they can go in good conscience.

18-18 True/False

While it is both illegal and unethical for a Canadian firm to bribe a Canadian government official, Canada currently does not have a law preventing firms from paying bribes when they operate overseas.

18-19 True/False

Canada does not offer a three-day 'cooling off period' to its citizens as many other countries do, and citizens must therefore live with the contracts they sign from high-pressure salespeople.

18-20 True/False

The seven principles for public policy toward marketing are based on the assumption that marketing's job is to maximize company profits and total consumption and consumer choice, not to maximize life quality.

Applying Terms and Concepts

Case#1   Biodegradable Diapers[1]

Some marketers have been criticized for being so concerned about their own interests they ignore all others. High prices, deceptive practices, high-pressure selling and poor service to disadvantaged customers are some of the practices critics bring up when charging that some firms are socially irresponsible. But now several firms have developed what appears to be the correct product for our times—biodegradable disposable diapers.

Over a half million babies are born each year in Canada. They are part of the "baby boom echo"—children of the postwar baby boomers. A baby in the house means bottles, baby food, and lots and lots of diapers. The average baby goes through between 8,000 and 10,000 diapers between birth and toilet training. For the country, that means 1.8 billion used diapers a year, which converts to a half million tonnes of waste filling up landfills and taking 2 to 500 years to dissolve. Concern about the impact of all these diapers has led to a different kind of boom—biodegradable diapers.

Biodegradable diapers are made with advanced plastics, most involving the binding of cornstarch polymers—molecules made up of repeating, identical subunits—with plastic

---

[1] *Principles of Marketing*, 3rd Edition, Kotler, Armstrong, Warren (Prentice Hall) – pg. 442.

molecules. The newly formed plastic is supposed to be readily broken down in the soil by a variety of microorganisms, such as fungi and bacteria that feed on the starch. As the cornstarch is eaten, the plastic's polymeric chains are broken down into smaller and smaller units, leaving behind only a plastic dust.

The condition of the nation's landfills has also contributed to the growth in the demand for biodegradable diapers. Many municipalities are finding their existing landfills must soon be closed because they do not meet federal guidelines for pollution control. Permits to construct new landfills are difficult to obtain and modern environmentally sound landfills are extremely expensive to build, maintain and monitor.

So far, most of the new diapers have been sold to well-educated parents who are willing to help the environment by paying an extra 5 to10 percent for a disposable diaper that actually does dispose of itself. Even though the industry is still in its infancy, brands such as Rocky Mountain, Tender Cares, DoveTails, Nappies, and Bunnies are starting to challenge major brands for supermarket shelf space.

But recently, some people have begun to question just how much disposable biodegradable diapers will do to alleviate the landfill problem. One researcher found the average landfill contains 36 percent paper, 20 percent yard wastes, 9 percent metal, 9 percent food, 8 percent glass, 7 percent plastic, and 11 percent other materials. And these proportions of materials do not change appreciably over time. Research also indicates once material is placed in a landfill, it remains virtually unchanged. Decades after it was buried, paper, metal, glass, and plastic remain. Even yard waste and food do not easily decay. It seems that in order for biodegradation to take place, water, oxygen, and sunlight must be present so that the microorganisms can break down the materials. Unfortunately, these conditions are not typically present in modern landfills. Also, the problem with landfills is not so much the type of material placed in them as the volume of that material. Some researchers suggest that the benefits of biodegradable plastics are illusory and that the solution to our waste problem is a combination of recycling, incineration, composition, and landfills.

1.   What is the philosophy of society marketing?

   _____

   _____

   _____

   _____

2. Explain why firms that make biodegradable disposable diapers could be said to be following a philosophy of society marketing.

_____

_____

_____

_____

3. What impact, if any will biodegradable disposable diapers have on landfills?

_____

_____

_____

_____

4. How are environmentalists likely to view biodegradable disposable diapers?

_____

_____

_____

5. Discuss any feasible alternatives to disposable diapers.

_____

_____

_____

_____

Case #2 Brown's Department Stores

Helen Mahon is the vice-president of security for Halifax-based Brown's Department Stores. She has become increasingly alarmed at the high rate of shoplifting and employee theft within Brown's store system. The current rate of loss is estimated at $2,600,000 per year.

Mahon is particularly upset because she realizes that everyone is hurt by the losses. Shoplifters, when caught, are prosecuted. Customers must pay higher prices to cover the loss, and cost of the security systems, and store managers are faced with an unpleasant, time-consuming activity that reduces the profitability of the organization.

Mahon was recently approached by Todd Roy Hill, the president of Hill Communications, Inc., with a proposal that has left her in a quandary. Hill Communications produces cassette tapes that contain subliminal messages designed to alter the behaviour of listeners. The listener hears music or "pink" noise such as ocean waves or rushing wind, while the subconscious hears the message (in this situation) "Do not shoplift." Hill explained that the message (any message) is recorded at about 5 decibels below the audible range. In time, the message embeds itself in the listener's mind, thereby affecting behaviour.

Hill produced evidence (studies he had conducted) indicating that losses were reduced by an average of 39 percent in similar settings. With a projected loss reduction of over $1,000,000, Mahon was interested, but she was uneasy because she wondered if it was right to manipulate people in this fashion. She also asked herself: "If subliminal messages can be used to reduce shoplifting, why not use it to stimulate sales at Brown's Stores?"

That evening Mahon came across an article in the magazine *Psychology In Action* by McGill University psychology professor Rene Alphonse, a specialist in the study of perception, who maintained that subliminal messages do not alter behaviour. Alphonse also went on to state that studies conducted to prove that they do were often flawed and unscientific.

The cost of the system proposed by Hill Communications is essentially what Brown now pays for background music in its stores. Hill has documentation from the provincial government that the practice is perfectly legal in Nova Scotia. He also stated that Brown's would be the first chain of department stores to use the service.

1. What would Mahon decide if she believed that issues of morality, ethics, responsibility and conscience should be made according to the free market or legal system?

   _____

   _____

   _____

   _____

2. What would Mahon decide if she believed that issues of morality, ethics, responsibility and conscience should be made according to managers' "social conscience?"

   _____

   _____

   _____

   _____

Case #3 Palmer Industries

Carl Palmer, President of Palmer Industries, recently startled the beverage industry with the introduction of a self-cooling can. The technology, pioneered by Palmer, allows a slightly modified can to cool itself within 20 seconds of opening. Cooling is accomplished by a carbon dioxide cartridge encased in an aluminum sheath surrounding the beverage container. When the container is opened, the carbon dioxide cartridge is pierced. As the carbon dioxide escapes from the cartridge, it freezes the outer sheath, thereby cooling the beverage. Variations in temperature can be achieved by increasing or decreasing the volume of carbon dioxide in the cartridge. Beer will chill to 3 degrees and soft drinks to 5 degrees, the ideal temperature.

The self-cooling can will have the same outer dimensions as a standard can. However, there will be approximately a 75 mL liquid displacement to accommodate the cooling mechanism. The outer sheath will be bonded to the top and bottom of the can with the inner container wall 2 mm from the outer wall. The carbon dioxide will escape through the aperture created when the can is opened. The self-cooling can will cost approximately $.05 more per unit than a conventional can.

The technology is protected by 16 Canadian and US patents, foreign patents pending. Palmer Industries will license manufacturers to produce the containers and sell them to various bottling companies. Bay Street responded enthusiastically; with Palmer Industries posting a 12% gain. An additional 6% was posted when the Consumer and Corporate and Agriculture Canada approved the technology as safe for sale.

Palmer plans to start with the beverage industry, but sees this technology applied to any packaged food consumers prefer chilled prior to consumption, including canned fruits, vegetables, desserts and meats. To date, the only group to express doubt about the new technology is the manufacturers of refrigerated soft drink vending machines, who will find demand for their machines declining as the self-cooling cans gain widespread distribution.

_____1. Critics may charge that development of a self-cooling can to replace regular cans is an example of _____.
    A.   unfair competition
    B.   planned obsolescence
    C.   deceptive packaging
    D.   high pressure selling
    E.   price gouging

_____2. Palmer Industries has utilized patent protection as a(n):
  A.   barrier to entry.
  B.   unfair competition.
  C.   unfair political protection.
  D.   high pressure selling.
  E.   planned obsolescence.

_____3. Consumers may view Palmer Industries as practicing _____ marketing.
  A.   antisocial
  B.   enlightened
  C.   production oriented
  D.   sales oriented
  E.   product oriented

_____4. If in a promotional campaign, Palmer Industries advertised the self-cooling would chill soft drinks to 5 degrees when it would only chill them to 14 degrees, Palmer would be engaged in _____.
  A.   high pressure selling
  B.   puffery
  C.   deceptive advertising
  D.   creating false wants
  E.   deceptive pricing

_____5. The self-cooling can is best classified as a _____ product.
  A.   deficient
  B.   decadent
  C.   desirable
  D.   pleasing
  E.   salutary

Case #4   Ancaster Aluminum

As an old company in downtown Vancouver Ancaster has been getting away with the same production facilities for the past fifty years. Their business is aluminum siding and they make and sell their product to consumers in the surrounding area. Through the years they have been written about in local newspapers as producing shoddy workmanship, producing an inferior product and using unethical salespeople to force their product on consumers. They continue to turn a profit but their days are numbered as government legislation makes it more difficult to get away with their old practices. In the early 1990's they were even fined for disposing of byproducts into the Vancouver sewer system. Their revenues have been generated from two sources: one from sale of the product and two from repair work to their own product.

Question #1 –What is the biggest threat facing this company?

_____

_____

_____

_____

Question #2 –What is its owner's social responsibility?

_____

_____

_____

_____

Question #3—How is planned obsolescence used as a revenue tool?

_____

_____

_____

_____

Multiple Choice Answers

1.	Correct Answer:	3	Reference:	pg. 746
2.	Correct Answer:	5	Reference:	pg. 746
3.	Correct Answer:	1	Reference:	pg. 746
4.	Correct Answer:	2	Reference:	pg. 747
5.	Correct Answer:	4	Reference:	pg. 748
6.	Correct Answer:	3	Reference:	pg. 750
7.	Correct Answer:	2	Reference:	pg. 751
8.	Correct Answer:	5	Reference:	pg. 753
9.	Correct Answer:	3	Reference:	pg. 753
10.	Correct Answer:	4	Reference:	pg. 754
11.	Correct Answer:	1	Reference:	pg. 755
12.	Correct Answer:	5	Reference:	pg. 756
13.	Correct Answer:	2	Reference:	pg. 758
14.	Correct Answer:	3	Reference:	pg. 760
15.	Correct Answer:	4	Reference:	pg. 762
16.	Correct Answer:	1	Reference:	pg. 762
17.	Correct Answer:	2	Reference:	pg. 763
18.	Correct Answer:	5	Reference:	pg. 768
19.	Correct Answer:	3	Reference:	pg. 768
20.	Correct Answer:	5	Reference:	pg. 769
21.	Correct Answer:	2	Reference:	pg. 753
22.	Correct Answer:	1	Reference:	pg. 754

23.	Correct Answer:	2	Reference:	pg. 755
24.	Correct Answer:	4	Reference:	pg. 767
25.	Correct Answer:	2	Reference:	pg. 766
26.	Correct Answer:	3	Reference:	pg. 767
27.	Correct Answer:	1	Reference:	pg. 766
28.	Correct Answer:	4	Reference:	pg. 768
29.	Correct Answer:	5	Reference:	pg. 759
30.	Correct Answer:	2	Reference:	pg. 747

True/False Answers

1.	TRUE	Reference:	pg. 746	Topic: Marketing's Impact on Individual Consumers
2.	TRUE	Reference:	pg. 746	Topic: Marketing's Impact on Individual Consumers
3.	FALSE	Reference:	pg. 747	Topic: Deceptive Practices
4.	TRUE	Reference:	pg. 746	Topic: High Prices
5.	FALSE	Reference:	pg. 747	Topic: Deceptive Practices
6.	FALSE	Reference:	pg. 751	Topic: False Wants and Too Much Materialism
7.	FALSE	Reference:	pg. 752	Topic: False Wants and Too Much Materialism
8.	TRUE	Reference:	pg. 753	Topic: Too Much Political Power
9.	FALSE	Reference:	pg. 754	Topic: Citizen and Public Action to Regulate Marketing
10.	FALSE	Reference:	pg. 750	Topic: Poor Service
11.	FALSE	Reference:	pg. 756	Topic: Environmentalism

12.	TRUE	Reference:	pg. 756	Topic: Environmentalism
13.	TRUE	Reference:	pg. 756	Topic: Environmentalism
14.	FALSE	Reference:	pg. 768	Topic: Marketing Ethics
15.	FALSE	Reference:	pg. 766	Topic: Societal Marketing
16.	TRUE	Reference:	pg. 766	Topic: Societal Marketing
17.	TRUE	Reference:	pg. 768	Topic: Marketing Ethics
18.	TRUE	Reference:	pg. 769	Topic: Marketing Ethics
19.	FALSE	Reference:	pg. 748	Topic: High Pressure Selling
20.	FALSE	Reference:	pg. 771	Topic: Principles for Public Policy Toward Marketing

Applying Terms and Concept Answers

Case#1   Biodegradable Diapers

Question #1
- An enlightened company following the principle of societal marketing makes marketing decisions by considering consumers' wants, the company's requirements, consumers' long-run interests, and society's long-run interests.
- The company is aware that neglecting the last two factors is a disservice to consumers and to society.
- Alert companies view societal problems as opportunities.
- A socially oriented marketer wants to design products that are not only pleasing but also beneficial.
- Therefore products can be classified according to their degree of immediate consumer satisfaction and long-run consumer benefit.
- Desirable products give both high immediate satisfaction and long-run benefits.

Question #2
- Biodegradable disposable diapers could be seen as a product that meets both of these criteria.
- Disposable diaper producers were responding to the consumers' environmental interests.
- The disposables are still completely functional and more beneficial to the environment.

- In addition, parents and consumers feel at ease knowing that the diaper won't be around in 100 years.

Question #3
- The impact will likely be negligible. In order for a substance to biodegrade, sunlight, water, and oxygen must be present, and these elements are typically absent in modern landfills.
- Researchers like Dr. William Rathje, an anthropologist at the University of Arizona, have found that most material put into a landfill does not decay.
- Decades after they were buried, paper, metal, glass and plastic remain. Even yard waste and food do not easily decay.
- This is because biodegradation is accomplished by microorganisms that need sunlight, moisture, and oxygen to do the job.
- The problem with landfills is not so much the type of material placed in them as the volume of that material.
- Some researchers suggest that the benefits of biodegradable plastics are illusory and that our waste problem will only be solved by a combination of recycling, incineration, composting, and landfills.

Question #4
- While consumer advocates look at whether the marketing system is efficiently serving consumer wants, environmentalists look at how marketing affects the environment and at the costs of serving consumer needs and wants.
- Environmentalism is an organized movement of concerned citizens and government agencies out to protect and improve people's living environment.
- Environmentalists are concerned about damage to the ecosystem caused by strip mining, forest depletion, acid rain, and loss of the ozone layer in the atmosphere, toxic wastes, and litter; about the loss of recreational areas; and about the increase in health problems caused by bad air, polluted water, and chemically treated food.
- Environmentalists are not against marketing and consumption; they simply want people and organizations to operate with more care for the environment.
- The marketing system's goal should not be to maximize consumption, consumer choice, or consumer satisfaction. Rather, it should be to maximize life quality.
- And "life quality" means not only the quality of consumer goods and services, but also the quality of the environment.
- Environmentalists want environmental costs included in producer and consumer decision making.
- Environmentalists are likely to endorse the marketing of biodegradable disposable diapers over regular disposables since the former are more compatible with their views.

Question #5

- There are always good old-fashioned cloth diapers.
- However, cloth diapers are not as convenient and simple to use. An alternative could be a cloth diaper service or business that would drop off clean diapers and pick up dirty diapers daily.
- This business would also clean and sterilize the diapers before their next use.
- Another alternative could be the production of the absorbing pads in diapers.
- Diapers are made up of the absorbing pads and the plastic outside shell.
- Diaper manufacturers could sell the absorbing pads and produce a re-useable plastic panty.
- This alternative would be less detrimental to the environment than disposable diapers.

Case #2   Brown's Department Store

1. The "Free Market and "Legal System" philosophies suggest that it is the responsibility of the firm to obey the law as it pursues rational and economic objectives and that the common good is best served when a business pursues its own competitive advantage. Therefore, it is Mahon's obligation to use the subliminal messages as a loss prevention mechanism to legally enhance Brown's competitive advantage and increase Brown's profitability.

2. The "Social Conscience" philosophy suggests that corporations exercise independent, noneconomic judgment in deciding what is morally and ethically right. It also calls for management to apply individual morality to corporate decisions. If Mahon was convinced that the system was legal and worked, she could decide to implement it because (a) the potential shoplifter is spared prosecution; (b) the cost of theft does not have to be passed on to the customers in the form of higher prices; and (c) store managers and owners avoid unpleasant situations and enjoy greater profitability. In this decision, her reasoning would be that manipulation of the would-be criminal through the use of subliminal messages is a small price to pay, given the benefits. In essence, the end justifies the means.

    However, Mahon might also decide that subliminal messages should not be included in the background music because it is an act of manipulation and subconscious behavior modification. Even though the act of shoplifting is wrong, the would-be criminal would not be acting of his or her own free will, therefore, the end, no matter how well intentioned, does not justify the means. In essence, it is morally wrong to engage in manipulation and subconscious behaviour modification.

Case #3   Palmer Industries

1.   B
2.   A
3.   B
4.   C
5.   C

Case#4

Question #1

Threats include :consumer groups, government legislation, fines, and loss of sales.

Question #2

Social responsibilities are: to make decisions based on customers wants and needs.

Sell product that satisfy customers over a long period of time

To stand behind their workmanship.

To meet consumer associations standards in response to quality and sales practices.

Appendix 4

Measuring and Forecasting Demand

Applying Terms and Concepts

To determine how well you understand the materials in this chapter, read each of the following brief cases and then respond to the questions that follow. Answers are given at the end of this chapter

Case #1   Clark Motors

Larry Clark is the president of Clark Motors, a network of six automotive dealerships in New Brunswick. Clark operates Chevrolet dealerships in Moncton, Riverview, and Sackville, a Pontiac/Buick dealership in Fredericton, and Toyota dealerships in Amherst and Oromocto. Each dealership operates in the black, although profits at the Toyota dealerships were limited because new automobiles were in short supply. Prior to 1990, the Toyota dealerships invariably sold out their allotment of automobiles because import quotas limited the availability of vehicles. However, with the increased availability of Toyotas, Clark estimates that he now receives approximately 150 additional Toyotas per dealership, per year.

Clark, while visiting relatives in Sydney, noticed that the community had no Toyota dealership. In fact, the majority of dealerships ignored imports, with the exception of the local Chevrolet dealership, which also sold Subarus. Clark, ever vigilant for an opportunity to make money, also noticed that an attractive building was available for sale or lease on the upper east side of Sydney located near Highway 4. It had formerly housed a Dodge dealership, which had gone bankrupt in the sales slump of 1983. Clark reasoned that with minimal effort, the facility could become a Toyota dealership.

Upon returning to his base of operations in Oromocto, Clark contacted Bobby Thompson, Toyota's zone manager, about the possibility of opening a dealership if the need could be justified. Thompson indicated that Toyota would support Clark not only with automobiles, but also with advertising allowances if he (Clark) opened a Toyota dealership in the area. Clark was especially pleased to hear of the advertising allowances because past experience showed that considerable consumer demand was generated by local, as well as regional advertising.

Clark quickly hired the market research firm of Gauthier and Nault to assess the needs for another dealership in the Sydney area and to determine the residents' interest in purchasing an imported automobile. Two weeks later, Clark also sent two of his dealership managers, three sales managers, and one business manager to the area to assess the attractiveness of the market.

Upon their return he gave them the report generated by the research firm and additional market information supplied by Toyota. He then instructed each manager to develop an estimate of sales potential for a dealership in Sydney.

Two weeks after the managers returned from Sydney, Clark brought them to Oromocto for a meeting. He instructed each manager to offer his/her estimate of sales potential and supporting rationale. Estimates of auto sales ranged from 600 to 900 vehicles per year, averaging 775. After each manager had offered their opinion. Clark instructed them to consider what the others had said. He also said he would reconvene the group in three days, when each manager would be expected to offer a revised sales estimate. During the next meeting, the estimates ranged from 640 to 830 vehicles per year, with an average of 750. Six weeks later, after financing had been arranged, a decision was made to open what eventually became Cindy Toyota (named after Clark's wife), the seventh addition to Clark's Motors.

_____1. Identify the factor that served to reduce Toyota sales prior to 1990.
   A.   consumer interest
   B.   access barrier
   C.   qualified buyers
   D.   available income
   E.   qualified available market

2.   From the evidence presented in the case, it is clear that Toyota faced a (n) _____ (expandable/nonexpandable) market.

_____3. Identify the approach used by Clark in forecasting the demand for automobiles in Sydney.
   A.   survey of buyer's intentions
   B.   expert opinion
   C.   Delphi method
   D.   composite of salesforce opinions
   E.   both (B) and (C)

_____4. The average estimate of 750 automobiles is an example of:
   A.   industry sales forecast.
   B.   economic forecast.
   C.   company sales forecast.
   D.   market potential.
   E.   time-series analysis.

5.   Comment on the process used by Clark in arriving at an average sales potential estimate of 750. Include in your comments, why the sales potential range of 600 to 900 with an average of 775 vehicles changed to a range of 640 to 830 vehicles with an average of 750.

   _____

   _____

   _____

   _____

Case #2   Xenephon Corporation

The Xenephon Corporation of Saskatchewan has just developed a radical new Concept in competition dune buggies. A new suspension system and drive chain provide much better acceleration and stability, while a special alloy frame gives the machine greater strength and lighter weight. Xenephon plans to charge a premium price for its offering.

The company believes that it can obtain immediate distribution in Canada, Mexico, and the US. Surveys indicate strong interest in an improved competition machine among residents of all three countries—because of the popularity of the sport of dune buggy racing. The countries have stringent age and licensing requirements for competition machines.

1. Keeping in mind that potential buyers for a product or service have four characteristics: interest, income, access and qualifications, define each of the following:

    A. Potential market

    _____

    _____

    _____

    _____

    B. Available market

    _____

    _____

    _____

    _____

    C. Qualified Available market

    _____

    _____

    _____

    _____

D.   Penetrated market

_____

_____

_____

_____

Case #3   Automobili Lamborghini USA

It has been said, "If you have to ask the price, you can't afford it." While that may have been true in the past, it is probably less so now. Exotic sports cars like the Lamborghini, Vector, Ferrari, Bugatti and McLaren priced to sell at 400 thousand dollars (CDN) or more are not as immune from the economy as they once were. Even the wealthy are becoming more value conscious. True, exotic sports cars are not bought for transportation; they are bought because they fit the lifestyle of the owner. They project a certain image with their seductive design and mesmerizing power.

Very few people will ever see a Lamborghini on the road and only a handful will ever purchase one. In fact, this partly adds to their mystique. But Megatech, the Indonesian investment group who recently purchased Lamborghini from Chrysler wants to change that. Lamborghini only sold 33 cars in the US in 1993, 89 in 1994 and approximately 100 in 1995. Megatech's plans are to eventually sell 1500 to 2000 units per year in the US. These ambitious sales goals will be achieved by expanding the product line to include a sport utility vehicle in the 100 to 140 thousand dollar range and a sports sedan priced below 280 thousand dollars. Aggressive marketing techniques designed to promote customer awareness are also planned. The activities include advertising in upscale business, travel and lifestyle publications, strategic partnerships with equally upscale products and organizations and allowing auto journalists to test-drive a Lamborghini for review in their publications. Lamborghini is also planning appearances at the PPG Indy Car races where prospective buyers can take one out for a test drive and perhaps run a few hot laps on the racetrack.

A new dealership network and lease program touted in both an advertising and direct mail program will complement other sales efforts.

1.   Explain what is meant by the concept of total market demand as it applies to exotic sports cars.

_____

_____

_____

_____

2.   What is the difference between primary demand and selective demand?

_____

_____

_____

_____

3.   Explain why the market for Lamborghini automobiles is expandable.

_____

_____

_____

_____

Sources: "Even Lamborghini Must Think Marketing" *Advertising Age,* May 7, 1995, p. 4. "1995 New Cars" *Motor Trend,* October 94, p. 41. *Vector Aeromotive Corporation Annual Report,* 1995.

Answers

Applying Terms and Concepts

Case #1   Clark Motors

1.   B (Import Quotas)   3.   E

2.   expandable   4.   C

5.   Clark used the expert opinion method to obtain the average sales estimate of 750 vehicles. In particular, he used the Delphi method when he brought the managers in for a second meeting where the managers offered their revised sales estimates. It is probable that the sales range converged during the second meeting because each manager had the opportunity to reflect on the opinions offered by the other managers. In essence, each manager now had a broader base of information on which to base the estimate.

Case #2   Xenephon Corporation

1.   a.   Xenephon's potential market consists of those consumers who have expressed a strong interest in their dune buggy.

b.   Xenephon's available market consists of those consumers who live in the company's three-country coverage area, are interested in a high performance dune buggy and are willing to pay Xenephon's price.

c.   Xenephon's qualified available market consists of those consumers who have expressed an interest, possess the necessary purchasing power and who can meet the legal requirements for purchase.

d.   Xenephon's penetrated market consists of those consumer who have all four characteristics. That is they are interested in the dune buggies, have the income to purchase them, have access to the dealership network and who also meet the age and licensing requirements.

Case #3   Automobile Lamborqhini USA

1.   The total market demand for a product or service is the total volume that would be bought by a defined consumer group in a defined geographic area in a defined time period in a defined marketing environment under a defined level and mix of industry marketing effort. Total market demand is not a fixed number but a function of given conditions including elements of the micro and macro environments. As these elements and others such as the level and types of competitive marketing activity change, so too will the level of demand.

2.   Primary demand is the total demand for all brands of exotic sports cars while selective demand is the demand for one brand such as the demand for Lamborghinis.

3.   Lamborghini has had a fairly steady increase in the sale of automobiles since Megatech purchased the company from Chrysler Corporation in 1994. The increase in selective demand for Lamborghini Automobiles can be attributed at least in part to an increase in marketing expenditures. Therefore, as Lamborghini and the other exotic sports car manufacturers increase their marketing expenditures, the total market demand can be expected to increase. Whether it will increase to the level that would allow Lamborghini to realize its eventual goal of selling 1,500 to 2,000 units a year in the US is debatable and remains to be seen.